# PROFILES

# PROBABILITIES

# AND

# STEREOTYPES

# PROFILES

# PROBABILITIES

# AND

# STEREOTYPES

## FREDERICK SCHAUER

The Belknap Press of Harvard University Press
Cambridge, Massachusetts
London, England
2003

All rights reserved
Printed in the United States of America
*Library of Congress Cataloging-in-Publication Data*
Schauer, Frederick F.
Profiles, probabilities, and stereotypes / Frederick Schauer.
p.   cm.
Includes bibliographical references and index.
ISBN 0-674-01186-4 (alk. paper)
1. Stereotype (Psychology).   2. Decision making.   3. Judgment.
4. Forecasting.   5. Justice.   I. Title.

HM1096.S34   2003
303.3'85—dc21                    2003048035

For
*Virginia*
indelibly

# CONTENTS

My aim in this book is to challenge the primacy of the particular. More specifically, I seek to defend an old-fashioned idea against the onslaughts of a more modern one. The modern idea is that *this* particular case, or *this* particular event, is what is most important, and that making the right decision for *this* case or on *this* occasion is the primary building-block of just behavior. Yet it was not always so. In this book I defend the morality of decision by categories and by generalizations, even with its consequent apparent disregard for the fact that decision-making by generalization often seems to produce an unjust result in particular cases. And because I defend the morality of decisions by categories and generalizations, I look more sympathetically than is fashionable nowadays at profiles and stereotypes, which are little more than generalizations in street clothes. This sympathetic look need not yield the conclusion that all stereotypes and profiles are desirable, and not even all of the ones that have a sound statistical basis. But we have lost something by our resistance to generalization, and by our excess sympathy with William Blake's opinion (in his *Annotations to Sir Joshua Reynolds's Discourses*) that "to generalize is to be an idiot. To particularize is the alone distinction of merit." Blake appears to be carrying the day, and in this book I try to recapture at least some of what we seem to have lost in our resistance to generalization and our sympathy for the particular.

This book grows out of but does not duplicate my previous work on rules. In expressing equivalently unfashionable sympathy with rules, even quite rigid ones, I departed from a widespread contemporary preference for taking cases (in law and elsewhere) one at a time, for looking at each person and at each event in full and rich detail, and for thinking of rules as obstacles to effective decisionmaking. Yet in thinking further about rules it became apparent that rules were merely the tip of the iceberg. Perhaps it is the conceit of the academic to believe that no problem is so deep or important that it cannot be seen as but an example of an even deeper and more important one, yet that conceit explains the provenance of the current book. As it became clear that rules were but one form of decisionmaking by generalization, and it became clear as well that even decisionmaking by generalization bore an important family resemblance to other forms of decision based on probabilities, profiles, stereotypes, and approximations, the current book took shape. Its aim is primarily to take a serious look at wholesale justice, unencumbered by the opprobrium that has attached to it from William Blake on up to current discussions of profiling and stereotyping. And if at the end of the day it appears that there is more to be said for generalizations than Blake and most others have thought, then the book will have been a success.

Going from an idea to completion has been possible only with generous support from various quarters. Most immediately, a Guggenheim Fellowship provided financial support as well as the impetus to crystallize the project. Additional financial support was provided by the Joan Shorenstein Center on the Press, Politics and Public Policy, which has generously supported much of my work for more than a decade, and whose support has been admirably open to projects both less and more closely related to issues of press and politics. Similarly, the support of the John F. Kennedy School of Government has been based on the admirable if old-fashioned idea that research support should not be tied to narrow agendas or specific outcomes.

This book began while I was serving as the academic dean of the Kennedy School, and thus owes much to the fact that Dean Joseph Nye and my faculty colleagues supported the idea that an academic dean could be a practicing academic, and were generous and tolerant about ensuring that I had the time to pursue academic inquiry in the midst of a seemingly all-consuming administrative position. And when the administrative duties came to an end, the Harvard Law School, the New York University School of Law, and a fellowship at the Radcliffe Institute for Advanced Study provided me with office space and stimulating colleagues during the intense period when the book was in its final stages.

I have benefited enormously from the opportunity to expose my ideas to constructive and generous criticism. Earlier versions of the basic idea were presented at the

University of Chicago Law School, at the New York University School of Law Colloquium on Constitutional Theory, at the University of North Carolina School of Law, at the Kennedy School of Government's faculty seminar, at the Carr Center for Human Rights Policy, and at the Radcliffe Institute for Advanced Study. Chapter 3 was presented as a guest lecture in Jonathan Zittrain's torts class at the Harvard Law School, chapter 2 at the Vermont Law School, chapter 9 at the University of Minnesota Law School, chapters 6 and 7 on several occasions at the Executive Program on Regulatory Reform at the Kennedy School of Government, chapter 8 at the Research School of Social Sciences at the Australian National University, a version of chapter 10 as the Donley Memorial Lectures at the West Virginia University College of Law, and parts of chapter 11 at the Columbia Law School. Walter Sinnott-Armstrong, in conjunction with the Rockefeller Center for Public Policy at Dartmouth College, organized an extraordinarily engaged and generous reading group around the entire manuscript, a group that also included Carol Bohmer, Susan Brison, Dick Brooks, Julia Driver, Bill Fischel, Ben Forest, Lynn Mather, Angie Means, Jim Murphy, David Peritz, Luke Swaine, and Dale Turner. In addition, good friends became even better colleagues and provided valuable written comments, paying me the compliment of taking time away from their own work to comment on mine. Kent Greenawalt, Sandy Levinson, Walter Sinnott-Armstrong, Bill Stuntz, and Ken Winston provided comments and critiques of virtually the entire manuscript; and Malcolm Sparrow, Michele Taruffo, Nick White, and Richard Zeckhauser helped me with chapters on which their expertise filled in large gaps in my own knowledge. Virginia Wise did the initial research on chapter 2 on the condition that I promise never to want a pit bull as a pet, a promise I have been happy to keep, just as with the promises I made when we were married eighteen years ago.

# PROFILES

# PROBABILITIES

# AND

# STEREOTYPES

# Painting with a Broad Brush

## Thinking like an Actuary

The scenario is familiar. A newspaper publishes an exposé. A government investigation issues its report. The exposé or report is about auto mechanics, for example, and reveals that many overcharge their customers, perform unnecessary repairs, and use secondhand rather than new replacement parts. Or perhaps the report is about funeral directors who prey on the bereaved, car salesmen who misrepresent the condition of used automobiles, surgeons who advise patients to have unnecessary but expensive operations, civil servants who are on the golf course rather than in their offices, stockbrokers who trade excessively with their customers' accounts in order to reap large commissions, or lawyers who commingle their clients' funds with their own. In these and countless other examples, the investigation concludes that members of the profession have persistently abused the trust that their clients and the public have placed in them.

The reaction is virtually automatic. A day after the report appears, the professional association of automobile mechanics—or the equivalent for funeral directors, automobile dealers, surgeons, civil servants, stockbrokers, or lawyers—issues its response. The conclusion drawn by the journalists or investigators is *unfair,* the association charges. It is unfair not because the instances of abuse that were discovered did not take place. Nor is it unfair because the individuals named are honest professionals. Rather, the report is unfair because not *all* auto mechanics, funeral directors, car salesmen, surgeons, civil servants, stockbrokers, or lawyers engage in such reprehensible practices. Although *some* do, the association admits (the evidence typically being so overwhelming as to make any other response laughable), these cases are the exception and not the rule. Every profession, after all, has its bad apples, and the association is now dealing with the small minority of individuals who are giving the entire profession a bad name. In fact, the response continues, the association has just issued new rules and hired more inspectors, these measures being designed to guarantee that a few ethically lax individuals cannot succeed in tarnishing the reputation of thousands upon thousands of honest professionals.

We typically treat such self-serving protestations of unfairness with the skepticism they deserve. Yet although we are skeptical, the argument made on behalf of the impugned profession resonates with many people. Even if 40 percent of the used-car dealers turn back odometers in order to make their wares look newer than they are, there then remain 60 percent who do not. These 60 percent, however, still suffer from the stigma created by the culpable 40 percent. Upon learning that a full 40 percent of any profession are corrupt, few of us could resist looking askance at the entire profession, including the 60 percent who have done nothing wrong. Moreover, few of us can avoid relying on such percentages as we make concrete decisions in our daily lives. As more and more cases of child molestation by priests (and also by scout leaders, baseball coaches, and day-care providers) are reported in the newspapers, many people place less trust in *all* priests, or even in all members of the clergy. As a result, the overwhelming majority of clergymen find themselves under a cloud, even though they are individuals for whom such behavior would be anathema. Or who among us would not prefer a retired federal judge to a former used-car salesman as an investment adviser? And most people think it perfectly sensible to guard their wallets and pocketbooks more carefully in Naples than in Helsinki, even as they know that the overwhelming majority of Neapolitans are every bit as honest as the overwhelming majority of Finns. Yet as we make such decisions, we may sometimes feel uneasy, for we are attributing to the many the sins of the few. Our intuitions are in conflict, because when we attribute the failings of the minority to the entire group we may sense that we are being simultaneously rational and unfair.

In stigmatizing an entire profession because of the behavior of a minority, or in engaging in similar attributions in other areas of decisionmaking, we undertake a process of *generalization*. "Painting with a broad brush," the slightly pejorative expression puts it. To refer to the practice as *stereotyping* intensifies the condemnation, and these days to describe it as *profiling* condemns more strongly still. Yet regardless of the label the structure of the decision is the same.[1] On the basis of a characteristic of some members of a class, we reach conclusions or make decisions about the entire class. When a teenage male acquires a driver's license, his family's insurance premiums will rise dramatically, even if their son is a paragon of caution less likely to be involved in an accident than even most adults. That this particular teenage male does not possess the traits possessed by many others in the class in which he is placed is, here and elsewhere, largely beside the point.

The phenomenon of the teenage male whose acquisition of a driver's license causes his family's insurance premiums to skyrocket reminds us that decisionmaking by generalization is the stock in trade of the insurance industry. Indeed, the insurance industry has its own name for this kind of decisionmaking. To be an *actuary* is to be a specialist in generalization, and actuaries engage in a form of decisionmaking that is sometimes called *actuarial*. Actuaries guide insurance companies in making decisions about large categories (teenage males living in northern New Jersey) that have the effect of attributing to the entire category certain characteristics (carelessness in driving) that are probabilistically indicated by membership in the category, but that still may not be possessed by a particular member of the category (this *particular* teenage male living in northern New Jersey).

Occasionally the actuarial generalizations of the insurance industry become controversial. One example is the use of generalizations about the comparative safety of different neighborhoods as a basis for setting the rates for homeowners' insurance or determining the willingness of a bank to give a mortgage. Normally these generalizations attract little attention, but they become controversial when they have a racially disproportionate effect, raising mortgage and insurance costs in predominantly black neighborhoods more than in largely white ones.[2] Similarly, there are protests at the prospects of requiring gay men to pay more for health insurance because as a class they have a statistically greater likelihood of contracting the HIV virus, and there is anger at the thought that people whose genetic makeup makes them more likely to suffer from cancer or heart disease would have to pay higher premiums for life insurance.[3]

Yet although examples like these generate controversy, in the vast majority of instances the actuarial behavior of the insurance industry is accepted simply as a fact of life. As a resident of Massachusetts, which has more than its share of bad drivers, I pay higher premiums for automobile insurance than I would were I a fulltime resident of Vermont. And this is so not only because the prevalence of bad drivers in Massachusetts increases the likelihood of my being involved in an accident that is not my fault. Rather, the principal reason my insurance premiums are so high is that I am actuarially saddled with the driving habits of my fellow Massachusetts residents, even though these are habits I do not share. And if as a safe driver I buy a high-performance sports car, my insurance premiums will again jump, even if the sports car has no greater monetary value than the staid station wagon I now own, and even if the sports car is no more attractive to thieves. When I buy a sports car I become actuarially encumbered with the risk-taking driving attributes of most sports car owners, attributes that again I do not share, and indeed that if given the opportunity I could prove to my insurance company I do not share. But the insurance company is stunningly uninterested in providing me the opportunity to demonstrate that the generalizations about Massachusetts drivers and sports car owners do not apply to me. I wish it were otherwise, but in the spectrum of life's injustices, both of these seem rather far down the list.

Insurance companies, of course, are not the only ones who operate actuarially. We all do, with far more frequency than most people typically acknowledge. We operate actuarially when we choose airlines on the basis of their records for safety, on-time performance, or not losing checked luggage. We operate actuarially when we associate personal characteristics such as a shaved head, a tattoo, and black clothing with behavioral characteristics, such as racist beliefs and a propensity to violence, that the personal characteristics seem probabilistically but not inexorably to indicate.[4] And we operate actuarially when we indulge in ordinarily harmless stereotyping by nationality, as in describing Italians as emotional and Scots as dour, even while recognizing that more pernicious stereotyping by race, by gender, by sexual orientation, and by ethnicity remains widespread. Still, once we see that insurance companies are in the business of systematic stereotyping, that employers stereotype when they assume that certain characteristics (good grades from a prestigious university) will predict successful job performance, that police detectives focus on suspects by aggregating stereotypes, and that most of us stereotype in much of our daily lives, we cannot so easily dismiss the practice of stereotyping—or profiling—as necessarily morally wrong. Nor can we dismiss as irrational the practice of generalizing even when the generalization produces errors in particular cases. This book tries to sort out when painting with a broad brush is desirable and when it is not, recognizing, for the time being, that the word "desirable" encompasses a wide range of considerations of prudence, efficiency, and, most importantly, morality.

## Generalizations Good and Bad

At the outset it is important to draw a distinction between those generalizations that have no statistical or factual basis and those that do. Following the statisticians, we can label the generalizations that are devoid of such empirical foundations as *spurious*. And although spurious generalizations will crop up at various points in this book, our primary concern will be not with the use of spurious generalizations, but rather with the use and misuse of those generalizations that do have a sound statistical basis. We can label the generalizations with a sound statistical basis *nonspurious*, but what it is for a generalization to have a sound statistical basis is a tricky question deserving some preliminary exploration.

Let us say that a generalization characteristically takes the form of "*x*'s are *y*." In this schematic form, *x* is some identifiable attribute or description, and *y* is an act, property, or behavioral propensity that the attribute or description is thought to indicate or predict.[5] "Scots are dour." "Ferraris are fast." "Golden Retrievers are good with children." "Swiss watches are well made." "Airline employees are rude." "Nonsmokers live longer than smokers." "Blondes have more fun." "German wines are sweet."

Sometimes these generalizations are *universal*, meaning that *all* of the *x*'s are *y*. In many cases universal generalizations are universal as a matter of definition. Philosophers often use the example "All bachelors are unmarried." Here the generalization is necessarily universal, because it is part of the definition of a bachelor that a bachelor be unmarried. If someone is married, he simply cannot be a bachelor. Thus the generalization "All bachelors are unmarried" is a universal generalization just because all the $x$'s—the bachelors—must by definition be $y$—unmarried.

Sometimes, however, universal generalizations are universal not for definitional reasons but for empirical ones. Some fact about the world and not about the word makes the generalization universal. For instance, it used to be believed that all swans were white. Even before the people who made the generalization that all swans were white realized that there were black swans (as there are in Australia, but nowhere else in the world, except in zoos or as Australian transplants), they probably recognized that something could have been a swan and have been a color other than white. It is just that there happened to be no nonwhite swans, or so they thought. So until black swans were discovered, "All swans are white" was a universal generalization; but the possibility remained open, even then, that there could be black swans, unlike the possibility, nonexistent by definition, that there could be married bachelors. Most people believe that the generalization "All human beings are less than nine feet tall" is universal, but the universality is again empirical and not definitional. Nothing in the defining characteristics of humanity requires that human beings be less than nine feet tall, although it is a contingent fact about the world that all of them are.[6] I would be astonished if I were to observe a person taller than nine feet, even more than people were astonished when they first encountered black swans, but my observation will not cause me to doubt that the nine-footer is a human being.

Universal generalizations, whether the source of the universality be definitional or empirical, tend to interest philosophers, but most of the generalizations that the rest of us employ and encounter on a daily basis are not universal. "Swiss cheese has holes." "Italians are demonstrative." "Philosophers are clever." "Volvos are reliable." "You get what you pay for" (inexpensive goods are poorly made). In using and understanding such statements, we recognize that they apply only to most cases, and although we could make things more precise by ensuring that we always prefaced each of the foregoing with "all," "most," "many," "a disproportionate number of," or some similar qualification, it is noteworthy that we rarely do so. Life is short, and time even shorter, and our language is consequently replete with unstated qualifications. As a result, it is an entrenched feature of linguistic usage that statements like "Swiss cheese has holes," "Volvos are reliable," and countless others are taken to be properly used even when not prefaced with the word "all," and even when it would be a mistake to do so. We know that some Swiss cheese has no holes, that some Italians are non-demonstrative, that some philosophers are dim, that some Volvos are lemons, and that some inexpensive products are well made. Nevertheless, the existence of particular cases in which the generalization does not hold rarely causes us to refrain from using the generalization, provided that the generalization holds true for most cases. As long as we remain satisfied that most Italians are demonstrative, it is an accepted part of everyday talk to assert that "Italians are demonstrative," even as we recognize that more than a few Italians are not.

Indeed, we often generalize, and are understood to have generalized appropriately, even when less than a majority of the $x$'s are $y$. When we say, "Bulldogs have bad hips," we do not necessarily mean that even a majority of bulldogs have bad hips. What we mean is that bulldogs have a higher percentage of hip problems than the category of dogs as a whole, and a higher percentage of hip problems than do other breeds. We would understand as sound the claim that bulldogs have bad hips even if only 30 percent of all bulldogs had bad hips, so long as the percentage of hip problems for dogs as a whole was, say, 5 percent, and so long as the percentage of hip problems for other breeds was lower than the percentage for bulldogs. And when on the basis of accident statistics or personal experience we actuarially castigate a group (males under the age of twenty-five, for example) as "bad drivers," we often mean only that the group has a noticeably higher percentage of bad drivers than some other group, or than the group of all drivers. To say that young men are reckless drivers is not to say that the majority of young men are reckless drivers, but only that the percentage of reckless drivers among young men is noticeably higher than the percentage of bad drivers in some comparison group (young women, for example) or in some background reference group (all drivers, for example). So when soccer aficionados conclude that English soccer fans are violent, they believe their conclusion is justified on the basis of there being a higher incidence of violence among English soccer fans than among their counterparts in other countries, even as they recognize that the number of individuals contributing to the higher incidence still falls far short of a majority.

Although there are several varieties of linguistically and empirically plausible generalizations, and although the use of nonuniversal generalizations is an entrenched feature of our linguistic and decisional lives, it still remains important to distinguish those nonuniversal generalizations that have a sound statistical basis from those that do not. Generalizations are of course statistically sound when they are universal, as in "Bachelors are unmarried" and "Human beings are less than nine feet tall." And generalizations are usually statistically sound when they accurately portray the traits of a majority of the members of the class, as in "Swiss cheese has holes." Moreover, as the example of bulldogs with bad hips demonstrates, generalizations are statistically sound whenever the generalization accurately portrays the members of the class as having a greater prevalence of some trait than has some larger class of which the group is ordinarily taken to be a part, even though the trait appears in less than a majority of the members of both groups. What makes "Bulldogs have bad hips" an example of a statistically sound generalization, despite the fact that a majority of bulldogs do not have bad hips, is that knowing that a dog was a bulldog would improve one's ability to predict hip problems relative to whatever information one had other than the information that the dog was a bulldog. As long as the probability of a dog's having hip problems given that the dog is a bulldog is greater than the probability of a dog's having hip problems given no information about the breed of dog, we can say that the trait of being a bulldog is *relevant*, and we can say that generalizing from that trait meets the minimum threshold of statistical (or actuarial) soundness.

The bulldog example illustrates not only that a generalization can be statistically sound despite the fact that the generalization applies only to a minority of members of the class, but also that a key feature of a sound generalization is its comparative dimension. Even if a generalization accurately represents the traits of even a majority of some group, we would think it misleading to use the generalization if the trait was no more present in the group we were talking about than it was in any other group. Suppose that by some measure of honesty— Would you turn in to the police an envelope of cash you found on the street even if you were absolutely certain that no one would ever know if you kept it for yourself?—60 percent of all human beings were honest. And suppose that by the same measure it turns out, not surprisingly, that 60 percent of Swedes were honest. Under these circumstances it seems misleading to say, "Swedes are honest," even though a majority of Swedes *are* honest. Only if Swedes were more honest than some other group would there be a point in making this statement. So although "Swiss cheese has holes" is accurate for most pieces of Swiss cheese, the significance of the statement lies in the fact that Swiss cheese generally has holes and most other kinds of cheese generally do not. If all cheese had holes, saying "Swiss cheese has holes" would be as odd as saying, in most contexts, that "Volvos have four wheels."

Yet even though generalizations can be statistically sound in a number of different ways, there *are* statistically unsound generalizations. Take the generalization "Capricorns are self-confident." If one is a Capricorn purely by virtue of having been born between December 22 and January 19, there is clearly a recognizable category of Capricorns. There is also a recognizable category of self-confidence, and we all understand that self-confidence is a trait that some people have more of than do others. "Capricorns are self-confident" is consequently a statistically sound generalization if all Capricorns are self-confident, if the trait of self-confidence appears in

Capricorns to a greater degree than it appears in the population at large, or if self-confidence appears in Capricorns to a greater degree than it appears in members of the population born under other astrological signs. To give this generalization the greatest chance of achieving statistical soundness, we can focus just on the possibility that Capricorns possess the trait of self-confidence to a greater degree than the population at large, independent of the absolute percentage of Capricorns who are self-confident. Thus, if Capricorns possess the trait of self-confidence in a higher proportion than the trait exists in the entire population, then the generalization that Capricorns are self-confident will be statistically sound, and we will have better information by which to predict whether a person is self-confident if we know that the person is a Capricorn than if we do not have that information.

Yet even taking the version of the claim that would be easiest to demonstrate, it turns out that the claim implicit in this generalization is almost certainly untrue. There is no evidence supporting the belief that the attribute of being a Capricorn is predictive of self-confidence, and in the absence of any such evidence it is highly likely that the relationship between being a Capricorn and being self-confident is spurious. In the language of the law of evidence it is *irrelevant*. Yet regardless of what we call it the conclusion is the same—we have no reason to believe that the trait of self-confidence appears more commonly in Capricorns than in anyone else.[7] If we want to know whether a person is self-confident, being told that the person is a Capricorn helps us not at all. In such a case, we can—and should—say that the generalization is irrelevant, that it is spurious, and that it is statistically unsound.

Another illustration of a spurious generalization is provided by the fortunately lost art of phrenology. Phrenology flourished in the middle of the 1800s, and the many people who believed in it believed that the contours of one's skull provided relevant evidence about a person's personality and natural talents. Because certain traits were fostered in certain parts of the brain, phrenologists and their followers believed, determining the size and location of external cranial features corresponding to those brain locations could provide valuable information about various mental abilities and traits of personality. One's acquisitiveness, self-esteem, combativeness, and facility with language, for example, were all thought to be reflected on a person's cranial terrain. As we know, however, it turned out that there was no evidence that any of phrenology's premises were actually true.[8] Phrenology is no longer practiced, chiefly because generalizations about personality and ability based on cranial features were exposed as simply spurious. It was not that phrenological generalizations, like most generalizations, were not universal. It is that these generalizations (like astrological generalizations, which still, curiously, persist) had no basis whatsoever in even probabilistic empirical fact.

Astrology and phrenology do not, unfortunately, exhaust the universe of commonly employed but statistically unsound generalizations. In Japan, and more recently in China, it is widely believed that one can generalize about the personalities of people on the basis of their blood types. Consequently, people sometimes are not hired for jobs for which they are otherwise qualified because of blood types, despite the fact that there is no more evidence of the relationship between blood type and personality than there is of the relationship between astrological sign or skull terrain and personality.[9] Closer to home, consider the often-believed generalization that gay men lack physical courage. Again, assume that we can distinguish gay men from their heterosexual counterparts. And assume as well that there is some measure of physical courage, such as the willingness to risk death for a cause one believes in, as with a soldier who does not break ranks and run even under direct fire from the enemy. The generalization that gay men lack physical courage would then be statistically sound insofar as gay men possessed the proclivity to physical courage in a smaller proportion than it was possessed by all men, or all people, or in a smaller proportion than it was possessed by heterosexual men. But once again there appears to be not a shred of evidence to support this proposition. The generalization that gay men lack physical courage, like the generalizations that Capricorns are self-confident, that people with bumps on the left front side of their skull are lacking in self-esteem, and that people with type O blood are loyal, is statistically unsound. The trait around which the generalization is constructed—sexual orientation—turns out to be completely irrelevant to the characteristic—courage—that we may often be trying to predict.

When applied to groups of people, statistically unsound generalizations are often castigated as *prejudices*. In common parlance, to have a prejudice is to have an unsubstantiated belief about a person because of his or her membership in a group. But this way of describing what it is to be prejudiced, no matter how common, is ambiguous. Some people might say that to have an unsubstantiated belief about a person is to subscribe to a statistically unsound generalization, such as believing that gay men are cowardly or that Scorpios lack self-confidence. Other people, however, often say that it is

"prejudiced" not only to rely on a spurious generalization, but also to apply a statistically sound but nonuniversal generalization to a particular member of the
group. Consider, for example, the case of people who
have been incarcerated for crimes and served their sentences—ex-convicts, in the common vernacular. We
know that many ex-convicts proceed to live exemplary
lives, never again committing a crime. Yet the percentage
of ex-convicts who commit subsequent crimes is much
greater than the percentage of the population at large
who commit crimes,[10] and thus someone who was "prejudiced" against ex-convicts would not necessarily be
someone operating on a mere superstition. On the contrary, a "prejudice" against ex-convicts might be the consequence of acting on a nonuniversal generalization that
actually does rest on a sound statistical foundation. To be
prejudiced against ex-convicts is quite different from being prejudiced against Scorpios, and the fact that the
same word is often used to apply to both forms of acting
on a generalization only compounds the confusion.

The people who apply the word "prejudice" to negative views about the class of ex-convicts are people who
understand that the word "prejudice" is pejorative. They
are unlikely to describe as a prejudice the belief that accountants are cautious, even though some accountants
plainly are not.[11] But when such people describe as "prejudices" the statistically sound generalization about the
propensity toward crime of ex-convicts, it is because they
believe it is usually wrong to prejudge people even on the
basis of statistically sound group characteristics. For such
people it is wrong to condemn or distrust all ex-convicts
on the basis of group characteristics not held by all
members of the group. As long as there are some or
many ex-convicts who will not commit further crimes,

being suspicious of *all* ex-convicts is wrong, so the argument goes, even if it is true that ex-convicts as a group are considerably more likely to commit crimes than the population at large. Because the word "prejudice" is pejorative, therefore, it is often used to refer not only to statistically unsound generalizations, but also to the inappropriate use of even statistically sound generalizations. But the fact that both of these quite different meanings of "prejudice" are widespread only serves to underscore the confusion.

Much the same can be said about the word "stereotype," which has an even more negative connotation. As with "prejudice," it seems wrong to use the word "stereotype" to refer to those cases in which a generalization is both empirically and morally appropriate.[12] But if stereotyping is wrong, and if condemnation is implicit in using the word "stereotype," we have the same ambiguity about whether stereotyping is wrong only when the stereotype lacks any statistical foundation, or whether it is wrong also when stereotypes that do have a sound statistical foundation are used to make decisions about entire classes, including the members of the class to whom the stereotype does not individually apply.[13]

All of this suggests that there are serious and unresolved definitional issues that surround the topic of generalization, and suggests as well that there is a great deal of loose language being thrown around, especially when we are generalizing about the characteristics of human beings on the basis of identifiable attributes. And although there is little point to thinking that we can answer difficult problems about the use of nonuniversal generalizations simply by defining our terms, we can make a start in avoiding confusion by recognizing some of the definitional issues before we get much further into the analysis. We should recognize, for example, that it may be misleading to describe both generalizations about the courage of gay men and generalizations about the recidivist tendencies of ex-convicts as prejudices, and that it may be misleading in a different way to describe generalizations about the self-confidence of Capricorns and generalizations about the meticulousness of accountants as stereotypes.

The reason we cannot resolve by definitional fiat the difficult issues surrounding the use of generalizations is that the relationship among universality, statistical soundness, and morality is exactly the matter at issue. That the terms in common usage, such as "prejudice," "stereotype," and "profiling," are ambiguous on the conceptual, empirical, and moral issues is not a solution, but a signal that we have a problem in need of analysis. This definitional detour, and the distinction it emphasizes between spurious and nonspurious generalizations, highlight the primary concern that pervades this book.

This primary concern, a concern that the definitional ambiguity between statistically sound and statistically unsound generalizations illuminates, is about the appropriate (and inappropriate) uses of statistically sound but nonuniversal generalizations. The problem of the statistically unsound generalization is not, to be sure, an unimportant one. Indeed, we will return to it repeatedly in considering when, if at all, it is appropriate to make decisions on the basis of even statistically sound generalizations. It is possible, after all, that a reluctance to employ even statistically sound generalizations will helpfully decrease the reliance on statistically unsound and dangerous generalizations. Nevertheless, our primary focus here will be on the statistically sound generalization, the generalization constructed around a trait or property that is relevant for the purpose at hand. In focusing on the statistically sound but nonuniversal generalization, we will examine a widespread feature of decisionmaking, for the problem of whether, and when, to rely on such statistically sound but nonuniversal generalizations pervades our decisionmaking experience. As one usage of the word "prejudice" indicates, many people believe it wrong to make individual decisions on the basis of nonuniversal group characteristics even if the group attributions have a solid statistical grounding. From this perspective it is simply always wrong to make actuarial decisions. All human beings—teenage males who drive cars, ex-convicts, used-car salesmen, Scots, accountants, and everyone else—deserve to be treated as individuals and not simply as members of a group, so the argument goes, and actuarial decisions about human beings are in most instances morally wrong. But although this belief in the wrongfulness of reliance on even statistically sound but nonuniversal generalizations is widespread, it still may not be correct. Indeed, it may not even be plausible. In any event, exploring the legitimacy of relying on statistically sound but nonuniversal generalizations in making decisions is the theme that connects all the specific topics addressed in this book.

## Is Particularism a Moral Imperative?

The goal of this book is thus to examine, and qualifiedly to defend, the practice of painting with a broad brush. In defending painting with a broad brush, I challenge an increasingly pervasive theme in contemporary thought. Sometimes this theme is described as "particularist," for the particular is the opposite of the general. Thus to make decisions on the basis of the characteristics of particular events or particular individuals, rather than on the basis of the characteristics of the groups or classes of which the particulars may be members, is often thought to be a moral imperative. Indeed it is often thought to define the concept of justice, and justice has long been thought necessarily to reside in particulars. When the philosopher Onora O'Neill maintains that "theorists of justice assume that interpretation will lead to differentiated action in differing cases," she describes an attitude not dissimilar to that endorsed by Thomas Hardy in *Tess of the D'Urbervilles* when he characterized Clare, Tess's husband, as having made the "mistake" of "allowing himself to be influenced by general principles to the disregard of the particular instance."[14] And perhaps most blunt was William Blake, who opined that "to generalize is to be an idiot. To particularize is the alone distinction of merit. General knowledges are those knowledges that idiots possess."[15] For O'Neill, for Hardy, for Blake, and for many others, maximum particularity is a characteristic of both justice and wisdom, and reliance on nonparticular categories or principles is at best a necessary evil, at worst an injustice, and all too often a demonstration of stupidity. Indeed, Blake's characterization of the generalizer as an idiot will be important to bear in mind, if only to make clear that the target is not one of straw. In countless walks of life, getting to the particulars of *this* situation or case or person is put forth as the ideal, with generalization seen as at best the lazy alternative. Lawyers celebrate deciding "one case at a time" and rail against the ways in which rigid rules interfere with the exercise of common sense in individual situations.[16] Philosophers extol the virtues of particularism in making moral judgments.[17] Feminist theorists often describe a qualified particularism as preferable to a traditionally male belief in the superiority of generalization and abstraction.[18] And psychologists frequently maintain that we should look at each person as an individual, with "going beyond categorization" being "the right thing to do in almost every case."[19]

Yet the distinguished recent and not-so-recent provenance of the particularist position may still not make the position right. Is reliance on generalizations simply the *modus operandi* of the lazy or the stupid? Perhaps so, but perhaps instead generalization is more inevitable and even more desirable than Blake and others have thought. Taking that possibility seriously is what joins the diverse topic considered in the following pages.

Because all the features of a particular event or decisionmaking occasion are commonly described as the *context* of that event or occasion, it is also common to refer to particularist decisionmaking as contextual. Looking at something in context is assumed to be good, and saying that someone has described a decision or a statement *out of context* is rarely a compliment. Nevertheless, part of what I seek to defend in this book is acontextual decisionmaking, decisionmaking that may deliberately ignore some of the context of the decision and some of the particular features of events or individuals, even features that may themselves be relevant to the decision to be made. As with the actuarial decisionmaking practices of the insurance industry, nonparticularist or acontextual decisionmaking is rarely defended. The fact that we have a battery of readily available pejoratives—*stereotyping, profiling, painting with a broad brush, ignoring the context, Procrustean, one size fits all*—shows just how strong the pull to particularism is. Yet on closer analysis it may appear that there is more to be said (and not only by the insurance companies) for actuarial decisionmaking than is commonly supposed. However often painting with a broad brush may be denied and condemned, it may still turn out on closer inspection to be an often inevitable and frequently desirable dimension of our decisionmaking lives.

To put it most starkly, and to set aside for now some of the definitional questions discussed above, part of my goal here is to defend the practice of stereotyping or profiling. But this, as will become apparent in later chapters, is not to defend the practice of stereotyping or profiling by, say, race, or gender, or sexual orientation. In most cases involving generalizing on the basis of race, gender, and sexual orientation, the stereotyping is simply statistically unsound, as with the stereotypes that blacks are lazy, that women are bad drivers, or that gay men lack courage. Not surprisingly, nothing in this book is directed toward the defense of statistically or empirically unsupportable generalizations. More importantly, however, we will see why even many statistically supportable generalizations—women have less upper-body strength than men—often ought not, for compelling moral reasons, to be the basis for decisions that affect people's lives. Just why this is so will occupy much of chapters 5 and 6. Yet a large part of the motivation for this book is the impression that we have moved too quickly from condemning stereotyping or profiling on the basis of characteristics such as race, gender, and sexual orientation to believing in the moral impermissibility of all stereotyping and all profiling. Perhaps people have too hastily taken the wrong of racial stereotyping, for example, as simply one instance of the wrong of stereotyping itself. It is this belief—that stereotyping and profiling and generalizing are *always* wrong—that this book will examine from numerous different angles, and it is this belief that in important respects this book will challenge.

Implicit in any defense of generality in decisionmaking is a defense of error. To make coarse-grained decisions is to make decisions in some particular cases that are less optimal than the decisions we might make in those cases if we focused only on the features of that case, and if we focused on all the relevant features of that case. Making such coarse-grained decisions—painting with a broad brush—is thus to make mistakes. Defending the making of mistakes is a formidable task. It may even be unwise. Yet as much of the philosophical and legal literature on rule-utilitarianism in particular and rules in general has shown,[20] creating a decisionmaking procedure predicted at the outset to make some number of errors will often lead to fewer errors in the long run than will creating a decisionmaking procedure that in theory produces no errors but that in practice produces many. Even more importantly, however, avoiding mistakes is often not the only goal. A decisionmaking procedure that makes more mistakes in the long run may serve other important goals and embody other important values.[21] Just as we refrain from pointing out all the errors that our loved ones make, and refrain even when pointing out these errors would reduce the total number of errors made, so too might we wish at times to adopt, in the service of accuracy-independent values, decision procedures that can be expected to make some number of mistakes, and even more mistakes of some kind that would be made by other plausible decision procedures. It is often the case that generality in decisionmaking is just such a procedure, and so while part of this book's goal is to demonstrate that such a procedure often produces fewer errors in the long run, another and possibly more difficult task is to show that the use of generalizations in decisionmaking—stereotyping—may sometimes be desirable even when it produces more and not fewer errors in the long run.

Although the analysis that follows is unavoidably a moral one, it is not the plan of this book to take off the shelf a moral framework or methodology and then apply it to the problem of generality. And it is certainly not the goal of this book to presuppose a strictly utilitarian or consequentialist focus on decisionmaking *efficiency* or *economy*. To show that it is often efficient to ignore individual differences is hardly a difficult task. Much harder, and much more important, is confronting the question whether ignoring individual differences is right, just, or fair even when it is efficient. Is ignoring individual differences unjust only when it is inefficient, and then only *because* it is inefficient? Perhaps efficiency does exhaust justice; but here we proceed on the assumption that it does not, and thus proceed on the assumption that there are important questions that must be asked about generality in decisionmaking that cannot be subsumed under efficiency-based or even more broadly utilitarian frameworks.

Instead of selecting a moral standpoint at the outset, we will explore a diverse collection of topics in which the problem of generality looms large. In examining the intuitions and arguments that might apply to these topics, we can generate a series of smaller moral propositions that might then be part of a larger moral framework. Rather than applying a moral framework to the problem of generality, therefore, this book proceeds on the assumption that more-particular solutions to the problem of generality might help compose that larger moral framework, rather than the other way around. Perhaps ironically, therefore, the approach here to the problem of generality will have a strongly particularistic flavor. We will examine problems as diverse as those of basing insurance rates and other social consequences on genetic differences; controlling vicious dogs and other dangerous animals on the basis of breed characteristics; identifying the targets of customs inspections, tax audits, airport searches, and police stops by reference to sets of characteristics commonly referred to as "profiles"; allowing statistics to be used as evidence in civil and criminal trials; imposing mandatory retirement for airline pilots and other forms of discrimination on the basis of age; taking gender differences into account in military and related contexts; criminalizing behavior not because it is intrinsically wrong, but because it indicates the likelihood that wrongful behavior has occurred; prohibiting the use of traditional methods of food production; and imposing sentences on those convicted of crimes not on the basis of whether the punishment fits the crime or fits the criminal, but instead on the basis of a predetermined guideline. From these and many other varied instances there will, it is to be hoped, emerge a greater understanding of the problem of generality in decisionmaking, a more sensitive appreciation of the relationship between generality and justice, and, most importantly, an increased awareness of the circumstances under which generality in decisionmaking is appropriate and the circumstances under which it is not.

# CHAPTER 1

# In Training
# with the Greeks

## Plato's Personal Trainer

Distinguishing appropriate from inappropriate uses of generalizations requires focusing on the nonuniversal dimension of even statistically sound generalizations. In other words, we must deal with the distinction between what is true generally of a class and what is true of each member of that class. Even if it is generally true that Volvos are reliable, that the class of Volvos is more reliable than the class of Buicks, and that the class of Volvos is more reliable than the class of cars, it does not follow that every Volvo is reliable. The generalization that Volvos are reliable, even if statistically sound for the class of Volvos, is almost certainly untrue for some of the Volvos that make up the class.

Long before there were any Volvos at all, however, the possibility that what is true generally for a class may still not be true for some members of that class was well recognized. Indeed, the distinction between the truth of the generalization and the truth of the particular has been understood and analyzed since classical times. Because these classical approaches have informed much of subsequent thinking on the topic, it may be helpful to start with the Greeks. Looking at what some of the classical philosophers thought about generalization, illuminated by some modern examples, will provide the historical foundations necessary to explore more contemporary topics in subsequent chapters.

Consider first an illuminating but preliminary section of Plato's often-ignored *Statesman*. In one part of this dialogue a visitor from Elea, sometimes called the Eleatic Stranger, is engaged in a conversation with the young Socrates. They are discussing the art of governance, and the Stranger is responding to Socrates' unconsidered defense of (general) laws.[1] As part of his response, the Stranger makes the case for "the superiority of rational expertise over written lawcodes."[2] He does this by observing that "law can never issue an injunction binding on all which really embodies what is best for each: it cannot prescribe with perfect accuracy what is good and right for each member of the community at any one time. The differences of human personality, the variety of men's activities and the inevitable unsettlement attending all human experience make it impossible for any art whatsoever to issue unqualified rules holding good on all questions at all times."[3] In criticizing law as a blunt instrument that is more general than the diversity of people and places that it seeks to control, the Stranger in this passage emphasizes *variation* as the key concept. People are different, places are different, times are different, and events are different. It would seem, therefore, that any form of decisionmaking about people and events should be as sensitive as possible to the variability of the observed and experienced world. Following Aristotle, we might say that like cases should be treated alike, and unlike cases unalike.[4]

Despite this natural impulse to tailor the law to the detailed richness of experience, and thus to make the law as nuanced as the world it seeks to control, the Stranger recognizes the impossibility of this degree of particularism. And he recognizes that total sensitivity to individual variation in people, places, times, and things would be especially difficult to embody in the decisionmaking methods of the law. Thus, "the legislator who has to preside over the herd . . . will lay down laws in general form for the majority, roughly meeting the cases of individuals . . . under average circumstances."[5] As with setting a speed limit that may be too slow for some drivers (and some conditions), too fast for others, and about right for most, the legislator described by the Stranger legislates for a group and not for individuals. The legislator thus aims to get it right for most of the group under most circumstances, even while recognizing the impossibility of getting it right for the entire group under all circumstances. As another contemporary example of legislating for "the herd," to use the Stranger's word, consider the minimum age established for activities such as driving, drinking, and voting. Although some people who are, say, fifteen years old are likely to be safe drivers, responsible drinkers, and knowledgeable voters, and although many people over the requisite ages (typically sixteen for driving, eighteen for voting, and twenty-one for drinking, at least in the United States) are not, the minimum ages we set for these activities take the "general form." They apply to all people under all circumstances even though these general rules may get it right only "for the majority," and then only under "average circumstances."

Plato recognizes that not all decisions can or should be made on the basis of large categories. He gives us the example of the captain of a ship, who operates successfully "not by writing rules," but by making the decisions that "at any moment [are] for the good of the vessel and the sailors."[6] The ship captain, in other words, stands on the bridge continuously aware of every variation in conditions, and makes his decisions on a moment-to-moment basis in such a way that none of those variations is ignored. But Plato uses the example of the ship captain precisely to emphasize that the model of the ship captain cannot be applied to all dimensions of human decision. The ship captain may not operate by writing rules, but written and general rules are in many contexts unavoidable. Legislatures cannot stand on the bridge of society, constantly monitoring every variation. As a result, it is often necessary for lawmakers, even if not for ship captains, to legislate for the herd.

The most noteworthy feature about the Stranger's claim, however, lies not in the way that legislation differs from the behavior of the ship captain. Nor is it even in the way that legislation prescribes for all on the basis of what is best for most, for this too is by now familiar terrain. Rather, what is particularly important for us here is the Stranger's argument that when there is an opportunity to avoid the error caused by the application of the universal and simple rule to some particular case, it would be "absurd," "evil," a "disgrace," and an "injustice" not to avoid the error. This language of powerful condemnation is especially striking in light of the examples that the Stranger uses to make his point. He asks us to consider both a physician and a training master, the latter being somewhat like today's personal trainer. Now suppose that the training master or the physician must be away, and accordingly must leave behind written memoranda of instructions for the regimen to be followed in his absence. If the training master or the physician should return sooner than expected, however, and if it should appear to the training master or physician upon his return that the prescribed regimen did not *then* appear at *that* time to be the best thing to do, then "nothing would be more unjust," the Stranger argues, than to refuse to make the necessary modification.[7]

By maintaining that the regimen should be modified in light of subsequent information, the Stranger could be understood simply to be making the point that rules made at one time might at a later time seem defective. When this happens, the Stranger might be arguing, the defective rules should then be modified or updated if it is at all possible to do so.[8] In this way, the rules we have would be the best rules possible given current understandings of current circumstances.

Recognizing that good rules might later be seen as defective is not unimportant. Keeping open the possibility of revising flawed rules is a valuable check on the limitations of human foresight. Moreover, recognizing the necessity of occasionally revising our rules is a useful reminder of the fact that rules necessarily prescribe for the future, of the way in which any estimation of future consequences or applications is beset by uncertainty, and of the conclusion that rules thus contain the conditions of their own obsolescence. Yet being open to the possibility that good rules made at one time might seem poor ones later is not the Stranger's immediate concern.[9] For the Stranger, the return of the training master is the occasion not for the training master to update the regimen, but for the training master to question the necessity of having a prescribed regimen at all. The regimen, after all, is general. That is just what a regimen *is*. And so the Stranger sees the necessarily general regimen as being what the training master prescribes precisely because he must be away, and precisely because he is consequently unable to act like a ship captain giving particularized and continuous instructions varying with the exact circumstances of the moment. Perhaps "fifty sit-ups a day" is what a modern-day training master prescribes for each of his many students for the month he is to be away, but if he is working daily with his students on an individual basis he might urge a hundred sit-ups for some students and ten for others, and even for particular students as many as eighty on days when the student is eager and fresh but as few as twenty for the same student on other days. This kind of condition-specific variability is not possible, however, when the training master is not present to evaluate and monitor each student in person on a daily basis. When he is away, therefore, the training master prescribes fifty sit-ups a day for everyone on every day as something that will be more or less right for the majority of students on the majority of days. When the training master returns, however, the regimen is no longer necessary. The fact that the training master abandons the regimen upon his return is thus a point not about the obsolescence of the regimen, but about the fact that regimens themselves are necessarily subject, *by virtue of their generality,* to the persistent possibility of being in error in individual cases.

The Stranger's point about the generality of any regimen is a valuable one. What remains curious, however, is the Stranger's characterization of the training master's refusal to abandon the regimen upon his return as "absurd," "ridiculous," "evil," "a disgrace," and an "injustice." And the language that the Stranger uses is all the more striking because in this context he is, after all, talking about a training master and an exercise regimen, and not something more morally consequential. Now it is true that exercise was probably more morally central (as a component of health) to Plato and his fellow Greeks than it is to most people today.[10] And the Stranger is using the examples of the training master and the physician to make a point not about health or physical exercise, but about lawmaking, about the irrelevance of general law or written rules to the ideal ruler, and about the relationship among various forms of expertise.[11] Moreover, it is likely that the Greek terms now commonly translated into English as "evil," "disgrace," and "injustice" carried different connotations for Plato than they do for us today. Nevertheless, the use of such morally heavy language even in the context of what appears to be a morally inconsequential decision highlights the nature of the problem: To what extent, if at all, does one make a *moral* error in refusing, when possible, to correct the general in order to take account of the particular, independently of the moral question of the moral consequences of that error? Or even if it is sometimes necessary as a practical matter to persist with the general even when it produces error in particular cases, does making a general decision and thus getting it wrong for some cases produce some moral residue—an occasion for moral regret, or for compensation or apology to those who have been mischaracterized—just by virtue of reaching some erroneous conclusions in particular cases?[12] In other words, does the fact of making decisions on the basis of generalizations by itself produce injustice in every case in which those generalizations produce the wrong result? Is particularism itself a moral command? Is generalization (and law) itself a moral flaw, at best—as Plato himself recognized in both the *Laws* and the *Republic*—an often necessary second-best accommodation to the realities of our existence, but even then an accommodation beset with morally problematic dimensions?

Consider another contemporary example. From the medical evidence that now exists it appears that women of eastern European Jewish (Ashkenazi) origin have a higher risk than women in general of becoming afflicted with breast and ovarian cancer. Specifically, some studies have concluded that approximately 2.3 percent of women of eastern European Jewish background have a genetic mutation (compared with somewhere between .16 percent and .5 percent for the population at large) that quadruples their likelihood of having breast cancer and increases by tenfold their risk of ovarian cancer; another study identified a different genetic variation in 7 percent of women of eastern European Jewish origin, a genetic variation that increased the likelihood of breast cancer by 50 percent.[13] On the basis of these and similar studies, it appears that the likelihood of becoming afflicted with breast or ovarian cancer is higher for a woman of eastern European Jewish background than it is for an otherwise identical woman not of eastern European Jewish background.

Given their increased risk of contracting breast or ovarian cancer, consider the hypothetical or not-so-hypothetical possibility, not unrelated to larger fears and debates about the use of genetic information in insurance, that women of eastern European Jewish origin might be denied health insurance, or be required to accept a breast and ovarian cancer exclusion from their health insurance coverage, or be charged higher insurance premiums than otherwise similarly situated women not of eastern European Jewish origin.[14] The question, then, is whether an insurance company's denial of coverage, or increase in the premiums it charges for the same coverage, works an injustice when based on the actuarially justified but nonuniversal generalization that women of eastern European Jewish origin are especially susceptible to breast and ovarian cancer. Is such a policy particularly unjust to those women of eastern European Jewish origin—well over 90 percent of them—who do not themselves actually possess any of the troublesome genetic mutations and thus do not themselves have any increased risk whatsoever of contracting breast or ovarian cancer?

Many people would believe that imposing insurance restrictions on all women with this background just because of a genetic variation that appears in only some of them is indeed unjust. But what are the reasons for such a belief? It appears that we can identify four possible reasons why it might be unjust to burden women of eastern European Jewish origin because of the greater statistical likelihood of their becoming afflicted with breast or ovarian cancer. The first is that health insurance is crucially important, and in the modern world a person without health insurance is at considerable risk of suffering a medical and financial catastrophe.[15] The second reason is that those who suffer from the generalization are women, and the fact that women are subject to financial discrimination in the workplace and elsewhere both compounds the magnitude of the financial risk and potentially exacerbates existing forms of gender discrimination.[16] Third, the statistically relevant factor, eastern European Jewishness, is one that may foster or entrench existing prejudices about the otherness of Jews, about

Jews as a distinct racial class, and about Jews as being in some way different from the bulk of the population. Fourth, and finally, using the generalization might be unjust simply because most eastern European Jewish women will not become afflicted with breast or ovarian cancer, and many will even have identifiable health factors or personal habits that lower the risk of such cancers substantially more than having an eastern European Jewish genetic background raises it.

Given these four different sources of concern, the case of Plato's training master helps us to isolate the question of the justice of generality—the fourth concern in the foregoing list—from other considerations. If the first, second, and third sources of concern in the example of women of eastern European Jewish origin—grave personal consequences, gender discrimination, and anti-Semitism—were absent, as they appear to be in the case of the training master, would people still believe, with the Eleatic Stranger, that there would be an injustice were a decision to be made on the basis of the generalization? And if people still believed this to be unjust, would they be right to believe it? Is the fourth concern, the nonuniversality of the generalization, sufficient by itself to warrant the charge of injustice whenever the nonuniversal generalization is used as a basis for decision even about the particular people and particular cases for which the generalization does not hold? This is the Stranger's claim, and the inconsequential (to us) nature of a training master's regimen, when compared with the highly consequential nature of denial of insurance coverage to women of eastern European Jewish origin, helps us to isolate the question about the possible injustice of generalized decisionmaking just because of its generality and not because of anything else.

In order to see further that the problem of generality is only one of four quite distinct problems in the example of insurance coverage for women of eastern European Jewish origin, let us return to the case of the English soccer (football) hooligans. Suppose there is good evidence that the probability that an English football supporter will commit an act of violence at a football match is 20 percent greater than it is for a randomly selected European. And suppose further that on the basis of this 20 percent increase in risk some football stadium on the Continent decides, as some countries and stadiums have in fact considered in recent years, to refuse admission to English spectators.[17] Does such an exclusion of all English spectators on the basis of the violent acts that only some of them might commit represent a case of injustice? Unlike the denial of health insurance, the consequences are not grave. Although many people enjoy watching football matches, being unable to do so is hardly comparable to being without health insurance. And unlike using a generalization in which those subject to the generalization are only women and only Jewish, here the generalization neither reflects nor exacerbates a morally and historically troublesome form of gender or ethnic discrimination. So if in the case of the exclusion of English football spectators the consequences of the exclusion are relatively small, and if a historically pernicious form of discrimination is absent, then the injustice, if there is one at all, consists solely in the nonuniversality of the generalization about English football supporters. Any injustice in this case would be solely a function of the way in which nonviolent English football supporters would be burdened with the statistically relevant but far from universal attributes of the class of which they are members.

Those who would claim that there is an injustice here would point to the stadium's possible unwillingness to look at potentially better predictors of football hooliganism than Englishness, and could argue that refusing to look at these better predictors is akin to the training master's refusal to abandon his regimen upon his return. If Plato's Stranger is right that this is an injustice in the case of the training master, then, so the argument would go, it is also an injustice in the case of the exclusion of the English football fans. The injustice would lie in the willingness of the stadium to impose the cost of the solution to the problem of football violence on those English football fans with no proclivities to violence. By excluding all the English football fans, the burden of remedying the problem is imposed on all the English and on no one else. Perhaps it would be fairer, therefore, to distribute the cost in a way that does not burden the many innocent English football fans, such as by employing greater security measures and increasing ticket prices—for everyone—accordingly. But if the stadium refuses to do this, has it committed an injustice, or are we now simply talking about the costs and benefits of various morally equivalent policies? This is exactly the question to which we will frequently return, and it is exactly the question that the morally lowered consequences of the case of the English football fans is designed to illustrate.

The case of the English football hooligans, as one in which the first three concerns identified in the case of women with eastern European Jewish origins are absent or greatly reduced,[18] exposes the fact that these three concerns—grave consequences, gender discrimination, and anti-Semitism—are independent of the questions of generality and generalization. Even if 100 percent of all women of eastern European Jewish background possessed the relevant genetic variation, and even if there were no way of determining further which of these women would actually contract breast or ovarian cancer (or even if all women with the genetic variation would contract cancer), the first three concerns would persist. Excluding all women of eastern European Jewish origin from insurance coverage, or charging all of them higher premiums, even were all of them at increased risk of contracting breast or ovarian cancer, would still raise concerns about grave consequences for a segment of the population, would still raise concerns about gender discrimination, and would still raise concerns about anti-Semitism. That this is so highlights the distinction between the possible injustice of singling out a group and the possible injustice of using an actuarially sound but nonuniversal generalization within the group. Although the concerns about grave consequences, gender discrimination, and anti-Semitism in the case of the eastern European Jewish women are real and important, they turn out on closer inspection not to be concerns about generalization at all. These concerns would be equally present were we dealing with universal characteristics of the group, and are not restricted to cases in which the characteristics appear in only some members of the group. Excluding this group from health coverage, even if it were certain that all members of the group would contract cancer, would still raise concerns about consequences, gender discrimination, and anti-Semitism, for these are concerns about exclusion and not about generalization.

Thus the concerns in the example of the eastern European Jewish women turn out not to be concerns about nonuniversal generalization within the group, but rather are concerns that relate to the history of how certain groups (here women and Jews) have been treated or that are a consequence of the magnitude of certain consequences (here the loss of medical insurance coverage). When these concerns about severe consequences and historically problematic discrimination drop out or are much attenuated, as in the example of the English football hooligans, the question of generality itself is isolated; and when it is isolated the instinctive negative reaction and the consequent sense that there is an injustice appears to be much less. There may still be a problem in the case of the English soccer fans, but it is now clearer what the problem might be, and, when isolated, it is not nearly so clear that there is a problem at all.

The point of comparing the case of the women of eastern European Jewish origin with the case of the English soccer fans is to illustrate the way in which Plato's example of the training master appears to be highly comparable to the case of the English soccer fans and less so to the case of the eastern European Jewish women, especially if we see the role of training and training masters in modern and not in classical context. As with the case of the exclusion of the English soccer fans, the consequences when the training master acts on the generalization in those instances in which the generalization is inaccurate are small. Also, and again as with the exclusion of the English soccer fans, in the case of the training master the standard forms of invidious discrimination are absent. So when concerns about severe consequences and historically invidious discrimination are excluded, the isolated question is before us: Is acting on a statistically sound but nonuniversal generalization morally worrisome in those cases in which the generalization does not hold? More precisely, is acting on the basis of such a generalization morally problematic because of the inaccuracy of the outcome itself (or because of the use of the generalization itself), independent of the severity of the consequences, and independent of questions of discrimination on the basis of race, gender, sexual orientation, and other forms of historically invidious discrimination?

Returning to Plato's training master, it is clear that the Stranger believes there to be an injustice even in a case of this sort. Less clear, however, is whether the Stranger is correct in so believing. In describing the case of the training master as one of injustice, the Stranger, at least in this portion of the dialogue, suggests that something is morally amiss every time we refuse to correct the general to take account of the particular. But it is far from self-evident that every failure to correct such an error is an injustice, and it is not immediately apparent what conception of justice and injustice produces such a conclusion. Plato's Stranger concludes that we have an injustice when the training master or the physician does not eliminate the regimen upon his return, but this conclusion stands largely without explanation. Plato has given us a valuable start in understanding our problem, but he offers less than we might have first thought by way of help in solving the problem.

## Aristotle and the Foundations of Equity

Plato's point, at least in the portion of the *Statesman* just discussed, is that ideal justice demands relinquishing general prescriptions when it is possible to reach better results in individual cases. For Plato the concept of justice appears to lie in the particulars.[19] Indeed, Plato's idea of justice as necessarily particular is consistent with our understanding of the story of King Solomon (to whom we shall return in chapter 10), and the way in which Solomon proposed cutting a baby in half in order to determine which of two claiming women was truly the baby's mother. We laud Solomon for his decision, and we take his solution as an exemplar not only of wisdom but also of justice. But we do so not because Solomon followed some preexisting rule about what to do in cases of contested motherhood. Rather, we praise Solomon because he devised the best solution to *this* problem, unique as it may have been. Solomon, like Plato's ship captain and like Plato's image of what the training master should have done upon his return, is someone who does justice precisely by doing the right thing at this time for this case.

This understanding of justice as particular is taken a step further by Aristotle. In both the *Nicomachean Ethics* and the *Rhetoric*, Aristotle argues for the moral necessity of locating and correcting the errors wrought by any generalization. Correcting the mistakes that are the by-products of generalization reflects the idea that Aristotle and others have since called *equity*, and Aristotle's argument for the necessity of an equitable supplement to the rigidity of law's generality is worth exploring in detail.

In explaining the idea of equity, Aristotle describes it as "a rectification of law in so far as law is defective on account of its generality."[20] He thus understands (and defines) law to be necessarily general, just as Plato did in the *Statesman* and subsequently in the *Laws*, and just as the Eleatic Stranger saw the regimen of the physician or the training master as necessarily general. Speaking through the voice of the Stranger, however, Plato was concerned with the circumstances under which the regimen might be discarded. Aristotle's concern is related but different: At times we have good reason, as in legislation, to lay down prescriptions in general form. But even then these legislative prescriptions might produce the wrong result in particular cases, as the Stranger recognized might happen in cases that were not average and in circumstances that were not normal. The Stranger says little further about such cases of legislation, except to hint that under nonideal circumstances it is better to accept the consequences of these mistakes than to have less-than-ideal rulers deciding everything by their own lights. Aristotle, however, believes that an approach to correcting such mistakes is required by justice; and for Aristotle that approach is equity.

> The explanation of this is that all law is universal, and there are some things about which it is not possible to pronounce rightly in general terms; therefore in cases where it is necessary to make a general pronouncement, but impossible to do so rightly, the law takes account of the majority of cases, though not unaware that in this way errors are made. And the law is none the less right; because the error lies not in the law nor in the legislator, but in the nature of the case; for the raw material of human behaviour is essentially of this kind. So when the law states a general rule, and a case arises under this that is exceptional, then it is right, where the legislator owing to the generality of his language has erred in not covering the case, to correct the omission by a ruling such as the legislator himself would have given if he had been present there, and as he would have enacted if he had been aware of the circumstances. . . .
>
> This is why equity, although just, and better than a kind of justice, is not better than absolute justice—only than the error due to generalization.[21]

Aristotle expresses much the same idea in the *Rhetoric:*

> For that which is equitable seems to be just, and equity
> is justice that goes beyond the written law. These omis-
> sions are sometimes involuntary, sometimes voluntary,
> on the part of the legislators; involuntary when it may
> have escaped their notice; voluntary when, being un-
> able to define for all cases, they are obliged to make a
> universal statement, which is not applicable to all, but
> only to most, cases; and whenever it is difficult to give
> a definition owing to the infinite number of cases . . .
> for life would not be long enough to reckon all the pos-
> sibilities. If then no exact definition is possible, but leg-
> islation is necessary, one must have recourse to general
> terms.[22]

As did Plato, Aristotle recognizes that general prescriptions—laws—might at times produce erroneous results. A speed limit that is designed for average drivers
under average circumstances will be too fast for some
drivers and some conditions, and too slow for others. A
prohibition on English football supporters will produce
the wrong results in all cases in which particular supporters with no tendencies toward violent behavior are
excluded; and fifty sit-ups a day, even if right for average
people in average conditions on average days, will be too
strenuous for some people in some circumstances and insufficiently challenging for other people in other circumstances. In all these cases there are relevant particulars
that the generalization ignores, and Aristotle properly
recognizes that excluding "ethically relevant particulars"
is a feature of all generalizations and of all laws.[23] Yet this
exclusion need not be final, Aristotle argues, and it is the
function of equity to rectify the failings of the general

law by including in a fully just decision those factors that the generality of the law has excluded. In this way, says Aristotle, equity serves the purpose of correcting the law and thus of providing "complete" rather than incomplete justice.[24]

It is possible to understand Aristotle's point as a claim about the nature of rules.[25] *De*scriptive rules are generalizations, and the phrase "as a rule" is another way of conveying the idea of a generalization. Norway is cold. Spicy food produces heartburn. Accountants are meticulous. But *pre*scriptive rules embody and build on generalizations as well. The "No Dogs Allowed" sign in a restaurant embodies the generalization that dogs will generally annoy other patrons and interfere with their dining enjoyment, even though some dogs—well-behaved guide dogs, for example—will produce no annoyance, and some animals that are not dogs—pet bears and pet monkeys, for example—will. By incorporating generalizations, therefore, prescriptive rules have the capacity to produce mistaken results, where "mistaken" is measured by the result that would have been produced by the direct application of the rule's background justification to the particular case. If in the case of the rule against dogs in restaurants we were to apply the justification of preventing annoyance directly to particular cases, we would not exclude well-behaved guide dogs and would exclude not only most pet bears and most pet monkeys, but also many poorly behaved children. Because the "No Dogs Allowed" rule draws upon a nonuniversal generalization about what creatures are likely to cause interference and what creatures are not, applying the rule instead of the justification will produce errors of overinclusion (excluding the guide dog) and errors of underinclusion (not excluding the child) that would not have been produced by direct application of the background justification. Importantly, all of this is not about gaps or uncertainties in the rules. The "No Dogs Allowed" rule is perfectly clear. On its face it plainly indicates what to do in these problematic cases: keep guide dogs out and let unruly children in. Thus the question is not one of dealing with "hard cases" in the conventional sense of that term.[26] It is not a problem of filling the gaps in the law or of clarifying the uncertainties of the law.[27] Rather it is a problem, as Aristotle was the first to recognize, of correcting the mistakes that law by its very generality necessarily makes.

Although Aristotle, with his language of "rectification," plainly recognizes the consequences of legislative generality, his point, both in the *Nicomachean Ethics* and in the *Rhetoric*, goes well beyond it. For Aristotle does not merely say that coarse rules, with the mistakes they inevitably will make, are a necessary evil in a world of nonideal decisionmakers. This is an observation that Plato makes in a later part of the *Statesman* and in the *Laws*, providing the underpinnings for Plato's central argument in favor of laws. Aristotle, however, is even less tolerant than Plato of the mistakes that are the inevitable by-product of general laws. As with the arguments appearing in the voice of the Eleatic Stranger, Aristotle sees these mistakes, the mistakes that are the invariable consequence of generalization, as cases of injustice, or at least of incomplete justice. And because they are cases of injustice or incomplete justice, Aristotle insists that the morality of complete justice urges creation of a mechanism or a procedure, or at least a state of mind, for alleviating these injustices. This approach is consistent with Aristotle's view that there is a distinction between law and the underlying "reality," with law being only an approximation of this underlying reality.[28] Because the rules often indicate one thing when the reality of the situation is something else, it is clear to Aristotle that a society committed to complete justice is in need of an institution or mechanism to reflect the reality. This mechanism is equity, the method (or attitude) by which someone can examine each individual case and, whenever necessary, correct the wrong done by mechanical application of general laws. Aristotle does not have much to say about the specific people or institutions that might serve this function, but he does suggest that "arbitrators" are the ones who "keep equity in view" and, unlike those who apply ony the law, are "appointed [so] that equity might prevail."[29]

So we see in Aristotle a foreshadowing of the two related points that dominate this book. First, any form of decisionmaking by generalization—and rule-based decisionmaking is one important form of decisionmaking by generalization—will produce some results that are different from and worse than the results that would be reached by an ideal decisionmaker accurately applying the rationales behind the generalization directly to particular cases. This is not a function of any imperfection in the procedure, but is a necessary consequence of making decisions according to generalizations. Second, although it is often necessary to make decisions according to generalizations, it is, says Aristotle, a mandate of complete justice that there be a way of rectifying these deficient results, so that in the final analysis the generalization is applied only in those cases in which the results it generates are accurate. As we examine a range of contemporary problems we will see these two themes repeated, and with some frequency I will be reinforcing the first while questioning the second. In other words, I will often side with Aristotle in recognizing that mistakes will necessarily be made when we rely on generalizations in decisionmaking, but will take issue with his conclusion that it is always or perhaps even usually necessary or desirable to establish a mechanism to ensure the rectification of these mistakes.

## Law, Equity, and the Law of Equity

We know little of the institutionalization of the idea of equity in ancient Greece, but we do know a great deal about the institutions of ancient Rome, and thus about the institutionalization of equity in Roman law. Aristotle's idea that there needed to be a mechanism for correcting the errors wrought by law's generality was reiterated by subsequent commentators in both Greece and Rome, most notably by Cicero.[30] Largely as a result of Cicero's influence, Aristotle's philosophical conception of equity became the basis for the introduction of *aequitas* in Roman law. Because Roman law was so formal and so precise, and thus because even the slightest deviation from the exact written law was fatal to an aggrieved party's ability to pursue a claim, there developed a mechanism—*aequitas*—to soften the rigidity of the law.[31] This mechanism was institutionalized by means of the "extraordinary jurisdiction" of the *praetors,* the Roman magistrates. In exercising this jurisdiction, the praetors had the power to correct inequities or moral wrongs done by rigid application of the written law (*ius civile*), and in doing so they could both add remedies when the formal law created none, and refuse to grant the remedies of the formal law when following the formal law would work an injustice. This power of the *praetors* can therefore be understood as the mechanism that gave effect to Aristotle's insight about the role of equitable correction of the law. Given that the law because of its generality is destined to produce injustices in particular cases, or is destined in its strict application to produce outcomes that would not have been desired by its drafters, then the Romans saw it necessary to create a means by which these mistakes, or injustices, would be corrected.

Similar ideas informed the original development of equity in English law. Starting in the thirteenth century and continuing until the early part of the sixteenth century, the king's chief minister, the chancellor, exercised the power to grant remedies not then available in the formal legal system, and to give relief on an individual basis to those who could not find it in the law. Originally the power arose because the law was far from comprehensive. In many instances large domains of controversy were simply not covered by the law at all, and the chancellor's jurisdiction—*equity*—added remedies that the law could not provide because of its incompleteness. But as the equity power grew, it came more and more to resemble Aristotle's basic idea of equity not so much as completing law but correcting it. As equity developed in England, the chancellor not only created new remedies in order to fill the gaps in law's power, but also took it upon himself, upon petition, to ameliorate the rigidities of the law. The chancellor was "trying to give relief in hard cases,"[32] and in many instances cases became hard cases precisely for the reasons first offered by Aristotle: that the inevitable generality of the law would produce outcomes inconsistent with the outcomes that would have been selected by a more particularistic decision-making procedure, and that would have been preferred by the lawmaker if only the lawmaker had been available to adjudicate the particular case. These suboptimal outcomes produced by law's generality were among the mistakes that the chancellor often took upon himself to remedy. As U.S. Supreme Court Justice William O. Douglas was later to put it, "The essence of equity jurisdiction has been the power of the Chancellor to do equity and to mold each decree to the necessities of the particular case."[33]

Over time the equitable jurisdiction of the chancellor, itself an exercise of the individual and discretionary royal prerogative, became further institutionalized in the form of the Court of Chancery. And thus the Court of Chancery continued to exercise the power described at the beginning of the sixteenth century by Christopher St. German in *Doctor and Student:*

> In some cases it is necessary to leave the words of the law, and to follow what reason and justice requireth, and to that extent equity is ordained; that is to say, *to temper and mitigate the rigor of the law.* . . . And so it appeareth that equity taketh not away the very right, but only that that seemeth not to be right by the general words of the law.[34]

Yet as the Court of Chancery became even more established and institutionalized, the nature of equity as a flexible power to correct the law decreased. Interestingly, the institutionalization of equity caused its equitable nature to decrease, with equity eventually becoming just another body of law, although a body of law dealing with the subjects and remedies—injunctions, specific performance, restitution, and others—that emanated historically from the chancellor's jurisdiction. This transformation of equity from the power to cure the defects of the law's generality to simply a separate body of law took place continuously from the seventeenth century to the present. Now, far from the idea originally set out by Aristotle, furthered by Cicero, and described by St. German, equity jurisdiction is such that commentators can say things like:

> It is very certain that no court of chancery jurisdiction would at the present day consciously and intentionally attempt to correct the rigor of the law or to supply its defects, by deciding contrary to its settled rules, in any manner, to any extent, or under any circumstances beyond the already settled principles of equity jurisprudence. . . . Nor would a chancellor at the present day assume to decide the facts of a controversy according to his own standard of right and justice, independently of fixed rules, . . . he is governed in his judicial functions by doctrines and rules embodied in precedents, and does not in this respect possess any greater liberty than the law judges.[35]

That the power of courts of equity to *do* equity, in the Aristotelian sense, has declined is as interesting as is its rise in the first instance. We can see from Aristotle and his successors why it would seem important to have an institution that could correct the mistakes that are the inevitable consequence of law's generality. Yet despite arguments such as those first made by Aristotle, that very power has been diminishing and not expanding. Ironically, courts of equity have become increasingly less equitable. One possible explanation for this phenomenon is that the need for a separate institution, such as a court of equity, is less if the primary interpreters of the law can exercise this correcting power in their own right.[36] If *all* judges and *all* interpreters have the power to rectify the mistakes occasioned by law's generality—and that is plainly a growing understanding of the power of American judges[37]—then the necessity of a separate correcting institution evaporates. Insofar as all adjudicators are empowered to find or create implicit exceptions in general rules when applying those general rules without exception would produce mistakes, then the equitable power exists within the law and need not be created outside it.

But although the acceptability of such correction by all interpreters has grown over time, this growth in the equitable powers of all judges does not appear to be the sole explanation for the legalization of equity. Another possible explanation is that the wide array of choices available to an equitable decisionmaker is simply too wide. Although people given too narrow an array of choices will typically try to expand the array, people given too wide an array will come up with ways of narrowing the range of their own choices. If life is not necessarily better when we are compelled to choose among 250 varieties of mustard, to take an example from a recent study documenting what one researcher has called the "tyranny of freedom," then so too might equitable decisionmakers see the same drawbacks to unlimited freedom.[38] If so, then equity may have become progressively more rulelike just because the total freedom or *discretion* that Aristotle envisaged in theory may have turned out to be too much freedom in practice.[39] For generations of equitable decisionmakers, the simple mandate to do equity, to do justice, to use their discretion, may have been too much freedom. The transformation from equity back to law, even accepting the mistakes that law by its generality necessarily makes, may have been the inevitable reaction to the tyranny of freedom or the paralysis of discretion.

Perhaps most important in explaining the legalization of equity, however, is the recurring concern with the potentially arbitrary and nonpredictable nature of the equitable power, regardless of who exercises it. The classic characterization of the concern comes from Lord Selden in the sixteenth century, who observed that "equity is a roguish thing. For law we have a measure. . . . Equity is according to the conscience of him that is Chancellor, and as that is longer or narrower so is equity. 'Tis all one as if they should make the standard for the measure a Chancellor's foot."[40] Similarly, Lord Pomeroy observed that if equity were to be understood "as the decision upon the facts and circumstances of a case which would be made by a man of intelligence and high principle," then "it needs no argument to show that . . . every decision would be a virtual arbitration, and all certainty in legal rules and security of legal rights would be lost."[41]

The history of equity as an institution thus foreshadows our problem. Insofar as there is no mechanism for correcting the mistakes that will inevitably be made under a procedure of decisionmaking by generalization, then there will be some decisions that at the very least are erroneous, and that will seem to some, as they did to Plato and Aristotle, ridiculous, disgraceful, absurd, or unjust. Yet insofar as the mechanism for correcting these mistakes is established, that mechanism will itself be the servant of the discretion of the error-correctors, a discretion that will seem to some to be the wise allocation of decisionmaking authority to sensible people, but will seem to others to be no less variable than the size of the chancellor's foot. This variability will also produce mistakes, even though the mistakes coming from excess discretion are of a quite different kind from the mistakes coming from the necessary generality of rules. When equity is unavailable, we will see all too clearly the errors that are a consequence of generalization. But when we seek to establish a mechanism for correcting these errors, we often see equally clearly the errors of a different kind that come from granting real people with real failings the discretion to determine when the errors of generalization should be corrected and when they should not.

# CHAPTER 2

# Pit Bulls,
# Golden Retrievers,
# and Other Dangerous Dogs

## Attacks by Pit Bulls and the Attack on Pit Bulls

The 1980s saw a dramatic increase in attacks by dogs on children, on adults, and on other dogs. Although attacks by all kinds of dogs contributed to the increase, it turned out that a disproportionate number of attacks, many quite severe, came from a single breed. This breed, the pit bull terrier, more simply the pit bull and less simply the American Staffordshire terrier, was thought to be more aggressive and tenacious in fighting than other dogs and because of the severity of its bite more likely to cause death or serious injury than other dogs. These traits, it was said, explained a rise in pit bull attacks far in excess of what could be accounted for by any rise in the total number of dogs or the total number of pit bulls. To Edward I. Koch, then the mayor of New York City, the pit bull was like "a great white shark," and needed to be dealt with in the same way.[1]

Mayor Koch's warning did not go unheeded. In the wake of increased pit bull attacks, many American municipalities listened to Koch and other exercised citizens by enacting ordinances prohibiting people from owning or keeping pit bulls. Some of these ordinances "grandfathered" existing pit bulls but others did not. Some, like the ordinance in Cincinnati, made pit bull ownership a crime, while others made it a civil offense, somewhat like a motor vehicle violation. New York imposed special registration and insurance requirements upon pit bull owners that were not imposed upon the owners of other breeds. But through numerous regulatory variants, the same idea persisted: pit bulls were to be eliminated, or at least were to be subject to more restrictions than other breeds.[2]

To the surprise of proponents of pit bull restrictions, adverse reaction to these restrictions followed immediately, and was as swift and as angry as the furor that had inspired the restrictions in the first place. Using inflammatory rhetoric such as "canine racism" or likening the banning of pit bulls to the imprisonment of AIDS victims, pit bull owners insisted that the vast majority of pit bulls did not attack people, and indeed did not have aggressive dispositions at all.[3] Although there were dangerously aggressive pit bulls, the pit bull owners and their sympathizers acknowledged, there were many docile pit bulls as well. Moreover, the owners argued, restrictions on pit bulls were not only overinclusive, restricting numerous nonharmful pit bulls, but were underinclusive as well. For not only were there also dangerously aggressive Rottweilers, Doberman pinschers, and German shepherds, as is well known, but one could also find dangerously aggressive cocker spaniels, Irish setters, and even golden retrievers. The incidents of dangerous aggression, so the argument went, were attributable to particular dogs and particular dog owners, but neither as a matter of fairness nor as a matter of empirical accuracy could these tragic incidents be blamed on entire breeds.

In opposing the various pit bull restrictions, the pit bull owners proposed instead a variety of "dangerous dog" or "vicious dog" ordinances.[4] Under these laws, no penalties, prohibitions, or restrictions would be imposed until after a documented incident involving the particular dog. Only those individual dogs found "guilty" of an attack would be subject to restrictions.[5] This approach, the pit bull defenders claimed, would precisely target particular problem dogs, and would not require reliance on inaccurate, prejudiced, and stereotypical generalizations about entire breeds of dogs. "We strongly believe that measures should deal with deeds, not breeds," proclaimed Noreen Rubin of the American Kennel Club, neatly encapsulating the fundamental theory of the alternative approach.[6]

The contrast between the two approaches presents clearly the difference between generalization and particularization. On the one hand we have actuarial generalization by breeds, with the characteristics of the breed as a whole taken to be the characteristics of each member of the breed. And on the other hand we have particularization, focusing on particular attacks by particular dogs. The aggregate characteristics of the class are of no consequence, for we pay attention to each individual dog and each individual act. Thus, insofar as the attribute of being a pit bull probabilistically (measured against the baseline of all dogs) but far from universally indicates the trait of viciousness, we confront again the question whether it is wrong to base our decisions on statistically relevant but nonuniversal characteristics of a class or category. May we act against all members of the class (breed) on the basis of traits that only some of them possess, as the breed-specific pit bull regulations would have it, or must we avoid the stereotypes even when they are statistically relevant and instead focus only on the particular acts or particular individuals that are our real concern?

As with the examples in the previous chapters, we have to start by getting our facts straight, and so the initial question must be an empirical one. Is the attribute of being a pit bull a statistically sound indicator of viciousness, or is the fact that a dog is a pit bull spurious to its viciousness, no more related to the viciousness of the dog than the terrain of the human cranium is related to its owner's personality?

Looking at what evidence we have, it turns out that the generalizations underlying pit bull restrictions do indeed have the kind of empirical support that distinguishes them from purely spurious generalizations. Although there is some difference of opinion on the empirical question, there appears to be substantial evidence for the proposition that the probability of dangerously aggressive behavior (as well as the extent of injury from attack) on the part of pit bulls (and several other breeds, including chow chows, Akitas, and the aforementioned Doberman pinschers, Rottweilers, and German shepherds) is significantly higher than the probability of dangerously aggressive behavior on the part of the entire population of dogs. It also appears, however, that the probability of dangerously aggressive behavior on the part of pit bulls is still quite low. Pit bulls, chow chows,

Akitas, Doberman pinschers, Rottweilers, and German shepherds are more likely to be dangerously aggressive than dogs in general, but most pit bulls and most members of these other breeds are still not dangerously aggressive at all. Moreover, it appears that the training of the individual dog and the disposition of the individual dog may be better predictors of dangerous aggressiveness than variations in breed.[7]

Yet although most pit bulls are not aggressive, and although breed might not be the *best* predictor of aggressiveness, both breed in general and the pit bull breed in particular turn out to be statistically sound probabilistic predictors of aggressiveness. Many insurance companies, for example, have on the basis of their own actuarial studies imposed higher rates for homeowner's insurance (which typically includes liability for injuries caused by the homeowner's dogs) for homes with pit bulls, Dobermans, chow chows, Akitas, German shepherds, and Rottweilers, even though the companies do not otherwise impose higher rates for homes with dogs.[8] The actuarial behavior of the insurance companies is also consistent with other evidence supporting the conclusion that the percentage of aggressive dogs in general, and certainly the percentage of aggressive golden retrievers, is lower than the percentage of aggressive pit bulls. For example, a 1987 report by the Humane Society of the United States indicated that between 1983 and 1987 there had been twenty-eight deaths coming after dog bites, that twenty of these deaths were attributed to pit bull bites, and that pit bulls accounted during this period for only about one percent of all American dogs.[9] Similarly, investigations of dog bite incidents in Cincinnati, Ohio, and Riverside, California, concluded that pit bulls, again representing approximately one percent of the dogs in these communities, accounted for between 6 and 7 percent of the reported dog bites.[10]

So suppose on the basis of these rough data we hypothesize, purely for the sake of example, that about one in five pit bulls is dangerously aggressive, that about one in twenty of all dogs is dangerously aggressive, and that about one in forty golden retrievers is dangerously aggressive. The one-in-twenty probability for all dogs is thus the aggregate of a series of subprobabilities, including dogs with higher probabilities than one in twenty of being dangerously aggressive, such as pit bulls, and dogs with lower probabilities than one in twenty of being dangerously aggressive, such as golden retrievers.

The statistical soundness of the generalization that pit bulls are dangerously aggressive, however, is a slightly more complex question than just suggested, because there is undeniably considerable human influence not only over the aggressiveness of individuals dogs, but also over the aggressiveness of entire breeds. By selecting favored traits and deselecting disfavored ones, breeds may be bred and developed to emphasize certain behaviors and deemphasize others. There is much truth to the view, therefore, that pit bulls are as a breed more aggressive than golden retrievers because of centuries-old breeding patterns. In other words, pit bulls are more aggressive than most dogs partly because human beings have made them so. At least some of the contemporary pit bull problem, consequently, may stem from the way in which the practice of breeding pit bulls for aggressiveness has increased in recent years as the demand for pit bulls as protectors or as weapons (especially for those engaged in drug-dealing and other unlawful activities) has increased, and as pit bulls have become the dog of choice for illegal dog fighting. Moreover, and even apart from the way in which entire breeds have been bred to emphasize certain behavioral patterns and deemphasize others, the behavior of individual dogs is properly recognized as being substantially under the control of the dog's owner or handler. It is possible to train a pit bull to be more or less aggressive, just as it is possible to do the same, sometimes successfully and sometimes not, with most other dogs.

Still, there are reasons why we see few golden retrievers as guard dogs, and few pit bulls as pets in families with small children, and these reasons are not exhausted by training methods or even recent breeding patterns. The evidence makes clear that some breeds of dogs are simply more aggressive than others, and resistance to this conclusion appears to be, at least in part, a function of the proclivity of people to anthropomorphize the characteristics of dogs more than they do the characteristics of other nonhuman creatures. If we can believe that certain kinds of snakes are shy and others bold, and so too with birds and fish, then why do some people find it so difficult to believe the same of dogs?

Yet even though it is true that pit bulls as a class have a greater propensity to viciousness than do dogs as a class, and even though pit bulls as a breed have greater tendencies toward viciousness than the overwhelming majority of other breeds, these facts do not by themselves make the case for pit-bull-specific regulation. Because such regulations rest only on a statistical tendency and not on an inexorable relationship, any restriction on a dog simply because of its *being* a pit bull will restrict many pit bulls that, individually, are in no need of restriction. Conversely, any restriction targeted at pit bulls because they are pit bulls will fail to restrict many dogs that are not pit bulls but that nevertheless present precisely the traits that concern those who are worried about dog attacks. By using the attribute of being a pit bull as a *proxy* for the trait of viciousness, therefore, all the breed-specific regulatory approaches carry with them the inevitable consequences of both under- and overinclusiveness.[11]

As we examine the virtues and vices of this kind of regulation by proxy, it is worthwhile considering the alternatives. One of these alternatives, of course, would be to regulate *all* dogs and not just pit bulls. Although it is true that the alternative of regulating all dogs would regulate a larger class than regulating only pit bulls, and although it is also true that regulating all dogs would be more overinclusive than regulating all pit bulls, neither of these facts is determinative, for the question of the evil of "singling out" an individual or group for harsh treatment is analytically distinct from the question of the size of the category that receives the harsh treatment.[12] In his autobiography, former professional football player Jerry Kramer recounts a story in which an African-American teammate was asked how he was treated by legendarily demanding and abusive coach Vince Lombardi. Understanding perfectly the import of the question, and seeking to exonerate Lombardi from charges of racism while being truthful about Lombardi's style of coaching, the player responded, "He treats us all the same—like dogs."[13] As this comment so efficiently illustrates, the fact of bad treatment and the fact of morally culpable unequal treatment are different, and treating everyone equally badly, however bad that may be, fails as an exemplification of the fault of treating people unequally. Treating *all* dogs badly, therefore, or at least subjecting all dogs to regulation, would appear to eliminate the particular problem of stereotyping and overgeneralization to which the opponents of breed-specific regulations have so vociferously objected.

But would it? If all dogs were to be regulated or restricted because of problems attributed to dangerous or vicious dogs, then the same issue that had presented itself in the context of different breeds of dog would now resurface in the context of different kinds of animals. Most dogs are not dangerous, but some other animals are, including a few that are occasionally kept as household pets, such as pythons, crocodiles, piranhas, and the occasional monkey. If a special regulatory approach were adopted for all dogs and just for dogs solely because *some* dogs were vicious and dangerous, then this approach would be strikingly analogous to adopting a special regulatory approach just for pit bulls because some pit bulls are vicious and dangerous. And because there appears to be strong empirical evidence to support the conclusion that dogs are more likely to cause injury than most other categories of household pets, and more likely to cause injury than the class of household pets generally (a class that includes not only the occasional python and crocodile but also millions upon millions of cats, canaries, rabbits, hamsters, gerbils, tropical fish, and countless other nondangerous creatures), then singling out dogs because of their proclivity to dangerousness, at least relative to other household animals, is strikingly similar to singling out pit bulls because of their proclivity to dangerousness relative to other dogs.[14] Just as the regulation of pit bulls but not other dogs produces substantial regions of both under- and overinclusiveness, so too would the regulation of dogs but not other household animals have the same effect. Yet regulating all dogs not only seems benign to most people; it is even the alternative of choice for those who object to breed-specific regulation.

It is curious, therefore, that many people who would not be troubled by singling out dogs for special treatment but not gerbils and other noncanine household pets are severely exercised by singling out pit bulls but not other dogs. As long as the singled-out class (pit bulls and dogs, respectively) possesses the feared trait (viciousness) to a greater extent than some larger class (dogs and household pets, respectively), then the two cases are structurally identical. To be consistent, anyone who objects to the special treatment of pit bulls because the special treatment inappropriately generalizes about pit bulls should also object to the special treatment of dogs because the special treatment inappropriately generalizes about dogs.[15]

But perhaps analogizing the pit bull/dog comparison to the dog/household animal comparison does not get to the real objection of the dog lovers. After all, those who have opposed the various pit bull regulations might very well also oppose the idea of general dog regulations. They could argue that the proper response to their concern about breed stereotyping is not to broaden the category of regulation, which would only make the stereotyping more pervasive by stereotyping all dogs and not just pit bulls. Instead, they would probably insist, the solution is to impose restrictions only on the particular dogs who have actually caused particular and identified problems. Only in this way, so the argument would go, would we achieve the fairness and justice that come from treating each dog as an individual, and from evaluating each dog on the basis of *its* behavior, and not on the aggregate or average behavior of the class—whether it be the class of pit bulls or the class of all dogs—to which the individual dog just happens to belong.

There are two ways in which we could pursue the goal of treating each dog as an individual and not as a member of a stereotyped group. The first would be to tailor the restrictions to even narrower predictive indicators. Suppose we could give each dog a test, much as we give each prospective entrant to college or university a Scholastic Aptitude Test (SAT) or American College Test, but in the case of dogs the test would be designed to identify traits indicating viciousness or aggressiveness. So rather than asking dogs to do analogies or arrange shapes in order, animal control officers might require the dogs to relate to lifelike dolls, to react to human sounds, or to interact with other dogs. In this way the authorities could determine just which individual dogs were vicious rather than assuming that dogs were vicious just because they were pit bulls, or just because they were dogs, or just because they were a member of some other class.

Yet although individualized testing would probably reduce the degree of imprecision of using breed as an indicator or predictor of likely viciousness, the differences would be differences of degree and not differences of kind. Assume (a very big assumption, as we shall see in later chapters) for the time being that there are no errors in the more individualized (clinical) assessment of potential viciousness.[16] Thus we assume that every dog identified by the clinical tests as potentially more vicious than most other dogs really is potentially more vicious than most other dogs. Even with this assumption, however, the components of that seemingly individualized assessment are still probabilistic predictions based on various proxies. Just as the individualized testing of prospective college students remains a process of probabilistic prediction of college performance based on how one performs on a test that is not itself identical with what is expected in college, so too in the dog example is the testing of a particular dog still based on nonparticularized and nonindividualized assessments of the likelihood that certain performances and certain attributes will predict viciousness. Suppose, for example, that the test entails putting each dog we are testing in a room with a lifelike doll of a seven-year-old child. If how a dog reacts to the doll is the basis for determining which dogs should be restricted and which not, then this assessment must necessarily be based on nonindividualized prior knowledge of the relationship between a dog's reaction to a doll and a dog's reaction to a real human being. And if in response to this objection the test were changed so that it involved putting the dog in contact with a real human being, there would still need to be a background assumption about how much an attack (or a nonattack) in controlled conditions indicated an attack (or nonattack) in the noncontrolled conditions that are the ultimate concern. Most significantly, and here we get to the crucial point, this background assumption is based on a probabilistic relationship—a generalization—about what is usually but not necessarily indicated about real-life aggressiveness by aggressiveness under test or clinical conditions.

Once we appreciate that even the seemingly individualized clinical testing of particular dogs is itself based on generalizations about the relationship between test behavior and real-world behavior, we should understand that the act of using membership in the class of pit bulls as a predictor of the likelihood of aggressiveness under real-world conditions is not fundamentally different from using clinical testing of this pit bull as a predictor of the likelihood of aggressiveness under real-world conditions. Indeed, the argument that seemingly individualized testing is not so different from stereotyping or generalizing by breed becomes even stronger once we recognize that the ability to predict the behavior of *this* pit bull in real conditions from the behavior of *this* pit bull under controlled conditions will necessarily be based on experience with other pit bulls, just as the ability to predict the performance of this student at university on the basis of this student's standardized tests is necessarily based on experience, in other settings, with other students. Once we are in the realm of prediction, it turns out that even so-called individualized assessment is far less individual and far more general than may be apparent at first glance. Looking at each dog as an individual dog, therefore, unavoidably involves assessments based on generalizations and based on what we know, probabilistically, about the behavior of other dogs under other conditions.

Having recognized that the conditions of testing—such as reacting to a doll—are not the ultimate concern, it then becomes apparent that even evaluations that may at first look individualized are nothing more than probabilistic predictions of future behavior based on the possession of certain characteristics or traits, with the clinical test serving only to identify the presence or absence of these particular traits. Accordingly, the so-called individualized test is not different in kind from making a prediction based on a dog's being a pit bull. Although it might be more readily apparent that a dog is a pit bull than that a dog is a doll-attacker, in both cases it is aggregate evidence from past events involving other dogs in other situations that leads us to say that possession of the relevant trait is probabilistically predictive of engaging in the relevant—that is, vicious—behavior.

It is true, at least in this example, that the "trait" of attacking a doll in a clinical test is probably a stronger predictor of a proclivity to attacking humans than is the trait of being a pit bull. But that the seemingly individualized clinical test is a stronger predictor than the seemingly less individualized possession of a trait that is obvious without testing turns out to be only an artifact of the example. Suppose we were to refine the nonclinical actuarial generalization "Nonneutered male pit bulls previously owned by people convicted of narcotics offenses are presumed to be dangerous." And suppose we were to make the clinical test cruder: all dogs that react aggressively to being beaten with a stick are assessed as being more aggressive than dogs that do not react aggressively under these conditions. Now it is no longer so clear that an individualized clinical test is a better predictor of actual aggressiveness than an observable attribute. If this version of an actuarial generalization is compared with this version of an individualized clinical test, it could very well be that nonneutered male pit bulls previously owned by drug dealers were substantially more likely to engage in unprovoked attacks than were dogs who reacted aggressively when provoked.

It turns out, therefore, that even analyses that look individualized are less so than they initially appear, because even individualized analyses are based on aggregate data about the relevance of certain traits. What distinguishes the individualized examination from the so-called stereotype or the so-called profile, therefore, is only the fact that the latter is obvious without closer inspection while the former is not, and that in some, but by no means all, of the cases the individualized analysis will provide a better predictor of the relevant behavior. But what appears to be an individualized analysis is simply an aggregate of stereotypes, and when we make a prediction based on this dog's being a pit bull previously owned by a drug dealer and being male and being three years old and having a proclivity to growl we are not doing anything fundamentally different from what we do when we make a prediction based solely on this dog's being a pit bull.

One response to the conclusion of this analysis represents the second form of individualized assessment, and it is close to the alternative seemingly suggested by the American Kennel Club representative who urged punishment of "deeds and not breeds." The proposal that appears to be behind this slogan would be an approach that would impose restrictions not on the basis of any advance prediction at all, but instead would impose punishment or liability only after the fact of an attack. Under this approach, it appears as if there is no prediction involved at all, for this alternative would impose the punishment or liability only on actual perpetrators. We could assume all dogs to be innocent, and then punish those dogs (and their owners) who were determined actually to have transgressed, just as we assume all citizens to be innocent of, say, burglary, and then punish only those who actually commit burglaries. One way of treating each dog and each owner as an individual would thus be to establish a system of after-the-fact liability for dog attacks. This system would protect by punishing all and only the guilty, and would thus be a system that would impose no restrictions, at least no restrictions designed to prevent dog attacks, in advance of any attack.

This alternative does appear to diminish the extent of predictive generalization, for by restricting only those dogs already determined to have committed an attack it eliminates the possibility of overinclusiveness, at least if we continue to assume no mistakes in the process of determining which dogs are guilty. But even if this system of after-the-transgression liability is successful in avoiding the problem of generalization, it does so at a cost that few societies are willing to pay. Consider, for example, the common highway speed limit. Although people are not punished unless they have actually violated the speed limit, the speed limit itself is a uniform restriction imposed on all drivers and is thus itself a generalization. The speed limit on the typical American interstate highway is sixty-five miles per hour, yet there are licensed drivers for whom such a speed exceeds their driving abilities, and there are drivers who have the ability to drive safely at considerably higher speeds. Even with the variability of road, traffic, and weather conditions set aside, it is clear that the typical speed limit, which is concerned not with excess speed as a problem in itself, but with speed as a producer of accidents, generalizes about all drivers and their abilities from what we know about most drivers and most of their abilities. More broadly, the speed limit generalizes about a class of drivers under a class of conditions in a class of locations, rather than being tailored, even were this possible, to particular drivers in (more) particular locations under particular conditions. If I am stopped for driving at seventy-five miles per hour on a good and straight highway on a clear dry day with light traffic when the speed limit is sixty-five, it will avail me not at all to claim that I am a far better than average driver and that it is unfair to stereotype me with the driving characteristics of those whose driving abilities are merely average.

The typical highway speed limit is thus but one example of a restriction that is based on generalizations about the behavior of people without recourse to individualized testing. The fact that I am not permitted to drive at a speed in excess of sixty-five, and the fact that people who are fifteen years old are not permitted to drive at all, are generalizations not different in kind from the generalization that leads to special restrictions on pit bulls. Similarly, the fact that all lawyers and all physicians are required to have a certain number of hours per year of continuing professional education is a restriction on all physicians and lawyers, a restriction that could be eliminated in favor of the more individualized method of imposing malpractice liability on those whose failure to keep up with changing methods caused injuries or losses. Indeed, we could even go so far as to say that the very act of licensing lawyers and physicians is an attempt to impose controls in advance of transgressions, and thus an attempt to predict, on the basis of imperfect generalizations, who should hold these positions and who should not. We could simply let anyone at all practice law and surgery, and impose liability and restrictions only on those who have at least once done it incompetently; but the fact that we attempt to control for expected as well as actual bad behavior is a common feature of social control. So to return to the speed limit example, we could say that people are free to drive as fast they wish and are liable only if they cause an accident; but the fact that this is a solution virtually no society has adopted is evidence of the unwillingness of societies to rest all of their social control on after-the-fact liability alone.

Thus, a policy of controlling "deeds and not breeds" would be a policy much like letting all people practice surgery or law until something goes amiss, and like letting people drive as fast as they want to unless they cause an accident. The fact that we do not do this for surgery, law, or driving suggests that the argument that we should do so for dogs turns out to work better as a slogan than as a policy. Punishing "deeds and not breeds" might be possible in theory (although it still tends to assume that committing one attack is predictive of committing other attacks, itself a probabilistic assumption based on a generalization about canine behavior), but would be a form of regulation quite different from much of the rest of what we commonly take to be appropriate regulatory approaches. Yet the fact that these widely accepted regulatory approaches routinely rely on generalizations about people and their behavior, or classes of people and the behavior of those classes, strongly suggests that generalizing about classes is more prevalent, and more accepted, than is often appreciated. If there is something troubling about restricting pit bulls because they are pit bulls, and perhaps there is, it cannot simply be the fact that this approach is based on a generalization that might not hold in some, or even in many, particular instances.

## Dog Stereotyping Redux: The American Kennel Club Guide

Although breed-specific restrictions are not fundamentally different from other methods of regulation, the cries of unfairness have resonated with many people. The claim of unfairness may not, as we have just seen, make much sense, but it has nevertheless hit home, and the opponents of breed-specific control have in many localities carried the day. Most of the breed-specific regulations have been repealed, typically to be replaced with just the kind of after-the-fact restrictions on "vicious" or "dangerous" dogs that the opponents of "dog stereotyping" have long advocated.[17] Despite the fact that regulation based on class characteristics—all fourteen-year-old drivers and all dogs, for example—is part of the stock of every society's regulatory arsenal, the rhetorical and consequently the political war has frequently been won by those who have managed to persuade the people who make our laws that there is something fundamentally unjust about singling out a certain class of dogs for special treatment.

Although surprisingly few breed-specific controls remain, the same controversy has resurfaced, only in slightly different clothing. In this case the issue was not formal regulation, but seemingly authoritative guidance to prospective dog owners. Those prospective (or current) dog owners can refer to any of a large number of published guides to dogs, but none is more widely used than the American Kennel Club's *Complete Dog Book*. Published since 1929, and now in its nineteenth edition, it has been almost since its first publication the authoritative reference work on purebred dogs. Used by both breeders and owners, it has sold over two million copies, and in its more than 700 pages contains highly detailed information about the characteristics of all the breeds recognized by the American Kennel Club.

The nineteenth edition, however, contained perhaps too much information. Published in 1998, it included for the first time "breed profiles" that described behavioral characteristics.[18] For more than a hundred breeds, the profiles were quite innocuous, including descriptions such as "affectionate," "friendly," "energetic," and "loyal." But 40 of the 145 breed profiles had a harder edge, characterizing the breed as "not good" for or with children. The description of the German shorthaired pointer, for example, included the assessment "Relationship with children—not good." Similar negative evaluations of a breed's compatibility with children were offered for toy poodles, borzois, Maltese terriers, whippets, Yorkshire terriers, Dalmatians, and more than 30 other breeds.

As with pit bull regulation a decade earlier, the reaction by dog owners to the *Complete Dog Book*'s breed profiles was immediate and irate. A veterinarian representing the Humane Society of the United States railed against what he called "breedism," which he likened to racism and sexism. It was "absurd" and "outrageous" to "discriminate" in this way, the Humane Society insisted, not because the breed profiles were statistically spurious, but because "we have to look at each animal as an individual."[19] In like fashion, others decried the American Kennel Club's willingness to make "blanket statements" or to rely on "stereotypes."[20] "Dogs are not vehicles stamped out of an assembly line. Each one is an individual," complained the incensed secretary of the Dachshund Club of America. And once again there were heard the cries of "canine racism," this time from Roger Caras, then president emeritus of the American Society for the Prevention of Cruelty to Animals.[21]

With respect to *The Complete Dog Book*, the victory of the objectors to "stereotyping" was even more dramatic than it was in the case of breed-specific pit bull regulation. The American Kennel Club recalled the entire balance of its first printing, approximately 10,000 copies, announcing that it "sincerely regrets the distress caused to dog owners and breeders," and offering the reassurance that "procedures have been put in place to prevent a recurrence."[22] Despite the fact that virtually none of the objectors had claimed that the breed profiles were statistically spurious, and had thus implicitly admitted that the stereotypes contained a kernel or more of truth, the existence of generalizations about breeds, and specifically the generalization about being not good with children, set in train a series of events such that the American Kennel Club could no longer, as a matter of politics and public relations, stand behind the profiles. As with attempts to target dangerous dogs by breed, even the attempts to describe negative behavioral characteristics by breed appears to have run afoul of the strong sense that nonparticularistic descriptions, even of types of dogs, were the functional equivalent of the most pernicious forms of racial stereotyping.

## Stereotypes Revisited

The continuing controversy about stereotyping dogs by breed illustrates two important lessons. The first is that what some people pejoratively call stereotyping is an essential part of our cognitive and decisionmaking apparatus. It is simply how we think. The fact that many people who are uncomfortable with breed-specific regulations remain comfortable with dog-specific regulations is powerful evidence of the way in which methods of decisionmaking employing no generalizations at all are a virtual impossibility. Even better evidence for the ubiquity of generalizing comes from the fact that many people who are uncomfortable with breed-specific regulations are comfortable with probabilistic predictions based on various other attributes, including behavior under simulated and therefore nonidentical clinical conditions. By exposing the way in which most objections to generalizations turn out merely to substitute another generalization, we have underscored the much larger point that avoiding decisionmaking by generalization, even nonuniversal generalization, is well-nigh impossible.

A few more examples may reinforce our understanding of the inevitability of nonuniversal generalization. When I travel from Massachusetts to New York I ordinarily take an airplane, and I do so because flying is usually faster than driving or taking the train. To my regret, however, I have not infrequently been delayed in flying to such an extent that in retrospect it is clear that it would have been faster to drive. Nevertheless, I persist in flying in most cases, and I do so because I believe that the generalization that flying is faster is a better guide for my travel decisions than any other decision procedure I can devise. Similarly, I evaluate the reliability of types or makes of cars or household appliances on the basis of nonuniversal generalizations, and I cannot imagine how it would be otherwise. People may not get as exercised about stereotyping Ford cars or Hotpoint refrigerators as they do about stereotyping pit bulls, but the processes are essentially the same. If I choose to buy Fords because they are more reliable, or refrain from buying Fords because they are less reliable, I am basing my decision on the belief that a car's being a Ford is a good predictor of its reliability, even as I recognize that some particular Fords are not reliable and that many other particular cars are. If reliability is for me an important criterion in choosing a car, therefore, the decision to buy or not to buy a Ford is essentially the same as the decision not to own a pit bull. One of the large lessons of the story of the pit bulls, therefore, is that decisionmaking by generalization, popular rhetoric to the contrary notwithstanding, appears to be an unavoidable feature of our decision-making existence.

Cars and household appliances share with dogs the property of not being human beings. But this banality points the way to the second lesson to be drawn from the case of the pit bulls. Because dogs, unlike cars, unlike appliances, unlike almost all other animals, and indeed unlike almost all other household pets, are often thought of in humanoid ways, the moral and rhetorical devices we typically deploy when we are talking about people come quickly, and perhaps too quickly, to mind. A few people might with a straight face be able to refer to "breedism," but no one has yet been accused of "brandism" for believing that Volvos are more reliable than Jaguars. Yet the social salience of the rhetoric and morality of antidiscrimination and antistereotyping makes it tempting to expand the moral rhetoric of antidiscrimination into other areas. Because the tendencies to see dogs in particularly humanoid ways are especially strong, the expansion of the moral rhetoric of antidiscrimination into the world of dogs is one that comes with particular ease.

Although moving from the rhetoric of antidiscrimination with respect to human beings to the rhetoric of antidiscrimination with respect to dogs is widespread, it still may not be right. One reason why subsequent chapters of this book will deal extensively with discrimination, with stereotyping, and with profiling is that these are the terms and the concepts that have been so effectively, and sometimes properly, used in cases involving generalizations based on race, on gender, on sexual orientation, and on other, to borrow the language of American constitutional law, "suspect" classifications.[23] But as the case of the pit bulls indicates, the presence of this antidiscrimination language in our public rhetorical space has made it easy—too easy—for any opponent of any classification to object that it is discriminatory, that it is a stereotype, that it is a case of profiling, and, as we saw with dogs, even that it is an example of racism. But as we also saw in the case of the dogs, on closer analysis the rhetoric is often seen to be misplaced.

Yet even as we recognize the way in which the rhetoric of unconstitutional, illegal, and immoral discrimination has seeped into far less morally problematic areas, the analysis of pit bulls may have created as many problems as it solves. For although the analysis cautions us against assuming that generalizations and stereotypes can (or should) ever be eliminated entirely, it raises questions regarding the distinction between permissible and impermissible stereotypes about people. If the principal argument against the opponents of breed-specific restrictions on dogs is that breed-specific restrictions are little different from a large number of inevitable and widely accepted bases for restriction, then is not the same true for people as well? If stereotyping dogs is permissible not only because dogs are dogs and not people, but also because stereotyping and generalizing are ineliminable, then what does this say about people, and what does it say about the distinction between permissible and impermissible stereotypes? It is this conundrum that will be the central focus of much of the rest of this book.

# CHAPTER 3

# A Ride on
# the Blue Bus

## Betty Smith and the Blue Bus Problem

On January 6, 1941, Betty Smith was driving her car from Dorchester to Winthrop, Massachusetts. Entering Winthrop at about one o'clock in the morning, she was crowded off the road by a bus, and collided with a parked car. Smith was injured in the accident, and sued Rapid Transit, Inc., in the Superior Court of the Commonwealth of Massachusetts.

Because the accident occurred in the middle of the night, because the bus that forced her off the road did not stop, and because she was preoccupied with trying to avoid the accident, Betty Smith did not see any of the identifying marks on the bus. At the trial she could testify only that the vehicle that forced her off the road was a bus, and that it was "a great, big, long wide affair." Smith was, however, able to prove that the Rapid Transit Company had been licensed by the City of Winthrop to operate buses on the very route on which the accident had occurred; that Rapid Transit's buses left Winthrop Highlands on the thirty-minute trip to Maverick Square, Boston, at 12:10 A.M., 12:45 A.M., 1:15 A.M., and 2:15 A.M.; that this route included the Main Street location of the accident; and that no other company was licensed to operate its buses on this route.

Despite this evidence in support of the proposition that the bus that caused the accident was operated by Rapid Transit, the trial court refused to let the jury even consider the case. The judge ruled that Betty Smith could not, as a matter of law, recover against Rapid Transit, because there was no *direct* evidence that the bus that hit Smith was one of Rapid Transit's buses. This ruling was upheld by the Massachusetts Supreme Judicial Court, which noted that Rapid Transit's exclusive franchise "did not preclude private or chartered buses from using this street; the bus in question could very well have been operated by someone other than the defendant." The court acknowledged that this was unlikely and that "perhaps the mathematical chances somewhat favor the proposition that a bus of the defendant caused the accident." But "this was not enough," the court said, concluding that the mathematical probability that the bus in question was the defendant's bus was not the type of "direct" evidence that could lead a jury to have an "actual belief" in the proposition that this was one of Rapid Transit's buses.[1]

Had this been a criminal case, the ruling would strike us as unexceptionable. After all, the evidence that the bus belonged to Rapid Transit was hardly of the quality and quantity that would establish "beyond a reasonable doubt" that this was one of Rapid Transit's buses, especially given the small but hardly inconceivable possibility that the accident was caused by a private bus or by a chartered bus. But Smith's lawsuit was a civil and not a criminal case. Accordingly, the required standard of proof was not that of "beyond a reasonable doubt." Instead, Betty Smith needed to establish her case only "by a preponderance of the evidence." And as the equivalent phrase in English law, "by a balance of the probabilities," indicates, we ordinarily understand the preponderance of the evidence to be the equivalent of just over a 50 percent likelihood that the proposition asserted is true.[2] Whatever the possibility might have been that a private or chartered bus caused the accident, no one claimed that the probability of such an occurrence was anything approaching 50 percent.[3] Thus there seemed to be no reasonable denial that the evidence presented by Smith established to a probability considerably greater than .5 that this was Rapid Transit's bus. But if that was the case, then why did Betty Smith not win?

Why not indeed? Smith's case is hardly unique,[4] and the Supreme Judicial Court's ruling is generally in line with the law as it was then, and as it is now.[5] Yet it still seems odd that if the plaintiff is required only to prove her case to a probability of .51 (to put it roughly), then statistical evidence that would do so is thought by itself to be insufficient, or so the courts routinely conclude. Indeed, it seems so odd to so many people that Smith's case has become a staple of academic teaching of evidence law in law schools, and the centerpiece of much of academic writing about what has come to be called the problem of "naked statistical evidence."[6] Commonly, the problem is made analytically crisper when presented as a hypothetical version of the *Smith* case known as the Blue Bus Problem: Suppose it is late at night, under one version of the problem, and an individual's car is hit by a bus. This individual cannot identify the bus, but she can establish that it is a blue bus, and she can prove as well that 80 percent of the blue buses in the city are operated by the Blue Bus Company, that 20 percent are operated by the Red Bus Company, and that there are no buses in the vicinity except those operated by one of these two companies. Moreover, each of the other elements of the case—negligence, causation, and, especially, the fact and the extent of the injury—is either stipulated or established to a virtual certainty. In these circumstances can the plaintiff recover in civil litigation against the Blue Bus Company, or, if not (as the overwhelming majority of American courts would conclude), then why not? Or consider a variation of the Blue Bus Problem even closer to Betty Smith's case: The plaintiff's car is hit by a bus late at night and all she knows about the offending vehicle is that it was a bus. Eighty percent of the buses in town are operated by the Blue Bus Company. Can the plaintiff win a lawsuit againt the Blue Bus Company on that evidence alone, assuming, as in the previous examples, that there is nothing in dispute about the issues of causation, negligence, or injury?

## The Generality of Statistics and the Statistics of Generality

Scholars have been debating the Blue Bus Problem for decades, sometimes in the highly technical language of mathematical statistics, and sometimes in a more commonsense way.[7] A few scholars have defended the legal system's skepticism about statistical evidence. Laurence Tribe and, later, Charles Nesson, for example, have pointed to the way in which explicit acknowledgment of the probability of error might, even if accurate, undermine confidence in the legal system. Other scholars urge increased acceptance of statistical evidence, sometimes arguing that a legal rule should not be premised on keeping jurors and the public in the dark about the actual nature and consequences of legal decisions. Yet regardless of the correct outcome of this scholarly debate, it is important to draw attention to the way in which the debate about naked statistical evidence links more closely than the literature recognizes to the superficially different questions about the role of generality in decisionmaking.

Recall the discussion of pit bull regulation in chapter 2. The problem (to some) with using the generalization "pit bull," which gathered up all the individual pit bulls with their diverse individual characteristics under the single category of pit bulls, was that one attribute of the category—a tendency toward dangerous aggressiveness—was not necessarily an attribute of each member of the category. The generalization about the danger of pit bulls is not spurious—the evidence plainly establishes that dangerousness exists in the class of pit bulls to a greater degree than it does in the class of all dogs, and to a greater degree than it does in almost all the subclasses that we call breeds—but there is still no disputing that many pit bulls, quite possibly the vast majority of them, are not dangerous at all.

Similarly with the Blue Bus Company. If the relevant attribute is ownership of a particular bus, as in the second version of the Blue Bus Problem, and if the Blue Bus Company owns 80 percent of all the buses, then the Blue Bus Company possesses the attribute of ownership of this particular bus to a higher probability than does any another possible defendant, just as pit bulls possess the attribute of dangerousness to a higher probability than most other breeds and to a higher probability than the class consisting of all dogs. Moreover, the Blue Bus Company possesses the attribute of ownership of the bus in question to a probability seemingly sufficient to justify liability in a civil lawsuit. If we were to hypothesize that 80 percent of the vicious dogs were pit bulls, then we could conclude, absent further information, that an attack by an otherwise unidentified vicious dog was 80 percent likely to have been an attack by a pit bull. Similarly, if 80 percent of the buses are owned by the Blue Bus Company, then we could conclude, absent further information, that an accident caused by an otherwise unidentified bus is 80 percent likely to have been an accident caused by a Blue Bus Company bus.

Casting the problem in this way brings to mind another famous hypothetical case, this one offered by the British philosopher L. Jonathan Cohen. In what he labels The Paradox of the Gatecrasher, Cohen hypothesizes a rodeo that charges for admission.[8] During the rodeo the organizers of the event count the spectators, and they discover that there are 1,000 in attendance. When at the end of the rodeo the organizers count the tickets collected at the ticket booth, however, it turns out that there are only 499 tickets in the ticket box. The mathematical corollary of this, of course, is that 501 of the 1,000 spectators at the rodeo were gatecrashers. So now suppose that the organizers of the rodeo bring a lawsuit against one—any one—of the 1,000 spectators for fraudulent entrance. No one saw this *particular* person enter fraudulently, and there is no other evidence connecting this particular defendant to a fraudulent entry. Yet still, absent any other evidence, there is a .501 probability that this person (or any of the other 999 spectators) was a gatecrasher. Why, then, cannot the statistical evidence by itself be sufficient to warrant a verdict, at least under the preponderance standard in civil litigation, in favor of the rodeo organizers? Cohen himself maintains that such a verdict would be profoundly unjust. For him the paradox consists not in the unwillingness of the courts to award a judgment to the rodeo organizers and against the alleged gatecrasher, because Cohen believes that this would be wrong. Rather, Cohen endorses the fact that courts would not award damages in such a case, but he finds it puzzling that courts continue to insist that the standard of proof in civil cases is a preponderance of the evidence, a standard that the .501 likelihood of gatecrashing by any one of the spectators appears to satisfy.

My aim is not to "solve" either the Paradox of the Gatecrasher or the Blue Bus Problem. It is, however, to show that both of these problems are best seen as variants on the larger problem of generality in decisionmaking. One way of doing this would be to start with seeing the problem of generality as an aspect of the problem of attempting to determine when we should and should not use statistically reliable but nonuniversal indicators. In this sense the problem of generality is "really" the problem of statistical inference, and thus the Blue Bus and Gatecrasher problems, which appear to be problems of statistical inference, resemble the problem of generality, because all are problems relating to the wisdom or justice of using nonuniversal but nonspurious statistical indicators.

Alternatively, and preferably, both the Blue Bus Problem and the Paradox of the Gatecrasher, which are typically presented as problems of statistical inference, are fundamentally problems about the use of generalizations. In each the issue is not simply a problem of statistics but instead a problem about the extent to which we can employ, at least for purposes of awarding damages in civil litigation, generalizations about rodeo spectators (most but not all entered fraudulently) and a generalization about the Blue Bus Company (owns most of the buses in this city). When the issue is framed in this way, the problems of generality and generalization become primary, and the problem of statistical inference is seen as but another way of describing what is at its core an issue about generalization.

The desirability of framing the issue as one fundamentally about generalization becomes even clearer once we understand that what the Massachusetts Supreme Judicial Court in *Smith* saw as the problem was not a problem of statistics at all. Rather, the court, although it did utilize the potentially confusing language of "mathematical chances" and "probability," was primarily focused on what it saw as the difference between so-called direct or actual evidence, on the one hand, and the kind of evidence that is based on the characteristics of the class of which the alleged perpetrator is a member, on the other.[9] This is even clearer in the Paradox of the Gatecrasher. Again, the fact that "statistics," in the numerical sense of that word, might have been part of the hypothetical rodeo organizers' case is largely beside the point. When the organizers bring a case against a particular individual, they base their claim on the attribution of nonspurious class characteristics—nonpayment of the admission charge—to an individual member of the class. In doing so, the organizers rely on the same process of generalization that Plato's training master relied on in attributing the characteristics of "the herd" to each of its members, that pit bull ordinances rely on in attributing the characteristics of the class of pit bulls to each individual pit bull, that insurance companies rely on in attributing the characteristics of the class of teenage male drivers to each teenage male driver, and that many of us rely on in attributing the honesty of the class of dealers in used automobiles to each dealer in used automobiles. In all these cases, the process, in the final analysis, is the process of basing decisions for all members of a class on nonspurious but nonuniversal characteristics of the class taken as a whole. This is the process of generalization, and this is the process of which the problem of so-called statistical evidence is but one component.

The conclusion of the immediately preceding paragraph notwithstanding, it may not be overly important whether it is statistical inference that is primary and generalization secondary, or generalization that is primary and statistical inference secondary. What is important is that we can appreciate that the seemingly disconnected issues of generality and statistical evidence are in fact remarkably similar, and that the resources that enable us to understand and negotiate the problem of generality are the same resources that can be used to understand and negotiate problems about the use of statistical evidence in civil and criminal trials. And once we understand this, there remains more to be said about these problems of statistical evidence and the light they shed on the issue of generality.

## Probabilistic Inference in an All-or-Nothing World

The Blue Bus and Gatecrasher problems are in an important way artifacts of the all-or-nothing manner in which most aspects of most modern legal systems operate. In much of nonlegal life people can act on their uncertainty by making decisions in accordance with the principle of expected value. In doing so, they value an uncertain outcome by multiplying the value of some set of consequences by the probability that those consequences will come to pass. The product is the expected value of those consequences. If you have a 50 percent chance of winning ten dollars, the value to you is five dollars. Just as a wager of eight dollars is therefore a good one if you are betting on a 10 percent chance of winning one hundred dollars, so too do we act in similar ways in much of our daily life. We invest less in risky investments than in more certain ones, we make shorter commitments when we are unsure of the value of what we are committing to than when we have greater confidence, we calculate how much insurance to buy on the basis of expected value (just as the insurance company does in determining how much to charge us), we plan travel times by factoring in the probability of delays, and we calculate expected fines in deciding whether it is worthwhile committing minor illegalities such as overtime parking, all of these decisions and more making the expression to "hedge one's bets" applicable in much more of our lives than the occasional trip to the racetrack. In these cases, and many more, an imprecise but serviceable conception of expected value guides many of our daily decisions.

Because statisticians understand and use the principle of expected value, to the statistician the Paradox of the Gatecrasher may be no paradox at all. If there is a .51 probability that any given spectator entered fraudulently, and if the purchase price of a ticket is $1.00, then the statistician sees the easy solution: the rodeo organizers recover 51 cents against each of the 1,000 spectators. In this way the rodeo organizers recover only their fair share of the proceeds, and each spectator is liable only to the extent of the likelihood that he or she entered without purchasing a ticket. And so too with the Blue Bus Problem. If there is a .80 chance that the bus that plainly negligently caused an indisputable $1,000 worth of damages to, say, Betty Smith, is a bus owned and operated by the Blue Bus Company, then the principle of expected value would indicate that Smith should recover $800 against the Blue Bus Company.

The law, however, does not operate this way. Perhaps oddly to the statistician, the law would give Smith all of her damages if she proved her case to a .51 probability, and nothing if she proved it to a .49 probability. And it would give her not a dollar more if she proved her case to a .90 probability than if she proved it to a .51 probability. With rare exceptions, the expected value of a plaintiff's claim, by which the extent of the plaintiff's proof would be multiplied by the extent of the plaintiff's damages, is not a principle of advanced legal systems.[10] These systems, we see throughout the world, are all-or-nothing affairs.[11]

In the context of a criminal case, our intuitions confirm the approach of the law. If there is a .70 chance that the defendant is the one who committed an aggravated assault, and if the penalty for aggravated assault is ten years' imprisonment, few of us, and not even the statisticians, would be comfortable imposing a sentence of seven years based on the principle of expected value. And perhaps that is so because of the strength of the maxim, first offered by William Blackstone, that "it is better that ten guilty persons escape, than that one innocent suffer."[12] The value we place on liberty, and thus the graveness of the error of denying liberty to the innocent, makes us uncomfortable with imprisoning those who are .30 likely to have done nothing wrong, and thus the principle of expected value is properly a stranger to the criminal law.

In civil cases, however, the aversion to expected-value verdicts seems less justifiable. After all, the plaintiff in a typical negligence case is claiming to have been injured through someone else's fault while doing nothing wrong. In such a case, it is not clear why erroneously denying recovery to a worthy plaintiff is any less harmful an error than erroneously awarding recovery against a nonnegligent defendant. To put it differently, the preponderance of the evidence standard presupposes that erroneous denials of liability and erroneous impositions of liability are equally regrettable.[13] The false positive is no worse than the false negative. And if this is so, if the Type I and Type II errors, to use the statistician's language, are equivalent, then it is by no means clear that the aversion to expected-value verdicts in criminal cases ought to be extended to civil cases.

The law, however, does not agree, and continues to be pervasively and perhaps perversely insistent on an all-or-nothing approach. The lessons of expected-value analysis notwithstanding, the law dismisses as too easy the statistician's solution to the Paradox of the Gatecrasher and the Blue Bus Problem. Most legal systems continue to resist expected-value outcomes, and as a result it is plausible to conclude that the difficulties presented by the Blue Bus Problem, the Paradox of the Gatecrasher, and other real and imagined examples are largely the products of the all-or-nothing character of most legal decisionmaking.

Once we see the relationship between the paradoxes of the law of evidence and the all-or-nothing nature of legal decision, however, we can understand the larger problem of generalization in a new light. For if the problem of statistical inference in the law of evidence is, as we have seen, little more than one instance of the problem of generalization, then the problems created by an all-or-nothing legal system parallel the problems created by the all-or-nothing parts of many other dimensions of our decisional lives. In numerous instances in which we employ probabilistically sound but nonuniversal generalizations in ordinary decisionmaking, it is because the nature of the decision makes an expected-value decision impossible or, at the very least, impractical. If I am looking for a pet, it is not possible for me to have a pit bull for one day out of seven and a golden retriever for the other six. Similarly, tax officials rarely conduct partial audits (even though some audits are more thorough than others), customs officials rarely conduct partial inspections, police officers cannot conduct partial stops, airlines do not believe that they can deal with the problem of pilots 10 percent more likely to cause an accident by having them fly 10 percent fewer flights, and hockey referees who are 75 percent sure that a player has committed a high-sticking infraction do not have the option of sending the offender to the penalty box for ninety seconds rather than the designated two minutes for that offense, any more than a football official unsure of whether a defensive lineman was offside can penalize the defense three yards rather than five. These and many more examples suggest that life as well as law is often an all-or-nothing affair, and that what looks at first to be the special all-or-nothing quality of the legal system may actually be found in much of nonlegal decisionmaking. In more cases than we or the statisticians might suppose, nonlegal decision-makers often understand themselves to be making all-or-nothing decisions (do I hire this person as a babysitter or not) in which the expected-value approach is just not available. The use of generalizations, therefore, appears to be not only an outgrowth of the frequent need to use generalizations as a time- and effort-saving heuristic in circumstances in which individual determinations would probably be too costly or too prone to the errors of discretion; it is also a function of the way in which expected-value decisionmaking is considerably more of a stranger to everyday decisional life than we may at first have fully appreciated.

## Individuality and Reliability

It is thus the nature of most of legal and more than we thought of nonlegal decisionmaking that requires us to engage in all-or-nothing decisionmaking. Consequently, if the nature of all-or-nothing decisionmaking pushes us toward what seem to many people to be unjust outcomes, then one way of understanding the instinct behind the *Smith* rule is as a desire to minimize the number of erroneous outcomes inevitably generated by all-or-nothing decision procedures. Perhaps the insistence on so-called direct or actual evidence, as the court in *Smith* naively put it, is explained by a reluctance to have the legal system forced into accepting the 20 percent error rate that giving Betty Smith 100 percent of her damages on an 80 percent chance of Rapid Transit's liability would entail.

Yet if this kind of error minimization is the goal, then it is hard to see how a supposed requirement of "direct" or "actual" evidence serves it. Initially, we can ask what the Massachusetts Supreme Judicial Court in *Smith* might have meant by the terms "direct" and "actual." Presumably the court had in mind evidence that comes from a perception of a witness, with that very witness then testifying to that perception in court.[14] Typically this would be a visual perception—an eyewitness—although there can also be perceptions by any of the other senses—hearing, smelling, tasting, and touching. But apart from sensory perception testified to under oath by the perceiver in court, it is difficult to see what the court could have meant by the terms "direct" and "actual."

If "direct" and "actual" refer to perceptual evidence testified to by the perceiver, then we must consider the reliability of this evidence as compared to the allegedly indirect or "nonactual" evidence offered in *Smith* and similar cases. Consider, therefore, another hypothetical variation of Betty Smith's case. Suppose Betty Smith testified that she saw what looked like the words "Rapid Transit" written in red letters on the side of the blue bus that hit her. But then suppose that on cross-examination the accuracy of her account is called into question by Rapid Transit's lawyer. Betty Smith, let us suppose, is forced to admit that it was foggy and rainy that night, that the eyeglasses she always wears were knocked from her head by the impact of the accident, that she first reported her observation of the words "Rapid Transit" not to the police officer who came upon the scene of the accident but only later after having consulted with an attorney, and that she saw the words only as the bus was heading away from her, at an angle to her direct vision, at a speed of no less than thirty miles per hour, and at a distance of no less than 200 feet. Yet despite all these reasons to doubt the accuracy of the hypothetical Smith's observation of the words "Rapid Transit," and despite the fact that it might be reasonable to place the probable accuracy of her observation of the words "Rapid Transit" at well less than .80, the very court that refused to let the real case go to the jury, even on a probability well above .80 that the bus in question was a Rapid Transit bus, would almost certainly have let the "fuzzy observation" case go to the jury on a probability well below .80 that the bus in question was a Rapid Transit bus. In this hypothetical case, the court would in all likelihood have said that these issues of credibility are for the jury and for the jury alone to determine.

Part of this anomaly of excluding more-reliable statistical evidence and admitting less-reliable personal testimony is explained by the widespread but empirically unsupported faith in eyewitness identification. Although there persists an aura of credibility historically attached to eyewitness accounts, a raft of serious psychological research has established that much of this historical faith in eyewitness testimony lacks a sound empirical foundation. People often see what they want to see, or see what they think they are expected to see, or see what they are positively reinforced in seeing. To put it slightly differently, people's perceptions are somewhere between usually and always filtered through their own biases, prejudices, and preconceptions; they simply forget or misremember what they saw; and they are afflicted with a host of other cognitive deficiencies that make eyewitness testimony much less reliable than the conventional wisdom would suppose.[15] If the preference for direct or actual evidence is based on a preference for perception over inference, then almost all of what we know about the deficiencies of human perception cast doubt on such a preference.

These doubts about perceptual abilities are exacerbated by the tendency of people not only to overweight perception as an empirical matter, but also to ignore what statisticians and psychologists call "base rates," thus leading people to make logical as well as empirical errors.[16] Consider an example made famous by Amos Tversky and Daniel Kahneman, an example that bears a close resemblance to the Blue Bus Problem.[17] Suppose that the Green Cab Company owns and operates taxis that are green in color, and the Blue Cab Company owns and operates blue taxis. Eighty-five percent of the taxis in town are the green taxis of the Green Cab Company, and the other 15 percent are the blue taxis of the Blue Cab Company. As in the *Smith* case, suppose a car is sideswiped or run off the road by a taxi, and a witness is 100 percent certain, presumably from the light on top of the cab, that the "guilty" car is a taxi, and is confident, but not certain, that the guilty taxi was blue. Suppose that the witness is 80 percent confident that the taxi was blue and thus that it was a taxi of the Blue Cab Company. On this basis, is it more likely that the taxi was a green taxi of the Green Cab Company or a blue taxi of the Blue Cab Company?

On these facts, most people would conclude, with the witness, that it is more likely that it was a blue taxi than that it was a green taxi and that the Blue Cab Company should therefore be held liable. But this conclusion gets it exactly wrong. The conclusion that the taxi was probably blue because the witness said so with a moderately high degree of confidence ignores the base-rate distribution of taxis. For most people, what they perceive as "evidence" overwhelms the underlying base rate. In other words, the conclusion that the taxi was blue ignores the fact that the witness's .2 likelihood of error must be applied to the actual distribution between blue and green taxis and not to a presumed 50–50 distribution when the distribution is not in fact 50–50. Thus the number of cases, on these probabilities, in which a witness said the cab was blue when it was green turns out to be somewhat higher than the number of cases in which a witness said the cab was green when it was blue. On these probabilities, in fact, the probability that the cab was green is .59

despite the fact that the witness was .80 certain that it was blue.[18]

The prevalence of ignoring the base rate, combined with the prevalence of overestimating the reliability of eyewitness testimony (which may be a contributing factor in people's willingness to ignore the base rate in cases like these), makes the legal system's prevailing skepticism about statistical evidence even more puzzling. As the above examples of fuzzy or otherwise uncertain observations are designed to illustrate, the kind of evidence commonly thought to be direct or nonstatistical is often far less reliable than the kind of evidence often thought to be indirect or statistical. Or, to translate this into the language of generality, it may frequently be the case that the inferences to be drawn from nonspurious but non-universal generalizations are empirically stronger than the inferences to be drawn from decisionmaking approaches that seemingly do not rely on generalizations or at least rely on smaller rather than larger ones.

There is an interesting parallel between the legal system's (and the public's) traditional but misguided preference for eyewitness testimony and the traditional and often equally misguided preference of many psychologists and physicians for clinical as opposed to actuarial assessments. Suppose the issue, a very common one, is trying to predict which offenders if released on parole will commit further offenses. Or suppose it is the similar issue of which people, having been found not guilty of some crime by reason of insanity, can safely be released into the community. In these and related cases the traditional view has been that a thorough and face-to-face psychological examination—a clinical assessment—is the most reliable method of predicting dangerousness. Yet much of the modern research has shown that actuarial assessments turn out to be more reliable than clinical ones.[19] If instead of performing a clinical assessment the authorities were simply to look at a group of actuarially tested but easily identified indicators—nature of the offense; age of the defendant; number of previous offenses; and so on—they would have more reliable indicators of dangerousness than if they were to rely on clinical assessments; and this is so even if the clinical assessments take into account these very same factors along with any others that the clinician believes relevant in the particular case. This outcome may at first seem surprising, but it is much like the problem with eyewitness testimony. Clinicians, even well-trained ones, often have excess confidence in their own perceptions, are sometimes influenced by biases and agendas that they themselves do not fully appreciate, and are frequently resistant to the base rates of dangerousness for the population they are evaluating.[20] For these and other reasons, therefore, relying on actuarial generalizations typically turns out to be more reliable than relying on the direct perceptions and intuitions of even highly trained professionals.

Whether we are talking about evidence in court or assessments of dangerousness by psychologists, the frequent empirical superiority of decisionmaking by generalization over direct individual perception may not be all there is to the matter. As we will explore in subsequent chapters, people may think that there is a moral imperative in maximal individuation in decisionmaking even if the actual practices of such individuation are less reliable than the alternative.[21] But at the very least the preference for individuation, of which Betty Smith's case is but one example, cannot plausibly be seen as resting on some overall greater accuracy of nongeneralized decisionmaking.

The possibility that relying on generalizations known from the beginning to be imperfect might still be empirically superior to relying on allegedly direct or individualized assessments also replicates important aspects of the debate about the virtues and vices of rules and rule-based decisionmaking. As prescriptive generalizations, rules necessarily entail the possibility that their strict application will produce suboptimal outcomes in some cases, where suboptimality is measured by reference to the outcome that would have been produced by accurate application of the background justification lying behind the rule.[22] To take a hoary example from the world of legal philosophy, if in order to prevent noise in the park (the background justification) we prohibit all vehicles from entering the park (the rule), we then produce a suboptimal result whenever we exclude nonnoisy vehicles (bicycles and electric cars) and whenever we fail to exclude noisy nonvehicles (musical instruments and loud radios).[23]

The inevitable suboptimality of rules, however, is premised on a supposition about the accuracy of individualized decisionmaking. We know, however, that this accuracy often does not exist, and especially when there are reasons of bias and mistake, among others, to distrust the reliability of the individualized decision. If there were grounds to believe that enforcement officers would make numerous mistakes in trying to determine which instrumentalities were noisy and which not, then in practice the suboptimal rule could very well produce fewer errors than the theoretically optimal individualized assessment.

The same question arises in a recent and very real context. In the face of evidence that many (possibly as many as a thousand a year in the United States) fatal automobile accidents have been caused by inattentive drivers talking on their cell phones when they should have been watching the road, the state of New York enacted a law prohibiting people from using telephones while driving, and many other states and a number of countries outside the United States are now considering similar laws. But as with the bans on pit bulls, people complained that focusing only on cell-phone users was under- and overinclusive, and therefore unfair.[24] Just as many pit bulls are nonvicious and many other kinds of dogs can be vicious, the cell-phone users and the cell-phone industry argued that for many people, talking on the phone while driving is no more distracting than listening to the radio or conversing with a passenger, making the law overinclusive, and that there were many sources of distraction, such as billboards, not covered by the law, making the law underinclusive. As a consequence, some states, such as New Hampshire, rejected cell-phone-specific regulation, and instead enacted laws prohibiting not cell-phone use, but driving while distracted.

As with the debates about both vehicles in the park and clinical assessments of dangerousness, however, the cell-phone issue presents the debate between the virtues of admittedly under- and overinclusive regulation by easily identifiable indicators—either you are on the phone or you are not, and it is not that difficult for a police officer to make that determination—and the virtues of more sensitive assessment by determining in each individual case whether the driver was distracted or not. But of course the sensitive determination of the police officer about which drivers are distracted and which not, like the sensitive determination of the clinician about which offenders are still dangerous and which are not, is also subject to mistakes. These are not the mistakes built into crude but simple actuarial measures; instead, they are the mistakes that come when police officers, like clinical psychologists, substitute the errors of misperception and bias, among others, for the errors that might be part of using a nonuniversal but statistically reliable and easily applied actuarial assessment, of which the actuarial assessment that cell-phone use is a common distraction for drivers is but one example.

The debate about statistical evidence, therefore, is like the debates about clinical assessments and much like the debates about rules, whether in cases involving pit bulls, vehicles in the park, or mobile phones. Each of these debates turns out to be about the advantages and disadvantages of relying on nonspurious but nonuniversal generalizations, and each of these debates then turns out to compel a focus on the advantages and disadvantages of relying on generalizations compared to relying on seemingly more individualized assessments. And when we look at the evidence, it is often the case that the aversion to generalization rests on erroneous empirical foundations. An aversion to generalization is typically based on an unwillingness to accept the mistakes that decisionmaking by generalization necessarily entails. But it is less often recognized that an aversion to large-scale generalizing must assume that the actual human beings who make more individualized decisions would in practice make fewer mistakes than those made in relying on the generalization. As the comparison of the record of unreliability of eyewitness testimony with the greater reliability of at least some statistical generalizations shows, however, and as the studies comparing actuarial with clinical psychological assessments reinforce, this assumption is often simply false. If there is something that is troublesome about relying on larger generalizations per se, it cannot be that there is good reason to believe that such reliance is necessarily or even typically likely to produce more errors than the alternative.[25]

## The Nonindividual Nature of Individualized Evidence

The objection to preferring so-called direct or actual evidence to other sorts of evidence, however, is not only an empirical one. Rather, the objection rests as well on understanding that the avoidance of generalizations is, with few or no qualifications, simply not possible at all. Put differently, even those decisions that appear initially to be maximally individual, that appear to be "direct" or "actual," in the words of the Massachusetts Supreme Judicial Court in the *Smith* case, may turn out to rely more on generalizations than many people suppose. The inevitability of generalization was the conclusion of our analysis of pit bull regulation, and considering what might possibly be meant by "direct" as opposed to statistical evidence makes the point even clearer.

Because most readers of this book are not visually impaired, it may be easier to see the issue by considering another hypothetical example, here one involving direct but nonvisual perception. Suppose there was a totally blind passenger in Betty Smith's car. And suppose as well that the Blue Bus Company owns all the buses in the city, and indeed all the buses in the county and surrounding counties. Because the possibility of buses owned by others is so minuscule, the defendant Blue Bus Company is prepared to concede that if Betty Smith's car was crowded off the road by a bus then it was crowded off the road by one of the Blue Bus Company's buses.

That Betty Smith was crowded off the road by a bus rather than a car, truck, or piece of construction equipment, however, is something that the Blue Bus Company is not willing to concede. Taking the position that Betty Smith's alleged visual observation of a bus was a fabrication (the Blue Bus Company being wealthy and well insured), the Blue Bus Company attempts at trial to cast doubt on the part of her story maintaining that it was a bus that crowded her off the road. In order to counter the bus company's strategy, Betty Smith's lawyer calls to the witness stand Smith's blind passenger, Walter Wilson. Wilson then testifies that he heard the sound of the offending vehicle approaching Betty Smith's car, that the vehicle approached the car to a distance of no more than two feet, and that the vehicle was definitely a bus. On cross-examination by the Blue Bus Company's lawyer, Wilson testifies to his previous experience with perceiving the sounds of vehicles and inferring their size, nature, and distance from the sounds. Betty Smith's lawyer, in further support of Walter Wilson's testimony, then introduces two expert witnesses who bolster Wilson's account by reporting that laboratory experiments bear out the ability of blind people to determine the proximity and nature of vehicles on the basis of hearing alone, which is just what Wilson claimed to have done.

There is, of course, nothing more or less "direct" or "actual" or "real" about Wilson's primary aural sensory perceptions than about Smith's primary visual ones. Yet in considering what to make of Wilson's perceptions, we would naturally think that the validity of these perceptions depends on a process of generalization and noncertain inference. Wilson has perceived certain sounds in the past, and they have turned out to be buses. He has perceived distances in the past, and they have turned out to be accurate. And so on. As a result, Wilson's inference from this sound to this conclusion (it is a bus at this distance) is an inference based on most but not necessarily all sounds of this type's having turned out in the past to be buses. This is a nonspurious but nonuniversal generalization—most but not all sounds like this are buses—that undergirds what appears to be a direct and thus individualized perception.

Though less obvious to those of us who are sighted, the process of making visual observations from what philosophers refer to as "sense-data" is conceptually no different in the case of visual observations than it is in the case of aural ones. And as the studies of the unreliability of eyewitness identification indicate, there may not be much of an empirical difference either, no matter how hard it is for those of us who are sighted to confront the possibility that, more often than we think, we should simply not believe our eyes. As a result, acknowledging the way in which seemingly direct observation involves a process of inference and generalization enables us to appreciate that even the processes that initially appear to us to be "direct," "actual," or individualized turn out to rely far more on generalizations from past experience than is often appreciated. Once we see that all evidence is in the final analysis probabilistic, the distinction between the probabilistic and the "direct," "actual," or "real" emerges as even more of an anomaly.

Not only are individualized assessments still based on probabilities and generalizations, but such individualized assessments are also always only partially individualized, omitting numerous dimensions of the particular case that might under other circumstances or other rules be relevant. Let us return to the real *Smith* case, and assume that what the Supreme Judicial Court was looking for was testimony by Betty Smith that she actually *saw* the words "Rapid Transit" on the side of the bus that crowded her off the road. But even if this evidence had been forthcoming, Smith would not have been permitted, under well-accepted principles of tort law and evidence law, to testify to how much she needed the money from a recovery against Rapid Transit, to how easily Rapid Transit or its insurer could have afforded to pay the judgment, to how exemplary a life she had lived in the past, to how many times Rapid Transit had been found liable for the negligence of one of its bus drivers, or to the positive effect that even a mistaken judgment for Smith would have on bus safety in the Town of Winthrop. Yet in a truly particularist account of the events, in which we are not applying a legal rule but are simply trying to reach the most just result or to achieve the result that will maximize utility, none of these genuinely "real" facts would be deemed irrelevant, and all of them would be components of a fully individualized consideration of all the equities of the case.

So what are we to make of the fact that Betty Smith would not have been allowed to testify to some number of facts that a fully individualized determination might have allowed into consideration? If we accept the inevitability and desirability of not allowing her to present evidence of her own need, the company's insurance, and the like, then we can see that most so-called individualized determinations are not as individualized as we suppose. Moreover, the exclusion of these facts is itself something that occurs by virtue of the operation of a rule (in this case all the combined rules of tort and evidence law), and that consequently operates by virtue of a generalization. We exclude evidence of the plaintiff's poverty, the defendant's wealth, the existence or terms of insurance coverage, and the defendant's past negligent acts, among others, because it has been determined at some earlier time that these facts would not *as a rule* promote justice, or increase utility, or whatever. But because these are rules, we exclude the evidence even in the face of a showing in the particular case that admission of this evidence might serve justice, or might increase utility, or might promote some other goal that can be seen as one of the background justifications lying behind the exclusionary rules.[26]

In many cases the parties on one side or the other will argue that the exclusionary rules should be overridden in a particular case, and the exclusion wrought by an exclusionary rule is best thought of in presumptive rather than absolute terms.[27] Nevertheless, every piece of unadmitted evidence is typically unadmitted, whether consciously or not, by virtue of a rule. The rule will itself be based on a generalization about the usual or probable, but not universal, irrelevance of the excluded fact, thus further underscoring the way in which decisionmaking in a totally individualized or particularistic manner is essentially impossible.

That all seemingly particular or individualized decisions turn out to have important dimensions of generality is not totally to deny the logical distinction between the particular and the general. Although pressing against this distinction has a distinguished philosophical provenance, there is no need for us to examine here the deepest questions of metaphysics and philosophical logic bearing on the nature and existence of the distinction between the particular and the general, or the relationship between particulars and universals.[28] For our purposes, the commonsense distinction between a thing and a group of things will suffice. The only point here, an important one, is that many of the things we perceive as particular objects or particular observations turn out to depend on the kinds of generalizations that, even if not on the same metaphysical status as true universals, are much the stuff of ordinary reasoning. This is still not to deny that there are important differences in degree between the more and the less particular and the more and the less general. Nevertheless, once we understand that most of the ordinary differences between general and particular decisionmaking are differences of degree and not differences in kind, we become properly skeptical of a widespread but mistaken view that the particular has some sort of natural epistemological or moral primacy over the general.

It turns out, therefore, that the Supreme Judicial Court's unwillingness to allow a jury to consider Betty Smith's case against the Rapid Transit company is a product of two significant mistakes: an overconfidence in the empirical reliability and even the very directness of direct evidence, and an underappreciation of the essential continuity between so-called indirect or statistical evidence and evidence that on its face appears to be more individualized and thus less statistical. The Supreme Judicial Court's skepticism about a "mathematical" case, therefore, even if the court was correct that this was a mathematical case, is, as we have seen, not so much a skepticism about mathematical or statistical evidence but a skepticism about resting legal decisions on nonspurious but nonuniversal generalizations.

Seen in this way, the Supreme Judicial Court's skepticism is of a piece with the skepticism of Plato's Stranger and of Aristotle about relying too heavily on what they called "laws," and with the inflammatory slogans of the pit bull sympathizers. In all these cases, the preference for particulars is seen as a moral imperative. But if particularism itself relies on generalizations, and if particularized decisions provide no guarantee of greater reliability, then the foundations for the preference for particularism are shakier than they often appear.

# CHAPTER 4

# Eighty-Year-Old Pilots and Twelve-Year-Old Voters

## The Actuarial Foundations of Age Discrimination

Commercial airline pilots in the United States are required by law to retire at the age of sixty. Under the Federal Aviation Administration's so-called Age Sixty Rule, it is unlawful for a person to pilot or copilot a commercial airliner after age sixty, and equally unlawful for the commercial airline to hire him or her to do so.[1] Underlying this rule is the premise that certain physical faculties are necessary for commercial airline pilots, especially during an in-flight emergency. Coupled with this premise is the belief that some of the most important of those faculties tend to decline after the age of sixty. In particular, it is believed that speed of reflexes, hearing (especially the ability to discern messages distinctly against potentially confusing background noise), and vision (especially in low light or high glare) all decline noticeably after age sixty, just as the risk of sudden and unexpected incapaci-

tation from stroke or heart attack is increasing. Because
the consequences of pilot error are often catastrophic,
the Age Sixty Rule, which functions as an exception to
the otherwise applicable Age Discrimination in Employment Act,[2] has been justified as a measure necessary
to maximize safety in commercial air transport.

As would be expected, most pilots, as well as at least
one of the pilots' unions, have objected to the Age Sixty
Rule.[3] Indeed, the vociferousness of these objections is
not much less now than it was some years ago when the
mandatory retirement age for pilots was originally proposed as fifty-five. Despite the fact that the age of obligatory retirement was set at sixty and not fifty-five, the
pilots have argued that even if a slowing of reflexes and a
decline in hearing and vision affect many or most people
after the age of sixty, they certainly do not affect all
people. As a consequence, so the argument goes, it would
be vastly preferable to institute individual reaction, vision, and hearing testing for all pilots in order to determine which pilots have good enough reflexes, vision, and
hearing and which do not. All pilots possessing sufficiently quick reaction times, sufficiently keen vision, and
sufficiently acute hearing, whether they be thirty-five or
seventy-five, should, the pilots and others argue, be allowed to continue in their chosen profession; and all pilots who fail to measure up to these physical standards,
again whether they be thirty-five or seventy-five, should
be excluded from the cockpits of commercial airliners.

A few preliminary issues will help to focus the question. First, we do not eliminate the problem by concluding that there should be periodic physical testing of pilots
after, say, age fifty. Such age-triggered testing, which is
now often proposed for elderly drivers, lessens the impact on those who are subject to the periodic testing, at

least relative to a total exclusion, but does not eliminate it. So long as periodic testing is required for, say, pilots over fifty or automobile drivers over seventy, and so long as periodic testing or retesting is not required for those under that age, a special burden, and an increased risk of exclusion, are imposed upon those over a certain age relative to those under that age. Instituting such an age-dependent differential may be the right course of action, and we will return to this possibility presently. For purposes of initially examining the issue of age stereotyping, however, the fact that a special test is imposed upon people precisely because of their age and precisely because age is considered a statistically reliable indicator of a decline in certain physical faculties makes this approach an instance of the problem we are addressing rather than being a solution to it.

Of course a policy of mandatory retirement at age sixty, whether imposed by law or voluntarily adopted by an employer even when the law is silent, may be objectionable simply because the traits that are allegedly age correlated are nevertheless immaterial to being an airline pilot.[4] Like the physical tests long used to exclude women from jobs for which the tested physical capacity was irrelevant (such as using upper-body strength as a qualification for the job of computer programmer), it is possible that the traits for which age is claimed to be the proxy are traits that have nothing to do with the skills that are properly demanded in a commercial airline pilot. If this were the case, then using even an empirically sound correlation between age and the decline in these traits as a way of making older pilots retire would seem to be profoundly unjust.

In the context of employment as a commercial airline pilot, however, the claim that quick reaction time, good low-light and high-glare vision, acute hearing against background noise, and low likelihood of sudden incapacitation are not among the desirable or necessary qualifications is implausible. There are, of course, numerous desirable traits in a commercial airline pilot other than quick reaction times, good vision, excellent hearing, and a low probability of having a stroke or heart attack. Experience, for example, is highly important, and correlates positively and not negatively with age. Still, and even apart from the risk of sudden incapacitation, the ability to understand rapidly delivered and potentially confusing messages from air traffic controllers, the ability to react instantly in case of an emergency, and the ability to see other airliners at night, when combined with the fact that failure to see danger or to hear instructions or to react with sufficient speed could cost hundreds of lives, makes it hard to argue that, other things being equal, a pilot with faster reaction times and better vision and hearing is not superior to one with slower reaction times and worse vision and hearing. Indeed, even with other things not being equal, it seems scarcely conceivable that quick reaction time and excellent vision and hearing are not among an admittedly larger number of traits that it is quite important for all pilots to have.

Yet although the faculties of quick reaction and undiminished visual and aural acuity are material to the job, and therefore to the decision (hiring or retaining pilots) to be made, it could still be argued that age is a spurious proxy for reaction speed and sound hearing and vision. As with taking homosexuality as a proxy for lack of courage, race as a proxy for industriousness, or gender as a proxy for business acumen (to take just three of the spurious proxies that have flourished for generations), it could be the case that there is a distribution in acute hearing, keen vision, and quick reflexes among people but no correlation between the distribution of these traits and the distribution of age. We would find slow reactors, for example, as proportionately well represented in the class of thirty-year-olds as in the class of sixty-year-olds, and we would be as likely to find a fast reactor in the population of those over sixty as in the population of those under thirty. If this were so for all the pertinent physical traits, then the actuarial basis for forcing pilots off the job at age sixty would be nonexistent, and the age-based mandatory retirement policy would be an example of pure empirically unsupportable prejudice, no different from excluding people with close-set eyes from positions of trust on the basis of the (totally unsupportable but often maintained) belief that people with close-set eyes are sneaky and not to be trusted.

In the case of using age as a proxy for diminished hearing, diminished vision, slowing of reaction times, and heightened risk of sudden incapacitation, however, it is clear that there *is* a substantial evidentiary foundation for taking age as statistically indicative of a decline in hearing acuity, of a slowing of reflexes, and of impairment of the other physical traits highly desirable in commercial airline pilots. Although there is much individual variation, the available evidence provides considerable empirical support for the proposition that a slowing of reaction times and a decrease in the ability to see clearly in low light or high glare or to distinguish sounds against background noise correlate with advancing age after the age of fifty-five, and that the correlation increases (the degree of individual variation decreases) as age increases.[5] Unlike the spurious and actuarially unsupportable generalizations upon which too many people rely, the generalization that people over the age of sixty have slower reaction times, worse hearing, worse vision, and a greater risk of sudden incapacitation than those below that age appears to be scientifically sound.

As we have seen repeatedly, however, the scientific soundness of an actuarial or statistical generalization is not inconsistent with that generalization's being both under- and overinclusive. None of the available evidence supports the proposition, for example, that slowing of reflexes or diminution of aural or visual capacity does not occur in those below age sixty. Nor does the evidence support the proposition that there are no or few people over the age of sixty who have suffered no loss in reaction time, hearing acuity, or visual perception, or who have no increase in the likelihood of sudden incapacitation. If age sixty is used as a proxy for diminished reaction time, worse hearing, worse vision, and greater risk of stroke or heart attack among commercial airline pilots, then no small number of commercial pilots are being forced to retire on account of the likelihood that their reflexes have slowed and their perceptive abilities have worsened when in fact nothing of the kind has taken place. It is against this empirical background that the debate about mandatory retirement has taken place.

## Are Age Limits Arbitrary?

The Age Discrimination in Employment Act prohibits "the setting of arbitrary age limits regardless of potential for job performance" and announces the purpose of the law as being "to prohibit arbitrary age discrimination in employment."[6] Similarly, commercial airline pilots have argued for decades in objecting to the Age Sixty Rule that its basic flaw is that it is "arbitrary."[7] Yet neither the law nor the pilots' advocacy has been very clear about what is meant by the charge of arbitrariness, and pausing over the different possible understandings of what it is for a rule or a law to be arbitrary will be helpful not only in understanding some of the issues surrounding age discrimination, but more broadly in understanding the larger issues of generality.

As utilized by the pilots, the charge of arbitrariness is largely a contention about the alleged mistake of drawing crisp and rigid lines in domains in which there are differences of degree and not of kind. It is especially problematic, the pilots appear to be claiming, to impose a rigid line on the nonrigid diversity of human experience. Thus, the pilots urge us to believe that it would be profoundly unfair to say to someone that he or she could be an airline pilot at age fifty-nine and 364 days but not one day later. Under one understanding of the common charge of arbitrariness in cases like this, a rule is arbitrary if it picks a particular point on a spectrum and makes falling on one side or the other of that line conclusive. When we hear about arbitrary lines, or arbitrary deadlines, or arbitrary cutoff points, we are often asked to consider the unfairness of making a crisp line so important when there is no basis for picking this point rather than some other.[8] In the case of the pilots, why could the age of mandatory retirement not be sixty-five (as it is now in Europe), or sixty-two, or even fifty-nine? In the absence of any conclusive reason to choose sixty rather than any of these or a number of other alternative retirement ages (including some that are not whole years, such as fifty-nine and a half), the choice of sixty as the date of mandatory retirement is simply arbitrary, or so the argument ordinarily goes.

If this is what is meant by the charge of arbitrariness, however, and much of the pilots' rhetoric suggests that it is, then the claim of arbitrariness is little more than one of the most common of shallow debater's tricks. If there is no good reason to pick age sixty rather than age sixty-one or age fifty-nine, the debater argues, then surely the selection of sixty as an absolute cutoff is arbitrary and thus irrational.

But of course it is not irrational at all. In numerous areas of life and decisionmaking we are compelled to select a point along a continuum as the trigger for action, and there is nothing the least bit irrational about doing so. The Greeks were the first to think carefully about this, and the notorious Sorites (The Heaper) Paradox was designed to drive this point home.[9] If there is a heap of salt, so the paradox goes, and if the removal of one grain of salt still leaves a heap, and so on for the next, and the next, and the next after that, and if there is no one grain the removal of which makes what has previously been a heap no longer a heap, then does this mean that there is no such thing as a heap? Or does it mean that there is a heap even when there are no grains left? Similarly, the Paradox of Falakros (The Bald Man), also of classical Greek origin but made famous by Bertrand Russell, uses baldness to make the same point, asking, rhetorically, whether the inability to specify the exact number of hairs the removal of which would convert a nonbald man into a bald one has the effect of saying that there is no difference between the bald and the thatched.[10] And Edmund Burke noted that "though no man can draw a stroke between the confines of night and day, still light and darkness are on the whole tolerably distinguishable."[11] Indeed, and with all due respect to Burke, Russell, and the Greeks, the pithiest observation comes from former Baltimore Orioles baseball player John Lowenstein, who observed, facetiously, that "they should move first base back a step to eliminate all the close plays."[12] Yet whether the examples be drawn from philosophy or baseball or ordinary experience—how do we distinguish the arm from the wrist, or frogs from tadpoles?—it is still clear that much of our language and much of our lives are dependent on the ability to distinguish concepts that have no crisp line between them. To claim otherwise is sophistry at its worst.

When a legal or other important consequence turns on the difference between night and day, bald and not-bald, or any other pair of extremes on a continuum, it is often necessary to fix a precise point between the extremes, that point then becoming the point of application or nonapplication of some rule.[13] And even though some other point could have been selected, there is nothing irrational, and thus nothing arbitrary in the ordinary sense of that word, in picking one point rather than another in the same neighborhood. A voting requirement of a two-thirds "supermajority" is not arbitrary because 65 percent or 70 percent could have been selected rather than 66.67 percent, a speed limit is not arbitrary because it is sixty-five rather than sixty-four or sixty-six, and a criminal jury of twelve, even apart from its historical provenance, is not arbitrary because the size of the jury could have been set at eleven or thirteen.

In all such instances of line-drawing, important consequences turn on being just on the right or wrong side of a line that could have been located elsewhere. A defendant convicted by a jury of eleven is entitled to a new trial, an impeached president who receives in the Senate two-thirds minus one votes for removal after impeachment gets to remain in office, and a person who is driving at sixty-six miles per hour rather than at sixty-five is liable to receive a ticket for speeding.[14] To set a mandatory retirement age for commercial airline pilots at age sixty, therefore, and thus to allow those who are a day younger to fly and require those a day older to retire, is no more arbitrary, in the sense of irrational or unreasoned, than are any of the other boundaries or cutoff points or deadlines that pervade our daily lives. If it is not arbitrary in this sense to say that those who are a day younger than thirty-five may not serve as president of the United States, then it is not arbitrary to say that those who are a day older than sixty may not serve as a pilot of a commercial airliner.

The statutory language of the Age Discrimination in Employment Act—"to prevent arbitrary age discrimination in employment"—could, rather than be understood as prohibiting the drawing of lines on the basis of age, be taken as condemning only those forms of age discrimination that turn out to have no empirical basis. Because there is no evidence of a decline in managerial abilities starting anywhere near age forty, for example, a mandatory retirement age of forty for corporate executives would be arbitrary in the sense that it would rest on a totally spurious claimed correlation between age and the material trait. But, as we have seen and as the evidence shows, this is not so in the case of mandatory retirement at age sixty for commercial airline pilots. In this case the selected age has precisely the empirical support necessary to distinguish it from the hypothetical mandatory retirement age of forty for corporate executives.

So if the mandatory retirement age for pilots is not arbitrary because it draws a sharp line at one point on a continuum, and if it is not arbitrary because it is spurious in the empirical and statistical sense, then it seems as if the only remaining plausible claim of arbitrariness is that the mandatory retirement age is arbitrary just because it uses a nonspurious but nonuniversal generalization to compel the retirement at age sixty of all commercial airline pilots, even those whose reflexes, hearing, and vision are every bit as sound as they were at age forty. If this is the argument, therefore, then we must confront directly the claim that this kind of statistically nonspurious discrimination on the basis of age is unfair just because of its overinclusiveness.

## From Maximums to Minimums

If one possible objection to mandatory retirement at age sixty for commercial airline pilots is that the age-sixty line is overinclusive, compelling the retirement of even those whose reflexes, hearing, and vision have declined not at all, then one way of putting to the test the objection that it is the very overinclusiveness that makes the rule unjust is to examine the other end of age discrimination, discrimination against the young. Consider, therefore, the typical minimum age for voting, which in the United States in the year 2003 is eighteen. What this means, of course, is that no one under the age of eighteen, even one day under that age on voting day, can cast a ballot, while everyone otherwise eligible who is at or over age eighteen, even one day over age eighteen, is entitled to vote.

For our purposes, there is no need to pause very long over the arguments to make the minimum voting age something other than eighteen. For much of American history, the minimum voting age in state and federal elections was twenty-one, but in 1971, prompted both by expansion of the franchise generally and by a concern that those who were eligible for conscription into the military could nevertheless not vote, the Twenty-sixth

Amendment mandated the reduction of the voting age in all federal and state elections to eighteen.[15] In some countries the minimum age is still twenty-one, and some have voting ages of nineteen or twenty. But whether the minimum age be eighteen, nineteen, twenty, twenty-one, or something else, the structure of the requirement is the same, allowing all (of those otherwise eligible) and only those at or above the specified age to vote.

There are a number of justifications for mandating a minimum voting age, and most of these justifications are obviously intertwined with questions about the age of majority generally and about the age of legal capacity as it pertains to issues such as the legal capacity to make a contract and the legal capacity to make various life decisions without the consent of one's parents. Moreover, using age as a marker for membership in the political community does not necessarily involve taking age as a proxy for various abilities in the way that it does when we use age as a proxy for excluding those thought too irresponsible to drive automobiles or to drink alcoholic beverages. Still, among the common justifications for a minimum voting age is the view that only those of sufficient wisdom, learning, judgment, and psychological maturity, among other things, should be permitted to exercise the franchise, because only those with such wisdom, judgment, and so on can exercise the franchise responsibly.

That those over the age of eighteen have the capacity to exercise the franchise responsibly is, of course, a generalization. The generalization is almost certainly not statistically spurious, for however we understand the capacities necessary for exercising the franchise it is highly likely that such capacities correlate well with age from the ages of, say, ten to twenty-five. Nevertheless, the minimum voting age is plainly both under- and overinclusive. There are undoubtedly numerous people under the age of eighteen who are sufficiently attuned to public affairs that they would exercise the franchise responsibly, and there are undoubtedly numerous people over the age of eighteen who do not possess sufficient maturity, wisdom, knowledge of public affairs, or sense of civic responsibility to exercise the franchise in a conscientious way.

So what would the commercial airline pilots say about minimum voting ages? We do not know exactly the answer to this question, but we do know that at the heart of the pilots' argument is the claim that it is somehow unfair or unjust to employ a nonspurious but nonuniversal generalization about the relationship between age and the physical abilities necessary to operate a commercial airliner safely. But if the injustice lies just in the imprecision of the generalization and the unfairness of not allowing individuals to demonstrate that they do not fall within the stereotype, then it must also be unfair or unjust to use a nonspurious but nonuniversal generalization about age and the mental abilities necessary to vote responsibly as the means of deciding who is entitled to cast a ballot. If, as the pilots often appear to be arguing, the injustice lies just in the imprecision, then the injustice lies in the minimum voting age just as surely as it lies in the maximum flying age. If justice resides in the particulars, then compelled nonvoting for those who are seventeen years old is every bit as unjust as compelled nonflying for those who are sixty-one.

Much the same could be said about other areas in which we employ minimum ages, such as the minimum ages for marriage, for driving an automobile, and for purchasing and consuming alcoholic beverages. At a much lower age, the same point applies to the minimum age for entering primary school. Yet in all these cases the minimum age can be seen as just another generalization, or just another stereotype. These stereotypes—those under six are too young to be able to benefit from primary school, those under seventeen are too immature for marriage, those under twenty-one are too irresponsible to drink, and those under sixteen are too careless to drive—are no less empirically grounded than the Age Sixty Rule is for pilots, but in none of these cases do very many people claim that justice demands that precocious four-year-olds be allowed to enter the first grade, that mature fourteen-year-olds be permitted to marry, that cautious fifteen-year-olds be authorized to drive, or that responsible nineteen-year-olds be eligible to purchase alcoholic beverages. Perhaps this is a mistake, and perhaps people should be angry that those not within the zone of accuracy of the stereotype or generalization should be allowed to demonstrate that in their individual case the generalization, however sound it may be in the aggregate, does not apply to them. But perhaps the lack of outrage about minimum ages demonstrates that whatever injustice some or many people feel about maximum ages for employment, whether in the cockpit or anywhere else, is based not on the injustice of stereotyping or generalizing itself, but rather on the injustice that surrounds only particular forms of generalization, and only because of something about the particular substance of the generalization. If this is correct, then justice does not necessarily lie in the particulars, and perhaps Plato's Stranger, Aristotle, and countless others have been too quick to conclude otherwise.

## Are Pilots like Pit Bulls?

One obvious way to reduce the degree of imprecision that comes from using age as a proxy for the traits necessary to vote responsibly would be to give every prospective voter a test, asking some basic civics and current affairs questions designed to separate the serious from the frivolous, and the informed from the ignorant. But even apart from the interesting question of democratic theory whether the frivolous and ignorant are less entitled to a voice than are the responsible and informed (a question not irrelevant to voting by those under the age of eighteen), such testing is, at least in the United States, no longer possible, that impossibility being a legacy of the history of using voting-ability tests not as a way of actually determining voting ability, but instead simply as a method of excluding African Americans from exercising the franchise.[16] Yet even assuming that with a different history such tests would have been legally permissible and politically possible, employing such tests would, as we saw in our analysis of pit bull testing, change matters only by degree. Whatever test we could devise would still use that test as a proxy—a generalization—for the actual trait we wish to see exercised in the voting booth. People who passed the test might still enter the voting booth uninformed on the particular issues before them, and people who failed the test might still in particular elections or in all elections vote with great responsibility and diligence. Although it is almost certainly the case that a well-designed test would reduce the degree of under- and overinclusion, at least relative to using age as the proxy, it would not eliminate it.

So too with pilots. Individual testing of all commercial airline pilots (of whom there are about 42,000 in the United States) would continue to involve some degree of overinclusion, for it is quite possible that some pilots who passed all the tests would still have deficiencies on the very traits tested (no test being perfect), or would still fail to test for relevant traits not part of the testing procedure; and individual testing would still fail to exclude those pilots who suffered rapid declines in reflexes, hearing, or vision in the intervals between tests. And in addition to these false positives, there would be a number of (though probably fewer) false negatives, some of these false negatives a consequence of imprecision in testing procedures, some a consequence of temporary impairments, and some a consequence of the failure to test for compensating traits. Indeed, the most important of these compensating traits are likely to be experience, which by definition correlates directly with age, and judgment, which correlates directly with age as an empirical even if not as a definitional matter. For those of us who would rather climb into an airplane commanded by a sixty-two-year-old pilot with 15 percent diminished reflexes, vision, and hearing than by a twenty-two-year-old male pilot with perfect reflexes, vision, and hearing, the traits that a test might not pick up could turn out to be more important than those that a test would capture.[17]

Yet although it might thus seem preferable to substitute a more complex algorithm, including factors such as experience and incidents of reprimand, for the coarser age cutoff, this substitution of the finer for the coarser avoids the central issue. For once we see, as we did in the case of pit bulls, that any test will itself build on probabilities and generalizations, and will as a consequence still run the risk of under- or overinclusiveness, we can no longer agree with the pilots that there is some fundamental question of justice distinguishing the age cutoff from individualized testing.[18] Rather, both involve generalizations, both involve under- and overinclusiveness, and the differences between them are differences of degree and not differences in kind.

Similarly, even the existing and non-age-based qualifications for being a commercial airline pilot are generalizations. A requirement of a certain number of flying
hours as a proxy for flying skill is a generalization, and so
too are requirements of military experience, education of
a certain kind, and even possession of a valid pilot's license. In all these cases, certain traits of selection stand
as proxies for certain skills we would like pilots to be able
to use when they are actually behind the controls, and
thus, again as in the case with pit bulls, and as we saw
when we noted the way in which dog-specific regulations were generalizations when compared with pet-
specific regulations, the elimination of the mandatory
retirement age would still leave a large number of under-
and overinclusive generalizations still in place.

Differences in degree, however, are no less real for being differences in degree and not differences in kind. To
believe otherwise is to commit just the kind of fallacy
that the Sorites Paradox is designed to illustrate, and
against which I railed just a few pages previously. It may
well be that in the case of commercial pilots, who are
fewer in number than voters or dogs, it would be conceivable to do just the kind of periodic testing that the
pilots and some of their unions have long urged. And
although such periodic testing would not, as we have
seen, eliminate the reliance on under- and overinclusive
generalizations, and although it might work better for
hearing, vision, and reflexes than for the age-correlated
increase in risk of sudden incapacitation, it is likely that
such testing would reduce substantially the amount of
overinclusion and reduce at least somewhat the amount
of underinclusion.

Yet although reducing the amount of under- and
overinclusion is not without its benefits, especially to the

particular pilots who would be overincluded under the Age Sixty Rule but would not be overincluded under, say, universal annual testing for vision, hearing, and reaction times, there remains an important point in identifying the fact that these differences, however real, are differences in degree and not differences in kind. For once we see that they are differences in degree, it becomes harder to see the fundamental injustice, as opposed merely to the possible inefficiency or possible miscalculated benefit-cost analysis, of choosing a coarser rather than a finer generalization. If it turns out that the coarser (and thus broader) generalization fares better on the benefit-cost analysis, the argument for its representing a case of fundamental injustice is much weaker once we see that the only plausible replacement is a finer (and thus narrower) generalization. Unlike those acts whose commission is taken to be wrong even when it is more efficient to commit them—torture, denial of freedom of belief, cruel and unusual punishment, racial discrimination, and so on—here we are not within the domain of acts that can be so easily isolated. Torture and government efficiency in rooting out terrorists are not measured on the same scale, so for all of those who do not see justice in simple benefit-cost terms, it makes perfect sense to understand torture and government efficiency as competing acts of a different kind. Their virtues and vices cannot simply be traded off against each other. Rather, torture, among other things, is one of those side constraints whose commission remains impermissible even when utility or efficiency would be increased, and thus the avoidance of torture stands as a value incommensurable with the values of utility and efficiency whose maximization it constrains.[19] And if this domain of moral incommensurables is the domain of justice,[20] then it may be that the discovery of the essential continuity of generality and so-called individual testing means that this is a domain that particularity, by itself, does not occupy.

## Generality and Its Consequences

That the Age Sixty Rule may not occupy the domain of fundamental justice (or, more accurately, fundamental injustice) does not mean that the rule is necessarily a wise one. Individualized testing may actually be less costly than the Federal Aviation Administration (FAA) supposes, especially given the small number of commercial airline pilots, at least as compared with the number of voters and, as we will address in chapters 6 and 7, the number of airline *passengers*. While it might not be plausible to decrease the under- and overinclusiveness of passenger searches by substituting close scrutiny of every passenger for some form of screening by generalization (commonly called profiling), it does seem plausible to consider such universal close scrutiny for commercial airline pilots, substituting more particularized testing for less particularized age screening. But to the extent that the FAA has examined just this alternative and found that its costs (including the costs of the underinclusiveness of even the best available tests, and including the costs consequent on the inability to test very well for the likelihood of sudden incapacitation) exceed its benefits (including the benefits of having more experienced pilots, and including the benefits to the nonimpaired pilots who would under individualized testing be allowed to continue to fly), the objections to this calculation would have to lie in the domain of empirical investigation rather than in the domain of fundamental justice.

If the issue is not one of fundamental justice, however, then the possibility of age-triggered rather than universal testing emerges as a serious possibility. Under such an approach, pilots could be subject to periodic testing upon reaching, say, age fifty but not before, just as some have proposed periodic testing of drivers upon reaching age seventy. Recall that we dismissed such proposals earlier in this chapter, not because they were unsound, but because, by still representing a form of age discrimination, albeit a less consequential one, they represented more an example of the problem we were addressing than a possible solution to it. But if we are now at the point in the analysis where we have recognized that age discrimination does not simply because of its under- and overinclusiveness and reliance on generalizations represent a case of fundamental injustice,[21] then we can return to the possibility that age-triggered testing might still be preferable to age-triggered exclusion. Age-triggered testing, such as a requirement that all pilots between the ages of fifty and sixty be tested every three years for hearing, vision, reaction times, and other possible sensory or cognitive disorders, that all pilots between sixty and seventy be tested annually, and that all pilots over seventy be tested semiannually, would of course be a form of age discrimination. Indeed, outside of the exceptions, of which the Age Sixty Rule for commercial airline pilots is one, such age-triggered testing would violate American law. But if we put aside the possible illegality of age-triggered testing (or assume that it would be legal for commercial airline pilots because it is less intrusive than the existing and entirely legal approach of total exclusion), age-triggered testing appears to be a plausible way of shrinking the degree of under- and overinclusiveness. As with the questions surrounding a total exclusion of those above a certain age, the questions here are likely to be largely empirical, and it could still well be the case, as the FAA has thus far concluded, that even age-triggered testing is too risky to public safety because the available tests produce too many false negatives and because certain age-correlated risks cannot be identified in advance by any existing test.[22] Nevertheless, it remains important to acknowledge that once we have passed the threshold of fundamental justice, and thus have concluded that the use of age is not automatically or necessarily unjust, then a range of age-based proposals less intrusive than total exclusion are open to serious consideration.

The relative merits of age-triggered exclusion and age-triggered testing turn out, more importantly, to implicate even larger issues about the distinction between appropriate and inappropriate forms of discrimination. When we explore gender discrimination in chapter 5 and airline passenger, immigration, and police screening using race as part of the screening algorithm (profiling) in chapters 6 and 7, we will consider the argument that certain forms of generalization, even if nonspurious vis-à-vis legitimate goals, are nevertheless morally repugnant because of the way in which they may stigmatize or isolate members of certain traditionally oppressed or marginalized groups. One possibility is that in many such cases the stigma is less if the trait at issue is used merely to trigger closer scrutiny and not to exclude. At this point in the analysis this is only a possibility, but a possibility suggesting that in some domains the intersection of the harms of stigmatization and isolation and the gains to be realized by employing nonspurious generalizations to serve legitimate goals are such that the best solution is to minimize the former without relinquishing all of the latter. Trait-triggered testing rather than trait-triggered exclusion could be just such a solution.

Whether this is the correct solution in the case of the Age Sixty Rule depends in part on the empirical issues already alluded to in this chapter. More importantly, however, it also depends on the question whether age is one of the characteristics that has so much stigmatizing and isolating potential that age discrimination ought to be classed with some other forms of discrimination whose stigmatizing and isolating potential best explains why we do not permit the use of even nonspurious generalizations. Because dealing in full with the issue of stigma and isolation as a basis for prohibiting even statistically sound generalizations would be getting ahead of ourselves, however, it will suffice merely to note the issue here, and to leave addressing it directly until later.

But whether age discrimination, for commercial airline pilots or anyone else, is the kind of stigmatizing and isolating generalization whose use ought to be condemned, legally and morally, even when it is statistically relevant to a legitimate end, is a question that may be illuminated by having considered, briefly, the question of minimum ages for voting and, even more briefly, the question of minimum ages for drinking, driving, and schooling. The minimum-age issue points up the fact that simply using age does not appear, by itself, to be especially problematic, even though, as in the case of voting ages, it is premised on a substantially under- and over-inclusive stereotype on the basis of age. But if, as we have seen, it is not simply the under- or overinclusion that creates a problem, if it is not the stereotype per se that creates the problem, then age may well be different from many of the problematic categories of stereotyping. This is certainly the case with minimum ages, and may be so with maximum ages as well. After all, it is not too far off the mark to observe that all of us fall into one of two categories: we are either old or hoping to get there. And if the universality of aging makes age different, as the Supreme Court of the United States has concluded in determining that age discrimination is not impermissible as a question of constitutional law,[23] then it may turn out that using age as a proxy for various legitimate interests is both empirically supportable and not nearly as connected with fundamental issues of justice as many people assume. And even if this conclusion is wrong, and it may well be, it should be clear that important issues of justice and policy, issues obscured rather than illuminated by unhelpful terms such as "ageism," would be issues arising from the irreversible status of the elderly as elderly, and not from the simple fact of using age as a proxy for other traits, and even more importantly, not from the simple fact of employing a statistically sound but nonuniversal generalization.

# CHAPTER 5

# The Women of the Virginia Military Institute

## Can Gender Be Relevant?

Unlike mandatory retirement for Capricorns but not for Scorpios, mandatory retirement for pilots at age sixty is not irrational. It may perhaps be wrong (but perhaps not), and it may perhaps be inefficient (but perhaps not). Still, age-based mandatory retirement for commercial airline pilots does rest on a genuine and demonstrable correlation between age and the decline of many of the faculties material to the decision at hand—determining who has and who does not have the physical capacities necessary to operate a commercial airliner.

The statistical rationality of a generalization is not, however, the end of the matter. As we began to glimpse in considering the Age Sixty Rule, there may be some statistically rational generalizations whose use ought nevertheless to be questioned. The Age Sixty Rule in particular and mandatory retirement in general may or may not represent one of these rational but impermissible generalizations, but having opened the issue we are now in a position to consider more broadly the possibility that using a nonspurious or statistically rational generalization as a decision rule is not under all circumstances right.

Yet if at times it is wrong to use a statistically rational generalization as a decision rule, we can now see that it is wrong not because there is something necessarily unjust about simply relying on a generalization. If that were so then it would be as wrong to generalize about the capacities of fourteen-year-old voters and sixteen-year-old drinkers as it is to generalize about the capacities of elderly pilots. Whatever injustice there is in the Age Sixty Rule, if indeed there is any at all, cannot reside simply in the making of important decisions on the basis of a statistically sound but nonuniversal generalization. There must be something else, and in this chapter and the two following we turn more closely to what that something else might be.

But we should not get ahead of ourselves. Once we are considering when it is wrong to use statistically sound generalizations, we are already in the domain of statistical rationality. Yet this domain of statistical rationality is a domain inhabited by neither of two distinct types of irrational generalization, and the discussion to follow will be furthered not only by distinguishing rational from irrational generalizations, but also by distinguishing these two importantly different forms of irrational generalization.

The first type of irrational generalization is the empirically sound generalization about an immaterial trait. Age statistically predicts hair loss for men, but it would be irrational to justify the Age Sixty Rule on the basis of wanting to avoid having bald pilots, for baldness has nothing to do with the ability to control an airplane. So even though the generalization that older men are on average balder than younger men is sound, the generalization is immaterial here, because baldness is not something we care about in airline pilots. A generalization is irrational, therefore, when it reliably predicts something in which we have no interest.

Second, generalizations are irrational when they are empirically unsound generalizations about a material trait. Unlike baldness, we do care about the vision of our pilots, but it would be irrational to use a generalization that was spurious with respect to good vision. Although age is a statistically nonspurious indicator of good vision, hair color is not. So it would be irrational in a quite different way to exclude blond pilots because of the belief that doing so would decrease the number of pilots possessing the admittedly material trait of impaired vision.[1] The second kind of irrationality, therefore, exists when the generalization is aimed at something we are indeed concerned about but has no tendency to indicate or predict it. Unlike the first kind of irrationality, which comes from hitting the wrong target, the second comes from identifying the right target but missing it.

The distinction between rational and irrational generalizations, and then the distinction between these two kinds of irrational generalization, present a number of important complications. These complications arise in many contexts, but especially often with respect to generalizations involving gender, the subject of this chapter. And although the issues discussed here apply not only to gender-based generalizations, generalizations based on gender are important both in their own right and as an illuminating beginning in considering the circumstances under which using even statistically rational generalizations might be wrong.

A useful vantage point for examining gender-based generalizations can be found in the 1996 decision of the U.S. Supreme Court holding unconstitutional the men-only policy of a state-operated military college known as the Virginia Military Institute—VMI for short.[2] VMI, founded in 1839 as a military-focused university, is in many respects similar to the U.S. Military Academy at West Point, the U.S. Naval Academy at Annapolis, and the U.S. Air Force Academy at Colorado Springs. Unlike West Point, Annapolis, and the Air Force Academy, however, VMI was and remains operated by the state and not by the federal government. And unlike its federal counterparts, students at VMI are not required, unless they voluntarily join the Reserve Officers Training Corps, to complete a period of actual military service upon graduation. But like the others, VMI historically restricted attendance to men. Moreover, VMI insisted on maintaining this restriction even after the U.S. Military, Naval, and Air Force Academies opened their doors to women in the 1970s.[3]

VMI's restriction of its student body to men need not have been based at all on generalizations about the relative capacities of men and women. The Institute could have believed simply that separation of the sexes in higher education was a moral mandate or social necessity, independent of the capacities of men and women.[4] Or it could have believed, and indeed did believe, that an all-male military or educational culture was desirable for any of a number of other alleged historical, social, psychological, educational, cultural, or moral reasons.[5] Like the governmental policies that have historically restricted marriage to a union between one man and one woman, or that mandate or permit gender-separated bathrooms, dormitories, and prisons, there are many policies of gender separation—some right and some wrong—that have little or nothing to do with generalizations about the relative physical, mental, or social capabilities of men and women.

There is strong evidence that what VMI really desired was an all-male environment.[6] Period. Perhaps strategically and perhaps more genuinely, however, VMI did not defend its men-only policy solely on these grounds, nor even solely on the grounds that single-sex education can offer distinct educational advantages. Instead, VMI to a significant extent justified the policy of offering its education only to men by recourse to generalizations about the respective educational capacities and preferences of men and women.[7] VMI claimed, especially in the Supreme Court, that its particular method of instruction required of students an array of physical skills and personal characteristics that women were less likely to possess than men. More specifically, VMI based its arguments on the unique demands of an educational method that was, to use VMI's word, "adversative." The adversative approach to education, which was at its most extreme in the experience of the "rat line" for first-year cadets, involved, to an even greater extent than is found at the other military academies, liberal doses of tormenting, screaming, berating, and belittling.[8] As described by VMI and acknowledged by the lower courts, the adversative method featured "physical rigor, mental stress, absolute equality of treatment, absence of privacy, minute regulation of behavior, and indoctrination in desirable values."[9] The results of its adversarial (some might say abusive) educational methods, VMI insisted, were immensely positive. Students educated in this manner, or so VMI claimed, became imbued with a high degree of discipline, with a respect for authority, with the ability to manage stress, and with a willingness to push oneself to the limits of one's capabilities. These abilities, VMI maintained, were especially important for military officers, and were to a great extent highly desirable even for people in other walks of life.

Not everyone appreciates being berated and belittled in a highly aggressive and combative manner. And not everyone benefits from the experience, even in the long run, and even if we concede that some do. Key to VMI's position, consequently, was the claim that the ability to stand up to personal abuse and then to benefit from that abuse were traits possessed by only a portion of the population of those around the age of eighteen (the typical beginning age for a VMI education). More importantly, VMI insisted that gender was a good, even if not perfect, statistical predictor of which individuals possessed the traits necessary to profit from an adversative education. At the heart of VMI's argument was the generalization that men were more likely to have the adversarial, combative, confrontational, and physical traits necessary to benefit from a VMI education, and that women, being more likely to have traits of empathy, compassion, and cooperation, would in general be ill fitted for the educational style that characterized the Virginia Military Institute.

Responding to a complaint from a woman who had been denied admission, the United States sued VMI, charging unconstitutional discrimination on the basis of gender by an instrumentality of the state.[10] At the trial VMI offered a raft of testimony from psychologists and other experts supporting the gender-based generalizations that VMI claimed justified the men-only policy.

And although the empirical basis of many of these generalizations is at the very least debatable, the trial judge accepted this testimony, concluding that there existed "gender-based developmental differences" between men and women. These differences, the judge ruled, reflected gender-based "tendencies" with respect to adaptability to a combative and adversarial educational environment. Because of these differential tendencies, conceded by even VMI's witnesses to be probabilistic and not universal, the all-male educational environment at VMI was, said the judge, constitutionally permissible.

The United States appealed, and eventually the case wound up in the Supreme Court. There the United States argued that courts should take a "hard look" at the kind of "generalizations or 'tendencies'" that had carried the day in the trial court. The federal government did not challenge the empirical basis for the generalizations, but nevertheless insisted that "state actors controlling gates to opportunity [may] not exclude qualified individuals based on 'fixed notions concerning the roles and abilities of males and females.'" Writing for a majority of the justices of the Supreme Court, Justice Ruth Bader Ginsburg agreed. "Estimates of what is appropriate for most women," she wrote, "no longer justify denying the opportunity to women whose talent and capacity place them outside the average description."[11]

Justice Ginsburg's reference to "the average description" strongly suggests that she, like the United States, accepted, at least for purposes of this case, the empirical underpinnings of this aspect of VMI's claim. Although a state practice of gender discrimination would surely be unconstitutional in the United States as a violation of the Fourteenth Amendment's guarantee of the "equal protection of the laws" were such discrimination found to rest on a simply spurious generalization—restricting admission to graduate school to men, for example, premised on the mistaken generalization that women as a class are less intelligent than men as a class; or restricting admission to cooking school to men because of the spurious generalization, still widely accepted in France, that women as a class lack the creativity to be serious chefs—Justice Ginsburg did not see VMI as one of those cases. Rather, she appears to have conceded for the sake of argument (and because of the difficulty of reevaluating lower-court factual findings on appeal) the factual basis of VMI's argument. For purposes of her opinion, therefore, Justice Ginsburg acknowledged that gender is a statistically nonspurious predictor of the ability to endure and to profit from VMI's adversarial method of education. With the majority of her colleagues, therefore, Justice Ginsburg accepted the empirical validity of the generalization that women were less likely than men to have the physical capacities and traits of personality that VMI sought. Yet for Justice Ginsburg the fact that a gender-based distinction was nonspurious and relevant to the state's goals was not sufficient to make the restriction constitutionally legitimate. The restriction to men was impermissible not because it was irrelevant, but despite the fact that it *was* relevant. And if that is what Justice Ginsburg had in mind, then we need to ask what it is that could justify such a conclusion.

### The Causes and Consequences of Gender Differences

Although Justice Ginsburg's opinion is not perfectly clear on the basis of the Court's conclusion that the gender-based classification was unconstitutional despite its statistical relevance, her reference to "fixed notions" gives a strong hint about one possible path the analysis might take.[12] By suggesting that these "fixed" notions may be less fixed than is commonly assumed, Justice Ginsburg offers the possibility that even a genuine statistical correlation between gender and the degree of tolerance for VMI's educational style, rather than being seen as a *justification* for discrimination, might better be understood as a *product* of discrimination. So although it would be implausible to believe that the decline with age in the vision and hearing of airline pilots (and everyone else) was solely or even largely the product of generations of age discrimination by the airline industry, such a conclusion might well be justified in the case of some forms of gender-based differences, including gender-based differences in tolerance for VMI's "adversative" method of college instruction.

Consider one of the very first of the Supreme Court's sex discrimination encounters, a case called *Reed v. Reed*.[13] The issue was the constitutionality of an Idaho law that, under certain circumstances, mandated a preference for men over women as administrators of estates. The Supreme Court did not inquire into the empirical basis for the discrimination, but we can suppose that in enacting the law the Idaho legislators subscribed to the generalization that the abilities required of an administrator of an estate—an understanding of accounting, a familiarity with the world of investments, and general knowledge of business, for example—were more likely to be located in men than in women. Yet even if this generalization were empirically sound, as it almost certainly was when the Supreme Court considered the Idaho law in 1970, it is extremely likely that the empirical soundness of the generalization was a product of women's having been prohibited or discouraged for generations from gaining just the kind of knowledge that Idaho concluded that they did not then have.[14] If in 1970 men were on average better trained and more experienced in business and finance than women, the reason was surely that generations of women had been steered away from the world of business and finance and in the direction of occupations thought to be more suitable for their gender. Thus in 1971, when the case was finally decided, the fact that women as a class were less likely than men as a class to have the financial training and experience necessary to succeed as the administrator of an estate was, we can say with considerable confidence, a product of social rather than biological forces.

It is distinctly possible that Justice Ginsburg had a similar view about the aptitude and preference of women for VMI's style of education. Although she accepted the generalization that men were, in 1996, better suited on average to VMI's pedagogical approach than women, she appears to have accepted as well the conclusion that the gender-based differential was a function of acculturation rather than of biological necessity. Moreover, it is highly likely that Justice Ginsburg believed that this differential acculturation was not simply a product of preferences, but was rather the consequence of a traditional view about the capacities of men and women that itself had little empirical foundation. When the Supreme Court in 1873 justified the exclusion of women from the practice of law by accepting the proposition that women's "timidity and delicacy . . . unfit[s them] for many of the occupations of civil life," it is likely that it imagined, with most of the culture within which it then existed, that this "timidity" and "delicacy" rendered women equally unfit for military training.[15] So even if it was true in 1996 that women were on average less suited for "adversative" training than men, the truth of this generalization, Justice Ginsburg can be understood as having concluded, was contingent rather than necessary, an effect rather than a cause. As a consequence and not a cause of sex discrimination, therefore, the nonspurious generalization was still, as a matter of law, insufficient to support a gender-based classification. Thus, Justice Ginsburg and her colleagues might have perceived the empirical underpinnings of VMI's men-only policy as akin to a policy of restricting tryouts for the violin section of the college orchestra to Jews or Asians or to a policy of prohibiting immigrants from Belgium from obtaining American driver's licenses. In each of these cases the generalization and the consequent exclusion probably have a nonspurious empirical basis, but the cultural contingency of that empirical basis, at least in the context of race or national origin, makes it wrong to translate the empirical generalization into public policy.

## Materiality Revisited

Yet even if the gender-based differential in tolerance for the adversative approach to university education was not culturally contingent, even if it reflected a deeper physiological differential in aggressiveness between eighteen-year-old men and eighteen-year-old women, it still might not follow that reliance on the generalization would be morally or legally permissible. Consider, for example, a hypothetical state university dedicated to the training not of military officers but of computer experts, including programmers, hardware engineers, software designers, and information technology policy specialists. And suppose that this university—call it the Virginia Computer Institute, VCI for short—excluded women on the grounds that women have less upper-body strength, on average, than men. Unlike a preference for aggressiveness and a tolerance for verbal abuse, as in the VMI policy, the VCI policy appears to be based on a generalization that is extremely unlikely to be socially contingent. That women as a class have less upper-body strength than men as a class is a biological and physiological fact rather than a social and cultural one. On the evidence now available, it appears that women as a class would have on average less upper-body strength than men as a class even were society to spend the next two hundred years steering women into occupations like stevedore and truck mechanic and men into occupations like flight attendant and librarian.[16]

Yet even if gender does statistically though imperfectly predict upper-body strength, using gender as the basis for admission to VCI appears wrong, and that is because it is fairly obvious that upper-body strength has little to do with the skills we would expect in our computer programmers, computer engineers, and computer designers. Gender is indeed relevant to upper-body strength, but upper-body strength is immaterial to computer expertise.

Because upper-body strength is immaterial to computer expertise, we might be properly suspicious of a claim to the contrary. One possibility would be that anyone who thought otherwise is just stupid. But what if a nonstupid justifier of the requirement talked about the necessity of lifting heavy desktop computers, about being able to pitch in at the loading dock of the computer company when necessary, and about the advantages of upper-body strength in moving furniture in order to gain access to cables and to the innards of computer hardware? Were this justification to be offered for VCI's men-only policy, we would be suspicious, doubting that these minor dimensions of some forms of computer industry employment were essential or even much desirable in computer specialists. As a result, we would suspect that the requirements had been added to the more obvious array of traits desirable in computer experts precisely in order to justify exclusion of women not because they would be, even on average, less capable of performing the necessary tasks, but because as women their presence was simply not desired.

The example is less fanciful than might at first appear, and there is indeed a long history of similarly immaterial requirements' being imposed to justify the exclusion of women from the workplace.[17] With some frequency we have seen requirements imposed not because they were important but because they were male, as with fire departments that imposed tests requiring considerably more upper-body strength than was necessary, or a transportation authority that required more aerobic capacity—another dimension in which men and women differ physiologically—than could plausibly be needed for any task that a transit police officer might be required to perform.[18] Against the background of this history, Justice Ginsburg's opinion in the real VMI case is best understood as displaying skepticism about VMI's claim that tolerance for the adversative method of instruction and training is material either to education or to service as a military officer. Perhaps, she and her colleagues may well have believed, VMI's instructional approach was not antecedent to the exclusion of women and not antecedent to VMI's views about the role of women in society or in the military. Instead, VMI's insistence on the desirability of the adversative method may have been more rationalization than justification, and more than anything a reflection of VMI's views about the desirability of all-male education and an all-male officer corps. Consequently, the adversative method of education might be seen as a less flagrant variation on the hypothetical VCI's understanding of the place of upper-body strength in the profile of the successful computer specialist. And if the Supreme Court thus suspected that an adversative education and tolerance for it were secondary to a true goal of excluding women just because they were women, then, in addition to the possibility that the Court viewed the differential abilities of men and women to endure adversative education as a product and not a justification of discrimination, there was also the possibility that the Court simply distrusted VMI's historical and current motives. For the majority of the Supreme Court, the desire to exclude women may have produced the adversative method much more than a gender-neutral preference for the adversative method may have produced the exclusion of women. To this extent, therefore, the Supreme Court's conclusion may have been based much more on the unconstitutionality of hostility to women, whether current or historical, than on the impermissibility of using a nonspurious gender-based proxy for a legitimate and gender-neutral goal.

## Gender as a Proxy

Although the possibility that the tendencies identified by VMI and endorsed by the lower courts are the products of discrimination is real, as is the possibility that VMI was being disingenuous about the motivations for its method of instruction, there are many instances in which neither of these is present. Because Justice Ginsburg's opinion in the VMI case suggests strongly that the VMI policy would have been unconstitutional even without a disingenuous justification, and even without the gender differential's being the product of historical discrimination, we must address directly why the use of gender as a proxy in such cases would be thought impermissible. Justice Ginsburg appears to be saying that any woman must as a matter of constitutional law be given the opportunity to demonstrate that even nonspurious and material generalizations about women's capabilities do not apply to *her*.

To help focus on the issue, consider an example less empirically contestable than the claim that men are more suited to adversative education than are women. Suppose an airline restricts the job of baggage handler to men. And suppose that the airline's policy is solely a product of its empirically justified beliefs that gender predicts upper-body strength and that upper-body strength is genuinely necessary to be an effective baggage handler. This example would resemble the VMI controversy if it had been the case that gender genuinely and not because of past discrimination predicts tolerance for adversative education, and if it had been the case that tolerance for adversative education is genuinely important in military training. This is probably untrue, but for now let us assume that it is, and under these assumptions the VMI case is analytically indistinguishable from the baggage-handler case.

The baggage-handler case, which though hypothetical resembles a host of real cases involving firefighters, police officers, and, in one case, hotel bellpersons,[19] is a "cleaner" example than the actual VMI case: in the baggage-handler case the difference is truly physiological, not even plausibly a product, as tolerance for an adversative education might be and as the ability to be administrator of an estate surely is, of historical societal discrimination. So if it can be established that upper-body strength is as important for baggage handlers as acute reflexes and vision are for pilots, if it can be established that gender is a good even if imperfect proxy for upper-body strength, if it can be established that the proxy is biologically and not culturally determined, and if it can be determined that the airline's use of gender as a proxy is based on efficiency rather than being a smokescreen for animosity toward women, then is it permissible to exclude women from the occupation of baggage handler, or is it instead necessary to give each person the opportunity to demonstrate that she, individually, has the requisite upper-body strength to do the job?

As a matter of American law, it is legally impermissible to exclude women from employment on the basis of even empirically sound but nonuniversal generalizations about the relationship between gender and a material qualification for the position.[20] There are a few exceptions for what are called "bona fide occupational qualifications"[21]—excluding women from the opportunity to play the character of Macbeth in a theatrical production, or excluding men from positions as counselors to female rape victims, for example—but by and large gender-based exclusions from employment are forbidden by law.

That even those forms of sex discrimination that are based on statistically sound generalizations about a material trait are illegal does not provide us a great deal of assistance, however. In part that is because our goal is to examine critically the foundations of the law itself. More importantly, even if the law is sound, the existence of the legal prohibition does not directly answer our central question: Are gender-based generalizations legally impermissible because of something important about gender as such, or are gender-based generalizations legally impermissible as an instantiation of a broader problem with basing employment and educational selection on even empirically sound generalizations, at least under circumstances in which the individuals who do not fit the generalization are not provided the opportunity to demonstrate that their own individual circumstances or abilities do not fit the generalization?

So although it would be illegal in the United States for the airline to exclude women from jobs as baggage handlers because of the airline's empirically justified belief that women were less likely to have a genuinely important qualification for the job, just why is this so? Part of the reason might have something to do with the way in which certain nonspurious proxies are selected rather than others. Upper-body strength is indeed important for baggage handlers, but so too are many other characteristics. Among them might be a tolerance for working outside in inclement weather, the ability to work as part of a team, the capacity to perform under great time pressure, and, especially after September 11, 2001, keen observation in order to detect suspicious-looking baggage. And although gender is a sound proxy for upper-body strength, there is no reason to believe that it is anything other than spurious for these other characteristics. There might, of course, be different proxies for job-related abilities other than lifting heavy pieces of luggage. Place of birth might turn out to be a statistically sound proxy for tolerance for extremes of weather, with those born in Florida and Arizona being on average better able to work in hot weather than those born in Maine or Oregon, and those born in Vermont or Minnesota better able to tolerate extreme cold than those born in Alabama or Texas. Military experience might be a good proxy for the ability to work as part of a team. Level of education might be a good proxy for observational abilities. And many other proxies might turn out to be as statistically sound for some of the other characteristics of a good baggage handler as gender is for the upper-body strength necessary to hoist heavy luggage.

Under these circumstances, what should we make of a policy that used gender as a proxy for an admittedly material ability, but that avoided using some number of equally relevant proxies for equally material abilities? To pick out only one from a large array of nonspurious proxies for material qualifications strongly suggests that the employer has a goal other than that of using efficient proxies in making employment decisions, for if that were the case than some of the other proxies would have been employed as well. Rather, as with what appeared to be some of the Supreme Court's suspicions about VMI's motives, in our hypothetical baggage-handler case the use by an employer of only the statistically sound gender proxy and none of the statistically sound nongender proxies provides strong evidence that seizing on the nonspurious gender proxy was a pretense, even if a subconscious one, rather than a sincere attempt to engage in a rational decisionmaking process. If gender as a proxy for upper-body strength had been part of a complex algorithm of multiple proxies, we would have had good reason to believe that some women had been excluded because, other things having been equal, they were likely to have insufficient upper-body strength to do the job. But when gender is the only proxy that is used, we have good reason to suspect that women are being excluded not because they are statistically likely to have insufficient upper-body strength, but simply because they are women.

If we look not at the hypothetical baggage-handler case but at the real controversies involving police officers, firefighters, and others in jobs for which upper-body strength is a genuine qualification, a similar pattern emerges. Police departments that provided individualized testing of each applicant for intelligence and suitable personality traits nevertheless often used the proxy of gender for the admittedly material qualification of upper-body strength. Fire departments that had numerous different qualifications for the job of firefighter selected only the qualification of upper-body strength for decisionmaking by large generalization and employed more particularistic approaches to most of the other qualifications. And in doing so, the fire departments and the police departments revealed that it was the exclusion of women and not the efficiency of the proxy that was the true determinant of their actions.

There could, of course, be instances in which gender did not stand out so starkly. Indeed, it is possible that under the Supreme Court's assumptions, the VMI case might be one of these. VMI, after all, excluded not only women, but numerous men whose array of pre-entrance qualifications—proxies—made them unlikely candidates for successfully negotiating VMI's adversative educational experience. Applicants with low test scores were excluded even though some of them would probably have been able to handle the academic work at VMI. Applicants presenting profiles showing them unlikely to respond well to discipline were excluded as well, even though again, as with test scores, the factors that would have predicted disciplinary problems were themselves generalizations.

So if it turns out that gender is not the only imperfect generalization that VMI employed, and if it turns out that physical strength as well as the personality to endure adversative education was one of VMI's justifications, then the issue becomes more complex.[22] To the extent that VMI's men-only policy was based on a physical and not on a psychological generalization, as in some part it was, the possibility that the generalization was the product of past discrimination evaporates. And to the extent that VMI used gender not as the only proxy but simply as one among many in determining the qualifications to enter the school, then, at least in theory if not in practice, VMI's use of the proxy might not have been the product of a desire to exclude women because they were women but only as a function of the desire to use efficient proxies for a wide range of qualifications necessary to succeed at VMI.

Yet even on this scenario, it appears likely that the Supreme Court would still have invalidated VMI's policy. And the best explanation for this outcome, or at least one strong explanation, goes back to the history of using gender-based generalizations, even sound ones, as exclusive factors rather than as simply one factor among many. Police departments and fire departments did not employ all the other generalizations empirically available to them, and Idaho, in enacting a statutory preference for women as administrators of estates, did not enact a statutory preference for college graduates, accountants, or people over the age of forty—all factors that were, as generalizations, as likely as gender to predict for the financial acumen desirable in the administrator of an estate. With this history, it should come as no surprise that both the law and the society it both shapes and inhabits has developed what we might think of as a *compensatory* generalization: Because most generalizations based on gender have, even when nonspurious, been used for purposes going far beyond the predictive capacity of the generalization, gender-based generalizations can be said to be, *in general,* suspect. In other words, a prohibition on the use of gender-based generalizations is best understood as based on the statistically sound but nonuniversal generalization that gender-based generalizations are typically used to mask empirically unsupported desires to exclude women just because they are women.

Thus, it is often the case that even nonspurious gender-based generalizations play a role in decisionmaking beyond what the relationship between gender and what we are trying to predict would justify. It is well documented that gender-based generalizations are certainly historically, and to a considerable extent still, routinely exaggerated and routinely overused.[23] And because of the historical and systematic exaggeration of the value of even sound gender-based generalizations, and because of the consequent overuse of even sound gender-based generalizations, the moral, legal, and constitutional prohibitions on sex discrimination, of which the Supreme Court decision in the VMI case is but one example, are best understood as the mandated *under*use of gender-based generalizations to compensate for the likelihood of their exaggeration and the likelihood of their overuse.[24] If accurate use is rare and overuse far more common than underuse, then a rule prohibiting all use will prohibit more inappropriate than appropriate uses of gender, and represents a rule-based solution to the problem of tendencies to overuse gender-based generalizations.

## Gender and Generalization

If prohibitions on gender-based generalizations operate in this compensatory way, then prohibitions on using gender are properly seen not (only) as prohibitions on spurious gender-based generalizations.[25] Although spurious gender-based generalizations—women are too timid to be lawyers or not analytic enough to be economists or mathematicians—are still common and still deserving of condemnation, the principle here is stronger. It is not that gender-based generalizations are condemned because they are spurious and therefore only *when* they are spurious. Rather, in order to compensate for the observed tendencies to overuse gender-based generalizations, we treat the use of gender-based generalizations as wrong even when those generalizations are statistically relevant and thus despite the fact that they are statistically relevant.[26]

Understanding the wrong of gender-based generalizations in this way produces a prohibition on the use of such generalizations that turns out to be more robust. For if gender-based generalizations are to be condemned only because they are spurious, then they will be condemned only when they *are* spurious, and nonspurious gender-based generalizations—women have insufficient upper-body strength to be police officers, firefighters, or VMI cadets, for example—will often emerge as permissible. But because this conclusion represents neither the law nor one common understanding of the prohibition on sex discrimination, a far sounder understanding is that such prohibitions, in order to compensate for tendencies to overuse even statistically relevant gender-based justifications, serve to condemn even statistically relevant generalizations, and thus serve to condemn even those gender-based generalizations that appear to rest on a sound statistical foundation. When Justice Ginsburg in the VMI case said that government "must not rely on overbroad generalizations about the different talents, capacities, or preferences of males and females," it is plain that by "overbroad" she meant essentially all nonuniversal generalizations about differences between men and women, and thus that she intended for the law to condemn not only those generalizations that are spurious, but those that are statistically rational as well.[27] Justice Ginsburg's opinion, therefore, was not a politically correct unwillingness to recognize the differences between men and women, especially from ages eighteen to twenty-two. Rather, it was a reflection and reinforcement of the basic principle of antidiscrimination, a principle that itself operates as a generalization not only to prohibit irrelevant discrimination but also, and more importantly, to prohibit relevant discrimination.

Understanding common legal prohibitions on the use of even nonspurious gender generalizations in this compensatory and generalizing way is not the only possibility. For some the prohibition on gender-based generalizations is a product of a desire to prevent the subordination of women and to compensate for its past effects.[28] For others the prohibition stems from the importance of guarding against dividing a society by gender (and thus isolating the socially nondominant gender) in the same way we think it important to guard against dividing it by race.[29] Still other possibilities have often been offered. For our purposes here, however, the roots of a prohibition on even rational gender-based generalizations are less important than the consequences. The major lesson for us is that the condemnation of gender-based generalizations is not simply an instantiation of a condemnation of generalizations, but is an outgrowth of something distinctive about the treatment of gender. If the prohibition of nonspurious gender-based generalizations were an instantiation of a larger problem with generalization, of the kind first identified by Plato, then gender-based generalizations would be on a par with generalizations about English soccer fans, juvenile drinkers, employment applicants with no college education, smok-

ers, college applicants with low SAT scores, Massachusetts drivers, drug addicts who sought employment as
drivers of subway trains,[30] and even pit bulls. The fact
that we routinely condemn even statistically rational sex
discrimination while not condemning discrimination
against Massachusetts drivers, English soccer fans, applicants for managerial jobs who have only a high school
education, smokers, drug addicts, college applicants with
low SAT scores, or pit bulls, however, shows that the issue is not generalization but gender. The relationship
between gender and generalization is not one of cause
but rather one of consequence. Relying on generalizations about gender is not wrong because relying on generalizations is wrong. On the contrary, the wrongness of
relying on generalizations about gender is the consequence of the wrongness of making (most) decisions on
the basis of gender. Because and when such decisionmaking is wrong, one consequence is that making decisions on the basis of even statistically sound gender-based
generalizations will be wrong as well. For too long too
many people have assumed that because generalization is
wrong then gender-based generalization is wrong. But
this reasoning is backwards. The truth is that it is because gender discrimination is wrong that gender-based
generalization, even when statistically rational, is wrong
as well.

# CHAPTER 6

# The Profilers

## The Ubiquity of Profiling

From 1996 until 2000, NBC Television presented a weekly series called *Profiler*. Part of the genre that for years has featured and celebrated physicians, lawyers, police officers, and occasional other professionals (such as medical examiners, construction engineers, and lifeguards, but never funeral directors, accountants, or librarians), the series had as its principal protagonist a woman named Samantha Waters, played by the actress Ally Walker. Waters, a forensic psychologist, was employed by the Federal Bureau of Investigation to examine unsolved crimes. More particularly, it was Waters' job to scrutinize all available information about the crime and then on the basis of this information construct a *profile* of the likely perpetrator. In examining the evidence at the scene and other available details of the crime (always a serial murder, and never shoplifting, pickpocketing, or insider trading), the profiler relied on psychological and criminological expertise, on her own experiences, and on the accumulated probabilistic learning from past solved crimes to make a highly educated guess as to the type of person who had committed the particular crime.[1] Armed with this profile, the F.B.I. would then greatly narrow the field of suspects and in short order identify the actual perpetrator from the profile-narrowed array.

At the time the television series was conceived, its creators did not imagine that there was anything controversial about the idea. Indeed, television's fictional profiler was created around a small cadre of actual professionals engaged in similar tasks. In the early 1950s, for example, New York City was plagued by a series of more than thirty bombings in movie theaters and railroad stations, the bombs planted by a mysterious individual dubbed by the newspapers as The Mad Bomber. Although none of the bombings was fatal, and only one produced a serious injury, the level of fear was high, as was the degree of frustration by law-enforcement authorities in not being able to identify or apprehend the perpetrator. The police sought help from a psychiatrist named James Brussel, who analyzed photographs of the bomb scenes, anonymous letters sent by the Mad Bomber, and various other available pieces of evidence. On this basis Dr. Brussel urged the police to look for a person with paranoid tendencies who hated his father and was obsessed by his mother, who lived in Connecticut, who had a serious heart condition, was probably overweight, and was a disgruntled current or former employee of the Consolidated Edison Company. In addition, said Dr. Brussel, the perpetrator was probably a middle-aged Roman Catholic born in eastern Europe, could conceivably live with a brother or sister, and was the type of individual who would wear a buttoned double-breasted suit.

Starting with the employee records of the Consolidated Edison Company, and assisted by information provided by the Mad Bomber in letters to the newspapers as well as by the profile compiled by Dr. Brussel, the police eventually focused on a man named George Metesky, whose grievance with Consolidated Edison stemmed from the company's refusal to compensate him for what he claimed was a work-related illness. When the police arrived to question Metesky, they discovered a single, middle-aged man with tuberculosis, born in Poland of Lithuanian Catholic parents but now living in Connecticut with his two sisters. Mestesky was in his pajamas when confronted by the police, and so he asked to be allowed to change clothes. Upon returning, Metesky was wearing a double-breasted suit. Buttoned.

The success of Dr. Brussel in helping the police home in on Metesky, who was committed to an institution for the mentally ill for seventeen years, and who after his release lived quietly in Waterbury, Connecticut, until his death at the age of ninety in 1994, was striking.[2] Equally important, however, was the way in which the publicity surrounding Dr. Brussel's eerily accurate profile of Metesky launched profiling as a serious specialty within forensic psychology. Professional profilers might, for example, determine that most child molesters had themselves been molested as children, and would thus narrow the field of suspects in a sexually oriented child murder case to a list of victims of molestation some years earlier. And if it was also the case that most perpetrators of a certain kind of child molestation had been well-off males between the ages of thirty and fifty, then this would narrow the field still more. That killings with a particular variety of excess violence often are committed by killers who know their victim would reduce the array of possible suspects even further. Other field-narrowing characteristics help reduce the number of possibilities to a point at which each suspect can be individually investigated.

The television profiler, following the model of real-life profilers, was thus engaged in a process of generalization, seeking to narrow the list of possible suspects by identifying an area of intersection among numerous generalizations. It is a generalization that most child molesters have themselves been molested as children, it is a generalization that most are between the ages of thirty and fifty, it is a generalization that most perpetrators of sexual crimes have had previous contacts with their victims, it is a generalization that most perpetrators of crimes live in the vicinity where the criminal act took place, it is a generalization that most molesters of young girls are men, it is a generalization that most of the people who pass unnoticed in wealthy suburban communities are white and well dressed, and it is a generalization that most of the well-dressed white males between the ages of thirty and fifty living in the vicinity of Hollywood, California, are in some way connected with the entertainment industry. If on the basis of these generalizations, therefore, a profiler initially narrowed the list of "prime" suspects to three people who belonged to all these categories, she would be doing what was expected of her, even though at least two and possibly all three of these individuals were not guilty of the crime being investigated.

The demise of *Profiler* on television was hastened by a raft of media attention to what appeared to many people to be the dark side of profiling. In many communities, it was discovered that ordinary police officers were also engaged in acts of profiling, and the profiles they constructed were far less scientific than those constructed by professional forensic psychologists working as profilers for law-enforcement agencies. They were even far less scientific than those constructed by the fictional profiler on television. Although the television profiler typically constructed her profile from multiple characteristics, and although real profilers always do, the profiles constructed by many police officers turned out to be based disproportionately on one characteristic—race.[3] Claiming that crime statistics, especially those related to narcotics offenses, justified a focus on African Americans, the profiling police officers would stop African Americans for questioning and investigation at a rate far in excess of what would have been expected on the basis of the percentage of African Americans in the population at large, and often in excess of what would have been expected on the basis of the percentage of African Americans committing the crime in question. And because many of the African Americans questioned were guilty of no crimes whatsoever, there developed an increasing suspicion that allegedly empirically justified profiles were simply a pretense for racial harassment. In the space of just a few years, "profiling" had moved in public perception from a description of an admirable and professional law-enforcement practice to a pejorative characterization of the worst form of police abuse.

It should come as little surprise, however, that profiling remains a widespread and necessary weapon in the law-enforcement arsenal. Tax inspectors use profiling to target certain taxpayers for intense audits, customs officials use profiling to determine which arriving passengers warrant close scrutiny, occupational safety and health officials use profiling to decide which businesses to inspect, and police detectives continue to narrow the focus of their inquiries by constructing profiles of likely suspects.

Are all these practices suspect? If not, is racial profiling different from other forms of profiling? And if this is so, is it because racial profiles are invariably spurious, little different from narrowing a field of suspects to those with a certain astrological sign on the basis of the mistaken belief that such people are more likely to have committed a crime of a certain sort? Or is racial profiling different not because it is always spurious, but only when it *is* spurious? Alternatively, is racial profiling different—and wrong—not only when it is spurious, but even when it is not? And if this is so, then why is it so?

These and related questions are the subject of this chapter and the next. In this chapter we examine the practice of profiling in the tax-audit process, then move to profiling at ports of entry by customs and immigration inspectors. In chapter 7 we take up the question of racial profiling, in the contexts both of the more traditional practice of including race as a factor in determining which people the police will target for close attention, and of the newer but even more salient—after September 11, 2001—practice of using racial profiling to determine which airline passengers are more likely than others to commit airborne acts of terrorism. Through all of this the goal will be not only to examine profiling—racial and otherwise—for its own importance, but also to connect the questions about profiling to the other questions about generalization that occupy the balance of this book.

## Profiling at the Internal Revenue Service

Every year Americans file approximately 130 million income tax returns. Not all the information reported on these returns is accurate, and, not surprisingly, the mistakes are more often in the taxpayer's favor than in the government's. Some people do overstate their actual income, but not nearly as many as those who understate it. Some taxpayers fail to take deductions to which they are entitled, but far more claim deductions to which they are not entitled. As a consequence, the Internal Revenue Service, not realistically capable of closely examining all 130 million returns in order to identify mistakes or fraud, appears to need some method of deciding which taxpayers to focus on and which to ignore.

The Internal Revenue Service only "appears" to need some method of focusing on some taxpayers and not others because there *are* other ways of dealing with limited enforcement resources and a massive volume of potential violators. Chief among these is the strategy of transferring the costs of enforcement to the violators themselves by a system of rare and random inspection coupled with draconian penalties for discovered violations. If the Internal Revenue Service were to pick totally at random one out of every 5,000 returns for close inspection,[4] and if those discovered to have understated their income or overstated their deductions were to face penalties of, say, one year in the penitentiary regardless of fault, it is fair to assume that the level of compliance would be extraordinarily high at a relatively low enforcement cost, at least if we assume that there was also an effective method of similarly deterring nonfiling.

Although the efficiency in some contexts of low-probability/high-penalty law enforcement is well-known,[5] it comes at a price that few populations are willing to accept. However genuinely random the selection procedures are, the public has at best a limited tolerance for the imposition of serious costs on people on the basis of what is perceived to be too much a matter of chance.[6] Subjecting all age-eligible males to conscription for one year is accepted in many countries, and subjecting approximately 30 percent of all age-eligible males to conscription for two years was (barely) accepted in the United States in the period from 1970 through 1972. But no amount of fairness in a conscription lottery would lead the public to accept a system imposing a 5 percent chance of conscription for ten years, despite the fact that a rational potential conscript should prefer a 5 percent chance of ten years' conscription, all else being equal, to a 30 percent chance of two years' conscription. Much the same applies to criminal penalties, and however efficient it would be to enforce the payment of tolls on limited-access highways by subjecting a small number of randomly selected scofflaws to hefty fines and a period of imprisonment, such a course of action is politically and socially impossible. As a result, what we actually have, instead of an efficient system of low-probability/high-penalty enforcement, is an inefficient system of low penalties coupled with an exceedingly costly array of cameras and counting devices.

For the same reasons, low-probability/high-penalty tax enforcement is politically and socially infeasible, despite its seeming efficiency. Accordingly, the Internal Revenue Service is faced with the task of devising a way to focus its limited enforcement resources on those taxpayers and those tax returns whose careful investigation by the authorities would be especially likely to uncover revenue-producing taxpayer errors. The method chosen by the Internal Revenue Service is the construction of an audit profile on the basis of what is known as a Discriminant Function (DIF) analysis. Every tax return is given a DIF score on the basis of those features obvious from the face of the return that indicate a disproportionate statistical likelihood of either taxpayer-favoring mistakes or outright tax fraud. Those returns with DIF scores above a certain threshold are then selected for manual inspection and likely audit.

The actual details of the audit profiling algorithms are a well-kept secret, but certain aspects of the system of deciding which taxpayers to audit have become moderately widely known.[7] Because people engaged in certain occupations—waiters, taxi drivers, casino dealers, and drywall contractors, for example—have shown themselves statistically more likely to underreport income than the median taxpayer, being engaged in one of these occupations increases the probability of audit, even controlling for every other aspect of one's tax return. Similarly, because people in certain other occupations—lawyers and physicians especially—are statistically more likely than most to overstate their deductions and to engage in tax-avoiding investment schemes of dubious legality, members of these occupations also find themselves more likely to be targeted for audit just because of their occupation. Because the Internal Revenue Service keeps track of average deductions—people with a certain income level average a certain amount of charitable deductions, medical deductions, and so on—those appreciably above the averages again have an increased risk of being audited. Geography plays a role—it is better to live in Minneapolis than in San Francisco, and in Milwaukee rather than in Los Angeles—and so does the willingness to claim certain kinds of credits and deductions. Inflating the number of dependents, for example, is a common tax-avoidance device, so people with large numbers of dependents come under close scrutiny. And although taking a business expense deduction for a necessary office in one's home is entirely permissible, the percentage of people unjustifiably claiming such a deduction is higher, controlling for all other factors, than is the percentage of people unjustifiably claiming deductions for real estate taxes or home mortgage payments. As a result, claiming the home office deduction, like some number of other "red flags," has an appreciable effect on the likelihood that one's tax return will be subject to close inspection.

Earning a high Discriminant Function score is no guarantee of being subject to an audit, but it is a guarantee that one's return will be carefully scrutinized by actual human eyes—as opposed to a computer. This manual scrutiny does not assure an audit, but it does increase the probability substantially. It turns out, therefore, that "fitting the profile" of a tax evader significantly increases the likelihood of being audited and, because approximately 80 percent of all audits produce increased tax assessments, significantly increases the likelihood of additional taxes as well. And even apart from the likelihood of an increased assessment, the audit itself is perceived by taxpayers to be a sufficiently costly, unpleasant, and altogether scary experience that most taxpayers would treat it as a penalty in its own right. Part of this fear of an audit is the consequence of the anxiety produced by the procedure, an anxiety that the Internal Revenue Service takes few pains to minimize; part is the possibility that those audited will deem it prudent to spend money for accountants and tax attorneys to assist them through the audit process; and part is the high probability that a person audited will be found to have underpaid her or his taxes, even as to items that the profiled characteristics did not indicate. Exaggerated noncash charitable deductions, for example, might be roughly evenly distributed throughout the taxpaying population, but those who are audited will get caught and those who are not audited

will escape. Consequently, even those who have high audit profile scores for reasons totally nonindicative of
charitable deduction inflation are at greater risk than
others of having their charitable deductions disallowed.

The entire process of compiling audit profiles through
the use of Discriminant Function analysis is of course an
exercise in generalization. Many waiters do not hide income, and most people who hide income are not waiters;
but being a taxpayer who is a waiter is a better indicator
of hiding income than is simply being a taxpayer. The
vast majority of orthopedists do not invest in legally
questionable tax shelters, and the vast majority of people
who invest in such tax shelters are not orthopedists; but
again the use of a nonspurious but under- and overinclusive generalization appears to increase the reliability of a
process of identifying potential tax avoiders. Just as targeting pit bulls helps to identify aggressiveness in dogs,
and targeting pilots over sixty helps to identify diminished hearing, vision, and reflexes, so too does targeting
waiters and orthopedists, as well as Los Angeles residents, home office deduction takers, and many others
help to focus scarce tax enforcement resources where
they will be used most productively. It turns out, therefore, that it is far better to be an honest Milwaukee
schoolteacher with two children than it is to be an honest San Francisco drywall contractor with six children.
Even the honest drywall contractor with six children—
just because of his occupation, place of residence, and
number of dependents—runs a much greater risk of audit than the person with a different occupation, different
place of residence, and fewer dependents.

Although some people do question the fairness of the
Discriminant Function method of tax enforcement, it
appears to be widely even if grudgingly accepted.[8] Most

likely, this degree of acceptance is due in large part to the seeming lack of any plausible alternative. That many people will cheat on their taxes if given the chance is pretty much a given, and so is the impossibility of examining anywhere near all 130 million returns. So if low-probability/high-penalty random inspection is also not feasible, then some method of focusing official attention on likely violators appears to be a practical necessity.

More broadly, the process of selecting tax returns for audit again illustrates the way in which generalization is as much a conceptual inevitability as it is merely a practical necessity. Even if every return were examined in detail, that examination would still need to rely on generalizations in order to conclude that a violation had occurred. Suppose every return is examined with care, and the tax return of a particular waiter shows that he reported gratuity income equal to 40 percent of his salary income, and suppose that such a percentage was less than half of what other similarly situated waiters reported. If this discrepancy were used to justify further investigation, it would again be the case that the further investigation was premised on a generalization. And even if there appeared to be even better evidence of underreporting income—high personal expenditures, or the eyewitness testimony of fellow waiters—this evidence, as we saw in examining the Blue Bus Problem in chapter 3, would itself necessarily rely on probabilities and generalizations. That a process of generalization is so widely accepted in the context of selecting tax returns for audit, therefore, appears to be less a function of anything specific to the tax enforcement system and more about people's willingness to understand and to accept—especially when characteristics such as race or gender are not an issue—that basing official decisions on probabilistic generalizations—profiles—is not something that can plausibly be avoided.

## "Would You Step over Here, Please?"

The problems faced by tax inspectors are similar in many respects to the problems faced by customs authorities. Although most people who enter the country are carrying no contraband, there are some who are. And although most travelers fully declare the value of all items acquired abroad, some do not. As a result, an important task of customs officials is to locate the small number of violators among the large number of travelers. As with the task presented by the sheer number of tax returns, the volume of airport traffic makes universal customs inspection impossible, for if every item in every suitcase of every passenger on every plane (to say nothing of ships, trains, and cars) were examined closely, the lines at airports would extend for miles and the time required to proceed through customs would be measured in days rather than in minutes or hours. Metal detectors and substance-sniffing dogs do make universal inspection for some forms of contraband possible, but for many others (ivory and knock-off Rolexes, for example) there remains no workable substitute for manual and visual inspection.

Because of the obvious practical necessity of narrowing the pool of returning passengers who will be subject to close scrutiny, customs officials routinely employ profiles not unlike those employed by tax inspectors, even though the characteristics identified in a customs profile differ from those identified in a tax profile. Although there are profiles for those likely to be transporting fake Louis Vuitton luggage or underdeclaring the value of goods purchased abroad, let us initially focus on the better-known profile, the profile of those who might be transporting illegal narcotics. Again, the full details of these drug-courier profiles are highly secret, but we do know that they include certain characteristics found to be indicative of those carrying illegal drugs.[9] Drug couriers are often coming from countries or regions known to be suppliers of drugs—Colombia and Thailand but not Estonia or Morocco—and are also often going to or from cities known to be centers of drug processing and distribution—Miami and Amsterdam but not Tokyo or Portland. Drug couriers disproportionately do not check their luggage; they disproportionately have a small number of carry-on bags, they disproportionately pay cash for their tickets; they disproportionately stay at their destination for a very short time; they disproportionately are not members of a frequent-flyer program; they disproportionately travel more than might be expected from their income or occupation; and they disproportionately travel alone.

In addition to the characteristics of current travel and previous travel history, there are characteristics of appearance and behavior. Drug couriers tend to wear sunglasses because sunglasses are thought to obscure a nervous demeanor or a disingenuous answer to questions. They tend to wear loose-fitting clothes, because such clothing can make it easier to hide contraband narcotics. And when questioned, drug couriers disproportionately appear nervous, disproportionately appear either overly polite or overly argumentative, and disproportionately claim illness.

None of these factors, each a generalization, represents anywhere near a perfect proxy. Although travelers wearing sunglasses are more likely to be transporting narcotics than those who are not, the vast majority of sunglass-wearing travelers are not drug couriers, and the vast majority of drug couriers are not wearing sunglasses. Like most of the generalizations that concern us here, the generalization that sunglass-wearers are more likely to be drug couriers is statistically nonspurious but still hugely under- and overinclusive.

When these individual factors are combined into a multifactored profile, however, the reliability increases dramatically. Like the Internal Revenue Service's Discriminant Function analysis with its fifty or more factors, in actual practice the U.S. Customs Service employs up to twenty dimensions in its profiling of drug couriers. Consequently, the question is not whether it is a good idea to subject all sunglass-wearers to extensive questioning and intrusive body searches. Rather, the question is whether it is sound law-enforcement practice to single out for special and admittedly intrusive attention those airline passengers who, say, are wearing sunglasses and loose-fitting clothing, are traveling alone with no checked luggage and only a small amount of carry-on luggage, who have just arrived from Amsterdam after a very short stay, and who argumentatively claim illness when asked the routine questions that are asked of virtually all passengers upon entering the country. When described and used with this degree of detail, according to customs authorities, the profile then provides a highly reliable albeit imperfect method of singling out for close attention those most likely to be transporting narcotics.

Totally apart from any question about the use of race or ethnicity as part of the multifactor profile, drug-courier profiling by the U.S. Customs Service has been controversial, in part because of constitutional questions about whether identification of a person for more-intrusive examination solely on the basis of a profile satisfies the "reasonable suspicion" standard that is well established in American constitutional law.[10] Yet in the most important case on the issue of customs stops, the Supreme Court has upheld the use of drug-courier profiles as a means of establishing reasonable suspicion. The key figure in *United States v. Sokolow* was Andrew Sokolow, who was targeted at the Honolulu International Airport after having paid $2,100 in cash from a roll of twenty-dollar bills for two airline tickets and after having traveled from Hawaii to Miami for a stay of only forty-eight hours.[11] In addition, Sokolow, who was twenty-five years old, was dressed in a black jumpsuit, wore gold jewelry, traveled only with carry-on luggage, gave a telephone number that was not listed in his name, and appeared nervous when questioned by the Customs Service. On the basis of all these observations, Sokolow was detained upon leaving the airport by the Drug Enforcement Administration, and as a consequence of this detention was found to have been transporting a large quantity of cocaine.

Sokolow claimed that merely fitting the profile was insufficient to establish reasonable suspicion, thus rendering the subsequent search unconstitutional. The Supreme Court, however, disagreed. The Court rejected Sokolow's argument, upholding the use of the profile to establish reasonable suspicion and thus supporting the sequence of events that led to the discovery of the cocaine in Sokolow's carry-on luggage. As in earlier cases, the Supreme Court concluded that comparing law-enforcement observations with a predetermined drug-courier profile was sufficiently connected to specific and articulable facts to satisfy any applicable constitutional requirements.[12] In so concluding, the Court rejected arguments by Sokolow that turn out to be quite similar to those accepted by the Massachusetts Supreme Judicial Court in Betty Smith's case against the Rapid Transit Company. Just as the Supreme Judicial Court insisted in that case on "direct" or "actual" evidence rather than on what it perceived as mere probabilities, so too did Sokolow insist that something more than the inherently probabilistic nature of a drug-courier profile was necessary to meet the demands of the Fourth Amendment.

In rejecting Sokolow's argument, the Supreme Court avoided the confusion that plagued the Massachusetts court in *Smith v. Rapid Transit*. If a police officer had testified that he had seen with his own eyes white powder coming out of Sokolow's luggage, Sokolow might have conceded that this testimonial evidence was sufficiently direct and sufficiently particularized to have established a reasonable suspicion. And even if Sokolow himself might not have conceded this or anything else, implicit in Sokolow's argument is that this kind of evidence is entitled to more credibility in establishing reasonable suspicion than are the probabilities used to make up the drug-courier profile, probabilities that started the chain of events that led to Sokolow's arrest. Yet given what we know about the numerous instances in which police officers have fabricated allegedly eyewitness accounts of observing a substance that appeared to be narcotics, and given the possibility that the white powder was talcum powder or coffee sweetener or something else other than cocaine, it is not totally clear that the reasonable suspicion that would have been provided by the police officer's account would have been stronger, at that time, than the reasonable suspicion offered by the profile.[13] Moreover, and again as we saw in chapter 3, the distinction between the use of the profile and the use of so-called direct evidence is far more illusory than real.

Inferences drawn from observations or from physical evidence are themselves based on probabilistic generalizations, and the cumulative set of inferences that produces a purportedly "direct" conclusion or observation is nothing more than a collection of inferences drawn from generalizations known to be reliable.[14] Just like a profile. Indeed, exposing the essential similarity between observation and profiling makes us question whether we can even be sure of what a profile *is*. The profiles constructed by the profiler on television and by her real-life professional counterparts are accumulations of probabilistic inferences, yet professional profilers typically do not reduce these inferences to a written formula. In the context of airport searches, however, we tend to think of a profile as a written formula provided to customs inspectors. When such a written formula is not provided to inspectors, however, what the inspectors necessarily do is draw on their own experiences in order to determine, on the basis of probabilistic generalizations from previous encounters, which travelers need further inspection and which do not. When customs inspectors do not have what in the customs context is known as a profile, therefore, what they use is what in a different context is called exactly the same thing.

This ambiguity about the very nature of a profile becomes even more apparent from Justice Thurgood Marshall's dissenting opinion in the *Sokolow* case. Objecting to the majority's allowance of reasonable suspicion to be based on the formula, Justice Marshall complained that, "In my view, a law enforcement officer's mechanistic application of a formula of personal and behavioral traits in deciding whom to question in detail can only dull the officer's ability and determination to make sensitive and fact-specific inferences in light of his experience."[15]

Here Justice Marshall went right to the heart of the matter. He recognized that the question of the profile is not about profiles as such, but is about *rules*. The issue is whether preexisting and general rules should be employed to determine which people to stop, as the majority was willing to permit, or whether that determination must, as Justice Marshall insisted, be made on a particularistic basis by individual officers using their own best judgment in each case, even if that best judgment can itself be seen as just another version of profiling. Once we understand that the issue is not about whether to use profiles or not but instead about whether to use (or to prefer) formal written profiles or informal unwritten ones, it becomes clear that this is not a question of profiles or not, but a question about discretion. Should individual customs officers have the discretion to create their own profiles, as Justice Marshall preferred, or is it at least permissible, even if not constitutionally mandatory, for formal written profiles to be used as a way of regularizing the process and limiting the discretion of individual officers?

Justice Marshall's objection to written formulas and his preference for the particularistic discretion of individual officers is thus one side of a debate in which, as with the famous hypothetical of vehicles in the park discussed in chapter 2, the question is whether and when we should prefer to make decisions according to predetermined and probably under- and overinclusive rules, and whether and when we should avoid such predetermined rules in favor of the possibly mistaken case-by-case discretion of enforcement officials.[16]

Once we understand the choice as being one between profiles that are constructed in advance and have the potential to be both under- and overinclusive, on the one hand, and profiles that are constructed on a case-by-case basis by law-enforcement officials making, in Justice Marshall's words, "sensitive and fact-specific inferences in light of [their] experience," on the other, we can see that the issue is not about profiling at all, for profiling is inevitable. Rather, the debate that masquerades as a debate about profiling is a debate about rules, and is a debate, therefore, that is centrally about the circumstances under which we will and will not rely on the unconstrained discretion of enforcement officials. The risks of this discretion are nowhere more apparent than in the area of race, and, as we shall see in the next chapter, it is the use of race that has caused the hitherto largely unobjectionable practice of profiling to become so laden with political, moral, and emotional baggage.

# CHAPTER 7

# The Usual Suspects

## Race at the Airport

In chapter 6 we spent considerable time examining the case of Andrew Sokolow, who was initially identified as a possible drug courier because he fitted a profile that included his appearance, his behavior, and his travel pattern. Yet one of the most noteworthy aspects of Mr. Sokolow's involvement with the question of profiling was that it arose in a context in which race was not an issue. Andrew Sokolow was a white male stopped as a suspected drug courier not because of anything to do with his racial or ethnic background, but because of his age, his clothing, his demeanor, and especially his travel behavior. It was Andrew Sokolow's black jumpsuit, gold jewelry, cash purchase, and quick trip from Honolulu to Miami that was his undoing, and in that context the controversy about profiling was a controversy about statistics and not about race. Or, to misappropriate Dr. Martin Luther King Jr.'s memorable words, Andrew

Sokolow was judged not by the color of his skin, but by the contents of his knapsack.[1]

Not many years have passed since Andrew Sokolow's case, but these days when profiling is the subject it is race that is the question. Issues of race and ethnicity have become inextricably connected with the issue of profiling, and debates focusing on race and ethnicity have irreversibly transformed the nature of the discussion about profiling.[2]

In the context of customs searches at airports, searches largely though not exclusively of those suspected of transporting illegal narcotics, some of the bad odor associated with profiling stems from the discovery that officials of the U.S. Customs Service were in the 1990s subjecting a disproportionately large number of African-American women to intrusive and humiliating body-cavity searches. Many of these searches took place at Chicago's O'Hare Airport, although there were incidents at other airports as well.[3] At O'Hare the vast majority of the women who were searched turned out to have been doing nothing wrong, and the subsequent investigation into these events made it clear that almost all the African-American women who were searched were initially targeted overwhelmingly because of their race.

The incidents at O'Hare intensified the condemnation of racial profiling, but were those events accurately described as racial profiling? We have to look more closely at what actually happened at O'Hare in order to understand exactly what it is that is being condemned. Although many people appeared to believe that the targeting of African-American women was a product of a formula that included race and gender among its elements, it turns out that at O'Hare this was not the case at all. As with the targeting of Andrew Sokolow, the customs officers at

O'Hare did indeed have a formula—a profile, in one sense of the term—but that formula made no mention whatsoever of either race or gender as factors whose presence increased the likelihood that the passenger was transporting unlawful drugs. And this is not surprising, because, according to the Customs Service, there was no evidence that either race or gender was statistically relevant to identifying drug couriers. A drug-courier algorithm or profile that added race and gender to the array of factors in the O'Hare profile, and indeed in the profile that snared Andrew Sokolow, would have made no incremental contribution to the effectiveness of the profile.

Race having been spurious in the underlying reality and nonexistent in any formal profiles that existed, the incidents at O'Hare were caused not by the inclusion of race or gender in a list of factors to be used in determining whom to search, but rather by individual customs officials' deciding on their own, or on the basis of collective but false folk wisdom, that African-American women were to be targeted. We do not know why they did so, but we can assume that it was some combination of two different motives. One was unalloyed racial hostility, not prompted by empirical beliefs of any kind, but rather by pure animosity toward African Americans. The other was a belief, but an unfounded one, that race and gender were somehow relevant to the ability to select likely drug couriers from the full population of passengers traveling through O'Hare Airport. But because the former motive did not even purport to be based on empirically reliable generalizations, and because the latter was based on generalizations that had no basis in fact or experience, it should come as little surprise that when the practice of targeting African-American women was halted, the effectiveness in locating drug smugglers actually increased.

When spurious factors were eliminated, therefore, a higher percentage of searches yielded contraband than had been the case when African-American women were being disproportionately stopped, which was only to be expected. The elimination of a spurious factor cannot help but increase the probability of successful identification of those with illegal drugs.

Although the events at O'Hare have commonly attracted the label "profile," the label seems inapt, for the targeting of African-American women was based either on no profile at all or on an empirically spurious one. What was transpiring at O'Hare was some combination of targeting a disliked group and reliance on a belief that was little different, statistically, from customs officials' stopping those with heads of a certain shape in the mistaken belief that head shape probabilistically indicates tendencies to illegal activity. The customs officials at O'Hare were neither following a written formula nor using a factor that had any statistical validity at all. It is no wonder that elimination of the practice turned out to increase efficiency.

The actual nature of the events at O'Hare and other airports should give us pause before we too quickly accept the lessons of Justice Marshall's dissenting opinion in the *Sokolow* case.[4] Justice Marshall, it will be recalled, objected to written formulas of the kind that led to the focus on Andrew Sokolow because Justice Marshall believed that the formulas would interfere with the ability of officers to make "sensitive and fact-specific inferences" in individual cases. At O'Hare, however, officers' practice of making sensitive and fact-specific inferences was precisely the problem. Given the discretion to make sensitive and fact-specific inferences, the Customs Service officials used that discretion to target African-American women even though there was no statistical basis for their doing so. Indeed, had the officers stuck mechanically and rigidly to the actual written formula for identifying drug couriers, the problem would not have arisen. Only when and because the officers were given the freedom to depart from that formula did they have the opening to introduce statistically spurious factors into the equation. The incidents at O'Hare, therefore, provide a strong argument against Justice Marshall's position. In a world of ideal customs officials, it might be better to rely on their sensitive and fact-specific inferences, for such inferences would enable the officers to avoid the inevitable under- and overinclusiveness of any set formula. But with the actual and decidedly nonideal customs officials who were operating at O'Hare, the wrong, we now see, was committed not because of a formula, but precisely because of the absence of one. As with the numerous studies showing the superiority of actuarial to clinical assessments of dangerous (as discussed in chapter 3), the exercise of individual discretion is often, though of course not always, inferior to decision-making based on more systematically compiled actuarial information.

Nor should this come as a surprise. For much the same reason that people typically ignore base-rate information, again as discussed in chapter 3, people are often inclined to overestimate the proportion of a particularly salient component within a larger population.[5] Because race is salient for most people, they are consequently likely to amplify the extent to which members of a race other than their own are represented in a larger population with negative attributes, such as the population of apprehended drug couriers, just because the observer is likely to focus more on the "out group" members of that population, and consequently take those "out group" members as being more representative of the group than they in fact are.[6]

If "racial profiling" is taken to mean the identification of people because their race appeared on a formal list of suspicion-raising factors, then it turns out that the O'Hare events provide us an example not of racial profiling at all, but of one or both of the two quite different pathologies just noted.[7] To repeat, one is simple racial animus, in which hostile acts against people because of their race are based on pure dislike of people of that race, with no pretense of an empirical basis for that dislike. For some people their dislike of people from races other than their own is no more empirically grounded than my dislike of anchovies and olives, dislikes that are based on no empirical facts about anchovies and olives other than that they do not appeal to me. It is more than likely that at least some of this type of nonempirical primal animus, possibly a function of the tendency of (too) many people to dislike people different from themselves, was the motivation behind the practices at O'Hare.[8]

In addition to stemming from outright racial hostility, the practices at O'Hare were also likely, as noted above, to be at least partially the product of mistaken beliefs on the part of the officers that race was a reliable predictor of narcotics trafficking. Subscribing to such an empirically unfounded belief may itself be the product of animus, or it may simply be a matter of negligence in relying on faulty sources of information; but once again the phenomenon is quite different from the reliance on race under circumstances in which race is a nonspurious indicator of likely criminal conduct. At O'Hare, however, the behavior of the customs officials had no such empirical grounding, and was probably a combination of pure animus and mistaken empirical beliefs, both of which need to be distinguished from an empirically grounded profile.[9] Rather than basing their actions on a genuine profile, therefore, the officers at O'Hare engaged in a series of acts that faithful adherence to a statistically sound profile could have done much to constrain.

The use of race in airport drug-courier investigation may be spurious, but the intellectually harder and potentially more important issues arise when race turns out to be nonspurious.[10] And although there may be such cases involving contraband at ports of entry (especially when there is a high correlation between race and nationality and a high correlation between nationality and country of narcotics origin, or when the groups engaged in certain kinds of unlawful activity are themselves organized along lines of national origin), and although there are probably such cases involving street-level narcotics offenses, the most salient example is that of suspected terrorists who would seek to bomb, hijack, or otherwise interfere with the operation of commercial airplanes. Unlike being a drug courier, here it appears that neither race nor gender is spurious. Those who commit acts of airplane terrorism, both before and after September 11, 2001, are disproportionately younger Muslim men of Middle Eastern background.[11] Unlike the case of stopping African-American women for suspected drug offenses, stopping men younger than middle-aged of Middle Eastern appearance for suspected terrorist activity seems hardly to be spurious. And if that is so, does that fact alone make the practice permissible?

In examining this issue, it is worthwhile recalling from chapter 6 the type of profiles used both by the Internal Revenue Service to determine likely targets for an audit and by the Customs Service in *Sokolow* to determine likely targets for a drug search. In each of those cases the official and statistically verified profiles contained multiple factors—as many as fifty in the computation of a taxpayer's Discriminant Function score, and approximately twenty in the case of the Customs Service profile of typical drug couriers. Although in neither case was any one factor either a necessary or a sufficient condition for further investigation, in both cases any of a large number of factors was relevant, and the profile was a complex algorithm of all the factors. Customs officials did not stop all nervous passengers, or all passengers traveling to Miami, or all passengers with sunglasses and loose clothing, or all passengers with carry-on luggage, or all passengers paying for their tickets in cash; but the combination of all of these—nervous cash-paying passengers traveling to Miami with sunglasses, loose clothing, and carry-on luggage only—would make one a prime target. The Internal Revenue Service does not audit all drywall contractors, all people living in San Francisco, all people with six dependents, or all people with substantial business expenses; but again the combination of these— San Francisco drywall contractors with six dependents and large claimed business expenses—will produce a significantly increased probability of audit.

In the context of searches for terrorists at airports, we see the same phenomenon. The currently employed Computer-Assisted Passenger Pre-screening System (CAPPS), the product of the White House Commission on Aviation Safety and Security, chaired by Vice-President Al Gore in 1997, has been used not for passenger searches but to decide which luggage, checked as well as carried on, should be examined with special care. Like all good profiles, the CAPPS system includes a multiplicity of factors but, following the explicit recommendation of the Gore Commission, does not include race among them. Specifically, the commission decried the use of race on the grounds that a profile must be based on "reasonable predictions of risk, [and] not stereotypes or generalizations."[12]

Yet although the Gore Commission announced that including race (as well as ethnicity, national origin, and religion) in the profile was improper, it said nothing about why that was so. By defining stereotypes and generalizations as representing a category distinct from the category of reasonable predictions of risk, the Gore Commission sidestepped the question whether using race was improper *because* it was statistically irrelevant or improper *despite* its statistical relevance. And in avoiding this question, the Gore Commission rendered itself unable to confront a host of post–September 11 issues that arise in a context in which race—or ethnicity—appears to be nonspurious. Of course the thoughtful defenders of using race or ethnicity as part of a careful airport screening process, whether in order to examine luggage or to search passengers, do not argue that race or ethnicity should be the only characteristic that is employed. So when officials insist that race or ethnicity should not be the "sole" factor in airport screening,[13] they are arguing against a straw figure. The serious proponents of using race or ethnicity do not claim that either should be the exclusive factor, but only that each is permissibly a factor that should be employed to the full extent of its statistical relevance.[14]

Proponents of ethnic profiling maintain, therefore, that when ethnicity is merely one of multiple factors employed in deciding whom to target, then there is, assuming statistical relevance, no good reason not to include ethnicity and, when justified, race, as part of the larger profile. The argument is thus not that all people of Middle Eastern appearance (which could include name as well as physical appearance) should be targeted, but that Middle Eastern appearance may be a permissible component of an algorithm that also includes gender, age, form of purchasing the ticket (cash or credit card, last minute or well in advance, direct or through a travel agent), membership in a frequent flyer program, time of check-in, type of luggage, presence or absence of a hotel or rental-car reservation at destination, demeanor, and all the other factors that are part of the current CAPPS system.[15] So although under this view it would be unwarranted to stop all Middle Easterners or all Middle Eastern men, or all young Middle Eastern men, it would not be unwarranted to detain for at least brief questioning all nervous young Middle Eastern men who bought their tickets with cash at the last minute and checked in late with only carry-on luggage even though not all nervous non-Middle Easterners who bought their tickets with cash and checked in late with only carry-on luggage would be stopped.

In order for this algorithm to make statistical sense, each of the factors would have to contribute something to the reliability of the full algorithm. In other words, for race or ethnicity itself to be statistically relevant it would have to be the case that stopping nervous Middle Eastern men who have bought their tickets at the last minute with cash and have only carry-on luggage would yield more terrorists (or the same number of terrorists at lower cost) than would stopping nervous men of all races who have bought their tickets at the last minute with cash and have only carry-on luggage. When we see race or ethnicity or national origin as components of a considerably larger array of factors, it may possibly turn out, therefore, that race, ethnicity, and national origin are less relevant than we suppose. Although most airplane terrorists have been young Middle Eastern Muslim men, it also turns out that most have been nervous people who have bought one-way tickets with cash at the last minute and have little luggage. Moreover, it would not be surprising to discover that most nervous people who buy one-way tickets with cash at the last minute and have little luggage are, if not terrorists, still up to no good in some form. In other words, it is possible that the fact of being a man of Middle Eastern origin is less contributory than many people suppose, and that an algorithm excluding race or ethnicity would be almost even if not quite as effective as one including it. To infer from the fact that most airline terrorists are Middle Easterners that Middle Eastern ethnicity is statistically relevant is a logical and statistical mistake, for even if Middle Easternness is nonspurious and genuinely contributes to the reliability of an algorithm including it, much of the predictive value may still be carried by other factors, even if not all of it is.

It appears highly unlikely, however, that race or ethnicity is as little relevant as this. On the evidence we now have, it is more than plausible to suppose that Middle Eastern ethnicity is a significant contributory factor, such that including it in the algorithm will make the algorithm substantially more effective than excluding it. In other words, it is likely that there is an appreciable number of cases in which the factor of race or ethnicity will push a case "over the line" from one not triggering scrutiny without the factor of race or ethnicity to triggering scrutiny with it.[16] If so, then even if we accept that using Middle Eastern appearance as the exclusive factor would be quite ineffective, and even if we accept that using a wide array of travel characteristics not including race or ethnicity would be more effective than using race or ethnicity alone, we must still confront the question whether it would be permissible to include race or ethnicity when it can be shown that including these factors would produce a noticeable improvement in the effectiveness of the algorithm compared to using all the other relevant factors but not including race or ethnicity.

When race would indeed substantially increase the effectiveness of the algorithm, it would appear that there is a strong argument in its favor. Especially when the consequences are catastrophic, as they are in the case of terrorism in the air, it strikes many people as obvious beyond question that the losses in safety from using a decidedly worse algorithm are costs that few societies should be willing to bear.

Yet recall our discussion of gender, and of the possibility that at times we may wish to impose a compensatory underuse of a relevant factor in order to account for an expected overuse. Just as we may at times prohibit the use of gender even when it is statistically relevant in order to prevent it from being more of a factor than it actually is, so too might the same apply to race or ethnicity. Suppose that airline counter employees and airport baggage screeners were given a list of factors to employ in determining when to trigger special security investigations and precautions. And suppose that these factors included all of the ones we have been discussing: gender (male), ethnicity (Middle Eastern), demeanor (nervous), frequent flyer membership (no), date of ticket purchase (last minute), time of check-in (late), form of purchase (cash), use of travel agent (no), and type of luggage (carry-on only). Now from what we know about the social psychology of race and ethnicity, it is quite possible that these attributes would be treated as the most important among many attributes of these factors even if they were not.[17] There are numerous reasons for this, but one of the most important is that race, gender, and age, and often ethnicity, unlike many other attributes, have a visibility and a consequent salience that makes them stand out more than other factors.[18] Such attributes thus have a tendency to be utilized more than their actual predictive contribution would justify. Because these attributes, unlike other personal characteristics and attributes, are "visually accessible, culturally meaningful, and interactionally relevant," such factors occupy more of the decisionmaking space than their empirical role would support.[19] In effect, race and ethnicity are, at least in part, encroachers on the terrain of other predictive factors, a feature of race and ethnicity that is not inconsistent with their being predictive factors in their own right. As a result, it is highly possble that airline counter employees would alert security when approached at the counter by neatly dressed Middle Eastern men checking their luggage who had purchased their ticket with a credit card a month in advance, but would not alert security when a jumpsuited and gold-jeweled Andrew Sokolow arrives to pay for his ticket in cash at the last minute and has only carry-on luggage. If this pattern existed, we might worry, on efficiency grounds as well as on moral ones, about the overuse of race and ethnicity and the consequent underuse of other relevant factors, and we might as a compensatory strategy prohibit the use of race and ethnicity just to ensure that they were not overused.

Consider, for example, the members of flight crews who in the first few months after September 11 insisted on the additional searching and questioning or at times even the removal from commercial airliners of various Middle Eastern men, all of whom turned out to have been doing nothing wrong.[20] Now even if it were true that the observable features of these men made them somewhat more statistically likely to be terrorists than others on the airplane, so too might, hypothetically, the characteristics of, say, a non–Middle Eastern man on the airplane who paid cash for his one-way ticket, whose profession was explosives expert, who belonged to a "militia" organization, and who had recently been released on parole from prison. But although the second array of characteristics is likely to be more predictive of terrorism than is the combination of male gender, age between twenty and forty, and Middle Eastern appearance, all of the latter features are visible and none of the former ones are. The flight attendants and pilots who were fearful of the youngish Middle Eastern men should have had much more reason to be afraid of the cash-paying, one-way-flying, militia-belonging, paroled explosives expert; but they had no way of knowing from their own observation that the man in seat 14C was the explosives expert, whereas they had an easy way of knowing that the man in seat 8D was Middle Eastern. The very visibility of race and, often, ethnicity, therefore, may produce, among other things, the conditions of their frequent overuse.

If the likely overuse was sufficiently large to suggest a compensatory underuse, the resultant prohibition on the use of race and ethnicity would probably produce a lowered level of effectiveness as compared to allowing race and ethnicity to be used in their proper proportion by ideal airline employees. But there is no reason to suppose that airline employees are, on average, less inclined to overuse race and ethnicity than are the customs officials at O'Hare Airport. So it could well turn out that, in a world of nonideal employees inclined to overuse race and ethnicity even when they are statistically relevant, mandatory underuse or nonuse would actually be more effective, not because race and ethnicity are not relevant, but because dramatic overuse of race and ethnicity might detract from the ability to examine closely those passengers with an even larger number of properly suspicion-raising characteristics and behaviors.

But again even this may not be so. Mandatory underuse may compensate for some overuse, but the net result may still be some loss of effectiveness in identifying potential terrorists. Although under some circumstances prohibiting the use of a nonspurious factor will be an efficient second-best solution that prevents more mistakes from its overuse than are created by its underuse, there is no reason to believe that this will always be the case. Under some circumstances race or ethnicity, even though likely to be overused, will be sufficiently statistically contributory that precluding their use may produce some net decrease in law-enforcement effectiveness.

Even under such conditions, the inclusion of race or ethnicity in the algorithm may still be unwise or unjust. If, for example, the accurate use of race or ethnicity produced more racial or ethnic separation than was morally or socially desirable, a particularly important consequence when people are taken out of a line and subjected to special attention, a society might decide that the loss of effectiveness was sufficiently small that it would be a price worth paying.[21] Or under circumstances of existing stigmatization by race or ethnicity for members of certain races or ethnic groups it again might well be worth paying a social price just in order to avoid any further racial or ethnic stigmatization.

Yet an increase in the actual amount of terrorism is a price that few people can be expected to believe is worth paying. So we need to examine more closely just what

the price would be. Still, even if the price of more terrorism is not worth paying in the way that the price of more
marijuana dealing or even more drunk driving might be,
it is a mistake to believe that the price must be paid in
more terrorism, or even in more crime of any sort. The
price of avoiding exacerbating existing racial or ethnic
isolation or stigmatization could more plausibly be seen
in the amount of time and effort necessary to produce
the same degree of scrutiny and security without the sav-
ings of time and effort that the inclusion of a nonspurious racial or ethnic factor in the profile would bring.
Because allowing the use of race and ethnicity imposes a
cost on those members of the targeted groups who are in
the area of overinclusion—Middle Easterners who have
done nothing wrong—it might be preferable to distribute the cost more broadly, and in doing so raise the cost
without lowering the degree of security. If excluding the
relevant factor of Middle Eastern appearance from the
algorithm made it necessary to increase the scrutiny of
everyone—if excluding ethnicity while still including
everything else increased waiting time at airports an average of thirty minutes per passenger—this might still be
a price worth paying.[22] So if the increase in waiting time
fully compensated for a suboptimal algorithm, the question is no longer one of ethnicity versus security, or ethnic sensitivity versus increased terrorism, but is the more
manageable one of time versus security. Put starkly, the
question of racial or ethnic profiling in air travel is not
the question of whether racial and ethnic sensitivity
must be bought at the price of thousands of lives. Rather,
it is most often the question of whether racial and ethnic
sensitivity should be bought at the price of arriving thirty
minues earlier at the airport.

## Driving while Black

The use of ethnicity in the context of airport security is a comparatively new concern, but the use of race and ethnicity in other law-enforcement contexts has been an issue for considerably longer.[23] And although the issue arises in many different law-enforcement settings, the most noteworthy has been that of automobile stops. Indeed, much of the current concern about so-called racial profiling stems from this very issue. When it was revealed several years ago that state police in New Jersey were stopping African Americans for allegedly routine or minor-violation checks at a rate far in excess of what could have been expected on the basis either of the percentage of African Americans in the New Jersey population or (and here the evidence is contested) of the percentage of African Americans committing traffic offenses, the African-American community was outraged but not surprised.[24] "Driving while Black" has long been the phrase used sarcastically by African Americans to describe the extent to which they are targeted for traffic stops predominantly because of their race.[25]

The incidents in New Jersey received the most publicity, but New Jersey was hardly unique in attracting complaints of this variety. Still, it is important to use our analysis thus far to try to determine just what New Jersey had done, and then to determine what was wrong with it.

In the first place, there is no indication that New Jersey had developed written formal profiles for determining which drivers were most likely to be committing offenses other than the ones that were visible from outside their automobiles. If one of the goals of stopping some but not all of those who exceed the speed limit or are driving cars with defective equipment is to identify those who might be transporting illegal weapons or narcotics or who might have outstanding arrest warrants, then one possible way to do this would be by use of a written profile. There is no indication, however, that New Jersey had performed the statistical analysis necessary to produce such a formal profile. Indeed, there is no evidence that the New Jersey state police had produced any kind of formal profile, whether statistically grounded or not. In an important sense, therefore, the so-called profiling in New Jersey was worlds apart from the profiling practices of the Internal Revenue Service in identifying potential tax cheats and the profiling practices of the Customs Service in identifying possible drug couriers, for in both of the latter cases there was, and still is, a formal list of factors that, taken together, constitute the profile. Indeed, the original New Jersey procedure ought not to be glorified by referring to it as a "profile," for it would be more accurate to call it a "guess."

The fact that a profile is not written down and promulgated officially, however, does not mean that it does not exist. A profile could exist as a shared norm, and thus it is still possible that the state police officers in New Jersey enforced an unwritten norm that took the form of a profile of drivers empirically likely to be transporting contraband or likely to be wanted for other offenses. Supposing that such an unwritten norm existed, however, as it almost certainly did, leaves open a range of possibilities about what the substance of this norm actually was.

One possibility was that this norm was not a profile at all, in the sense of a perceived probabilistic generalization designed, even if imperfectly, to locate those who had violated the law. It could well have been, as with one of the probable multiple motivations in the case of the O'Hare Airport customs officials, simply a norm of racial animus. Stopping African Americans may not have been a proxy for anything, and may have been, to some or many of the officers doing the stopping, an end in itself. As with the actions of some or many of the Customs Service officials at O'Hare airport, the actions of some of the New Jersey state police may have been more akin to those of a group of police officers wandering through a black neighborhood in a small southern town in the 1940s or 1950s solely for the purpose of asserting their authority and harassing the residents. Such actions are unqualifiedly reprehensible, but far removed from what people think of when they think of "profiling." "Targeting" is a bit closer to the mark, but "harassing" seems the most apt term of all, whether in Selma in 1963 or at O'Hare Airport in 1993 or on the highways of New Jersey in 1994. To describe this as "profiling" runs a serious risk of confusing the issue.

Alternatively, some of the New Jersey state police officers may have been following an unwritten norm according to which some officers believed that their goal was, in part, to stop those drivers especially likely to be carrying contraband or especially likely to be wanted on various nontraffic charges, and may have believed that race was an empirically sound proxy for these behaviors. For at least some of the police officers, rounding up what they perceived as "the usual suspects" may have been part of what they imagined to be an efficient and statistically justified law-enforcement tool. Indeed, the state police of New Jersey, while experienced at dealing with highway safety, were untrained novices at their newly assigned task of drug interdiction, and thus their immediate recourse to rounding up the usual suspects, whether empirically justified or not, may have been mostly a product of their inexperience.[26]

Thus, it is well within the realm of possibility that the New Jersey police officers acted not (or not only) on the basis of racial animus, but also on the basis of a mistaken belief about the role of race in predicting highway drug-related offenses.[27] Like the beliefs of presumably some of the customs officials at O'Hare Airport, the belief that the race of the driver was a useful proxy for illegal activities may have been totally without empirical foundations. And if this was the case (and without the results of more thorough empirical analyses than have yet been performed we do not know with certainty), then the norm of targeting African-American drivers, even apart from the moral issues, may simply have been, like the searches of African-American women at O'Hare Airport, both inefficient and counterproductive.

Yet what about those instances in which using race is not totally spurious? What if the race of the driver is in fact sometimes, even if not on the Garden State Parkway, a statistically sound predictor of illegal activity beyond what could be otherwise observed by a police officer in another car or at the side of the highway? If and when this is so, then we again confront the question of the strength of the factor as a component of a larger profile. There are, to be sure, some factors that even if taken alone are strong predictors. If our only goal is to prevent false positives—overinclusion—then gender by itself is a strong predictor of the ability to lift a two-hundred-pound weight, and age over age sixty is a strong predictor of the lack of quick reflexes. But there has not been a strong suggestion that race is anywhere nearly that good a predictor of any form of illegality. Even if race is a statistically nonspurious predictor of unlawful activity, and especially a statistically nonspurious predictor of serious unlawful activity within the group of those who are observed committing traffic violations, not even the staunchest defenders of using race as a factor in criminal apprehension would deny that it remains substantially under- and overinclusive in the context of identifying those who, without any other information, are likely to be carrying contraband, or are likely to be wanted for other crimes. In the context of using race to determine which traffic-offending drivers to investigate for possible nondriving offenses, race may be like wearing sunglasses while going through customs—statistically relevant but vastly under- and overinclusive.

If that is the case, then it turns out that there is, once again, a vast difference between a "racial profile" and what we might call a "profile that includes race." If race is part of a profile that includes numerous other components—nature of the traffic offense, type of automobile, number of people in the car, attire of the driver, condition of the vehicle, and many others—then using race and not all the others (assuming that race is not itself a sound proxy for some of the other factors) is like auditing all drywall contractors and waiters or stopping all people wearing sunglasses at points of entry.

On many of these issues the empirical evidence is spotty. Because what evidence we do have is based upon those who are stopped and not on a less biased (in the statistical sense of that word) array of all passengers or all drivers, we do not yet know with certainty whether Middle Eastern background is truly an independently statistically significant factor in identifying airport terrorists or whether being an African-American driver statistically predicts those with contraband or outstanding arrest warrants. Yet even if the racial or ethnic factors are statistically relevant, it again does not necessarily follow that they ought to be used. Especially when the statistical contribution of race turns out to be small, and when the use of all other statistically relevant factors except race does not involve giving up much in effectiveness, there may be good arguments in favor of the exclusion of race even when the race-excluding profile is somewhat less predictive than the race-including profile. If it turns out that race, even when it is a nonspurious indicator of criminal conduct, is being used far in excess of what its statistical contribution would justify, then a statistically legitimate "profile that includes race" is being converted at the point of application into something that focuses only on race and ignores the other indicators that would be part of the full array of indicative factors. And if this is true, then, once again, a compensatory overdiminution (in practice, a prohibition) of the use of race may again be necessary. Even if we define racial profiling in its narrowest and most justifiable sense—including race in a large list of mostly nonracial factors that when taken together provide a good even if imperfect indicator for some sorts of illegal activity in some locations—it may often be the case that in actual application race may take on a larger role than the underlying evidence may justify. And if it is suspected that this is likely to be the case, then the strongest argument against including race is not that race is irrelevant, although it may sometimes be, but that race, even if relevant, is so likely to be overused that it is necessary to prohibit its use—to mandate its underuse—just to ensure that things come out even in the end.

As with the discussion of race at the airport, however, we ought not to make empirical assumptions, in the absence of better evidence, that make the problem easier than it is. To put it more directly, we ought to take seriously the possibility that excluding race from the algorithm could come only at a high law-enforcement cost, a possibility that is not negated by the recognition of the fact that race is very likely to be overused.

Yet even when race is a substantial factor, and thus even when its exclusion would significantly decrease law-enforcement efficiency, the consequence of excluding race from the profile is an increase in crime only if we are holding cost and efficiency constant. But if we exclude race and are willing to suffer a decrease in efficiency but not in crime, as with for example increasing the number of roadblocks that would slow down and inconvenience all drivers without regard to race, but at more cost and annoyance to everyone, there need not be any reduction in the ability to apprehend criminals. As with the issue of increased waiting time at airports, the issue of when to refrain from using statistically justifiable racial factors in a larger profile in the service of avoiding isolation and stigmatization by race is not necessarily a conflict between equality and security or between racial sensitivity and crime control. In most cases the issue appears this way only because we take crime-control resources and citizen tolerance for minor inconvenience as givens. But if we do not, if we see the tradeoff not as one between crime and equality but as one between equality and inconvenience, the case for using even statistically well-grounded racial factors in policing and other forms of law enforcement becomes much weaker.

The major lesson of this chapter, however, especially when seen in contrast with chapter 6, is that the problems with racial profiling, problems that may justify imposing greater costs on society in order to avoid it, are not problems of profiling, with race being merely an example. Rather, and in parallel with the discussion of gender in chapter 5, the problem is about race and not about profiling. Once we comprehend the ubiquity and inevitability of profiling, we see that the objection to racial profiling, when valid, will treat the racial component and not the profiling component of racial profiling as crucial. We may often have good reasons for excluding race from the array of characteristics we use to focus on some potential suspects and not others, but this will not be because race is irrelevant, and it will not be because profiling is impermissible, but because there may be important and race-specific reasons for excluding race as a factor even when there are good empirical grounds for including it.

# CHAPTER 8

# Two Cheers for Procrustes

## On Treating Like Cases Differently

One of the more famous villains in Greek mythology is Procrustes (the "stretcher"). A roadside robber in the vicinity of Eleusis, Procrustes would invite passing strangers in for an evening meal and a night's rest, promising each guest that he would provide a bed that would fit them perfectly. What Procrustes did not disclose, however, was that there was only one bed. If the guest was shorter than the bed, Procrustes would stretch the guest to fit the bed. And if the guest was too tall, Procrustes would cut off his victim's legs (or, in some versions of the myth, his head) to the appropriate length. Procrustes kept this up for some time until he tried it on Theseus, the hero of the tale. Theseus turned the tables on Procrustes, cutting off his head to make Procrustes fit into his own bed, thus bringing the villainy of Procrustes to a fitting conclusion.

Procrustes was killed by Theseus but lives on as an adjective. To be Procrustean is to be irrationally committed to uniformity, seeking to make every situation fit the same mold, just as Procrustes made every passerby fit the same bed. To describe a person or a plan as Procrustean is no compliment, being much the same as describing an approach or technique, always pejoratively, as having "one size fits all" characteristics.[1] "One size fits all" may be good for socks, but to characterize anything else in those terms is invariably to condemn it. Those who have a "one size fits all" or Procrustean view, so the common charge goes, are the ones who are unable to recognize the importance of tailoring the particular solution to the particular problem.

This common belief notwithstanding, the ideas we have considered in this book, often sympathetically, can be understood as variations on the Procrustean theme. Again and again decisionmaking by generalization has emerged as an approach that ignores important differences, yet by now it should be clear that there is more to be said for the bed of Procrustes than many (including Procrustes' guests) have thought. At the very least, of course, Procrustes saved money and space, for he needed only one bed for the diversity of his guests. Procrustean solutions, more broadly, often bring the efficiency or economy that comes from avoiding the cost or effort of making new decisions for each case, just as Procrustes avoided the cost and effort of having to have a different bed for each guest. We all know that we cannot devote maximum time or effort to every decision, and forcing many decisions into a predetermined mold can be an efficient allocation of scarce decisional resources in a world in which some decisions are simply more important than others.

Yet efficiency and economy, however valuable each

may at times be, are not all that can be said for Procrustes. That Procrustean solutions sometimes bring even more than efficiency becomes apparent once we recognize that a Procrustean approach is often excoriated as a blind commitment to *equality* for equality's sake.[2] Unlike Procrustes, however, equality is usually understood in a favorable light: the Procrustean bed may have a bad reputation, but equality has a very good one. It is therefore time for us to look at equality, and to examine the relationship between equality and generality. Viewing generality through the lens of equality may cast generality and generalization in a still more favorable light, and, conversely, viewing equality through the lens of generality may expose important features of equality that are rarely fully appreciated.

A good place to start is the traditional maxim "Like cases should be treated alike."[3] We have glanced at this maxim earlier in this book, but it is now time for more than a glance. Initially, we see that the maxim of treating like cases alike is often expressed in conjunction with its supposed corollary, the principle that different cases should be treated differently.[4] Yet it hardly follows from treating like cases alike that different cases should be treated differently. If one student answers 90 percent of the questions on an examination correctly and receives an A- and another also answers 90 percent of the questions correctly and receives a B+, then the second student is rightly aggrieved. But if both a student who answers 92 percent correctly and another who answers 89 percent correctly receive a grade of A-, it is hardly clear that there is any grievance at all.[5] It may at times be right to treat different cases differently, but the principle that we should do so is neither a moral nor a logical corollary of the principle that we should treat like cases alike.

Even though treating different cases differently does not follow logically from treating like cases alike, the fact that the two are so often expressed together suggests that each has some role to play in thinking about equality. Yet treating different cases differently is just what Procrustes did not do. If the Procrustean bed is the repository of equality, then perhaps treating different cases differently is not even a component of the idea of equality, and may indeed be inconsistent with it. Over and over we have seen situations in which different cases are treated in the same way, squeezed together in Procrustean fashion by the force of some generalization that ignores material differences between the cases. Docile pit bulls are regulated in the same way as vicious ones, well-behaved English soccer fans are lumped together with the hooligans, fit older pilots are forced to retire at the same time as those whose skills are declining, and the profiles employed by both customs and tax officials ignore differences, at least at the initial inquiry stage, between the guilty and the innocent. In all these instances, and in countless others in which generalizations are employed, we are not only treating like cases alike, but are also, and more importantly, treating unlike cases alike as well. Does this then suggest that the idea and virtues of generalization are in some tension with a foundational precept of equality? Or might it suggest instead that generalization furthers equality rather than impedes it? Aristotle was the first to suggest a relationship between the moral idea of equality and the maxim of treating like cases alike, and he was one of the first to suggest a relationship between equality and justice.[6] But was Aristotle wrong? Is there anything to the idea of treating like cases alike, and, if so, how does that idea connect, if at all, with the concept of equality? We need now, therefore, to consider more closely the possibility that reliance on generalizations is problematic precisely because it conflicts with the principles of treating like cases alike and different cases differently. For although it is possible that a conflict between generalization and treating (only) like cases alike presents difficulties for generalization, another possibility is that it is not generalization but the principle of treating like cases alike that is the problem.

When we examine the principle of treating like cases alike, we perceive an immediate difficulty, not because it is a bad thing to treat like cases alike, but because the principle of treating like cases alike appears to be so vacuous as to be incapable of supporting the idea of equality, or indeed of supporting much of anything else. This is a familiar refrain, as we shall see; but what is less familiar is the possibility that treating *un*like cases alike is not only inevitable and often desirable but also that it, and not the more traditional maxim, is what lies at the heart of the idea of equality. The principle of treating different cases differently is typically conjoined with the principle of treating like cases alike, but, as noted above, treating different cases differently is not the logical corollary of treating like cases alike.[7] We could treat both like and unlike cases alike, and in exploring this possibility we will see the way in which the demands of equality frequently require not only the easy task of treating like cases alike, but the considerably more difficult one of treating different cases alike as well.

It is now widely accepted that Aristotle's prescription to treat like cases alike is essentially tautological, or, as Peter Westen puts it, empty.[8] As H. L. A. Hart explains the point, though "treat like cases alike and different cases differently" is a central element in the idea of justice, it is by itself incomplete and, until supplemented, cannot afford any determinate guide to conduct. This is because any set of human beings will resemble each other in some respects and differ from each other in others and, until it is established what resemblances and differences are relevant, "treat like cases alike" must remain an empty form.[9]

Although it is possible to treat truly identical cases in nonidentical fashion, doing so appears simply to be irrational.[10] And although the principle of rationality may have content, there is nothing that the "Treat like cases alike" maxim adds to this basic principle of thought, or so it is widely believed.[11]

Consider the recent statement of animal-rights activist Gary Francione, suggesting that the failure to grant the same rights to dogs and porpoises that we grant to humans has violated the principle of treating like cases alike.[12] To Francione and other advocates of animal rights, and in a more limited way to Jeremy Bentham almost two centuries earlier,[13] the fact that dogs, porpoises, and humans all share that degree of mental awareness and ability to experience pleasure and pain that we call sentience (something that paramecia and lobsters, among others, appear to lack) was sufficient to say that they are "alike" and should therefore be "treated alike."

Yet although there are plainly some respects in which we humans are similar to porpoises, there are just as plainly some respects in which the two species are different, something even the animal-rights advocates acknowledge. What some of the animal-rights advocates do not acknowledge, of course, is that these differences make a difference, especially on the question of rights. To them the difference between a human and a porpoise is like the difference, in most contexts, between a red car and a green one—different, to be sure, but not in any consequential way.

Those who believe that the maxim of treating like cases alike is empty observe debates such as this one and conclude that all of the work is being done by the decision about what is or is not a relevant difference, a decision that is assisted not at all by the "Treat like cases alike" principle. Perhaps the facts that most humans are smarter than most porpoises, and that most porpoises can swim better than most humans, are irrelevant differences; but determining whether the ability to do long division or swim a mile in ten minutes is or is not relevant to rights recognition is not something that the "Treat like cases alike" maxim helps us with one bit. Or so say the skeptics.[14] For the skeptics both the maxim of treating like cases alike and the principle of equality are empty, mere rhetorical flourishes that camouflage real issues about the identity of relevant and irrelevant differences and about the criteria we need to employ to determine which differences are relevant and which are not.

A more promising start is offered by a different version of the claim that there is something important about the maxim of treating like cases alike. To some legal theorists, treating like cases alike is a function of decisionmaking according to rules, for it is the rule that determines which cases are alike. H. L. A. Hart again puts it well:

> If we attach to a legal system the minimum meaning that it must consist of general rules—general both in the sense that they refer to courses of action, not single

actions, and to multiplicities of men, not single individuals—this meaning connotes the principle of treating like cases alike, though the criteria of when cases are alike will be, so far, only the general elements specified in the rules. It is, however, true that *one* essential element of the concept of justice is the principle of treating like cases alike.[15]

Hart is correct in recognizing that the precept of treating like cases alike must be supplemented by something else in order to determine the relevant indicia of likeness. And he is correct as well in concluding that one function of rules is to provide these indicia. The consequence of this connection between the incompleteness of equality and the formal nature of rules is that following a rule just *is* a matter of treating like cases alike, that being the logical corollary of what it is to follow a rule. Following a rule means treating all the cases falling under the rule in the same way, and consequently it is the fact of falling under the same rule that renders the cases alike.

Yet having taken us this far, Hart then stumbles in appearing to suggest that rules help us to treat like cases alike, as opposed simply to defining what likeness means. For Hart the principle of treating like cases alike is an independent value that decisionmaking according to rules both fosters and facilitates. Now it is true that the cases that are treated alike are alike because the rule makes them alike. But the fact that rules make the cases alike is why, and often only why, they are alike. As we have seen repeatedly, the generalizations that lie behind rules—the multiple courses of action and multiplicities of people that Hart properly says are encompassed by any rule— are not collections of like cases. Rather, they are collections of unlike cases that the rules force together. Following a rule is accordingly not a matter of treating alike cases that really are alike, but is instead a matter of treating alike cases that are, in at least some relevant respects, unlike. To repeat, because the point is crucial: rules do not simply or necessarily gather up cases that are antecedently alike in some relevant respect. By ignoring differences that the justifications or rationales lying behind those very rules would recognize, as with the differences between a wet and a dry road that the safety rationale lying behind the typical speed-limit rule would recognize, rules often treat as alike those cases that are relevantly different; and it is frequently only the fact of the rule itself that forces the rule-follower to treat the different cases similarly.[16] As we will see shortly, however, this conclusion about treating relevantly unalike cases alike is not just about rules, but is about the use of generalizations more broadly, and about the relationship between generalization and equality.

## Antidiscrimination as Generalization

In chapter 4 we spent some time with questions of age discrimination, especially in the context of the Federal Aviation Administrations's Age Sixty Rule. The Age Sixty Rule, it will be recalled, relies on group characteristics of older people—in particular slower reflexes, diminished low-light vision, diminished hearing acuity in the presence of background noise, and greater likelihood of sudden incapacitation—to mandate the retirement of commercial airline pilots when they reach the age of sixty, regardless of the absence of any such decrease in capabilities or increase in risks for an individual pilot forced to retire. Because of the Age Sixty Rule, and only because of the Age Sixty Rule, even the keen-hearing, quick-reflexed, and visually acute sixty-year-old pilot must leave the cockpit.

But now let us turn to a different dimension of discrimination on the basis of age. The Age Sixty Rule is important and interesting, but it exists as an exception to the prevailing rule of American law. In the United States, often to the astonishment of observers in other countries, mandatory retirement has been eliminated by the Age Discrimination in Employment Act (ADEA).[17] Commercial airline pilots, law-enforcement officers, firefighters, and high state officials remain exempt from the coverage of the act, but virtually all other employees in both the public and private sectors are now protected by federal law from being forced to retire just because the employee has reached a specified age. Employees can be forced to retire if the skills necessary to do their jobs have diminished, but age may no longer be used as a proxy for the diminution of those skills, regardless of how accurate that proxy may seem to be.

Although the ADEA was designed primarily to prevent the use of age-based generalizations, the ADEA itself, perhaps ironically, is premised on a generalization and operates through the use of a generalization. Lying behind the ADEA, and often lying behind the concerns of people who object to age discrimination, is the belief that age-based generalizations are unfair to the individuals whose own attributes are misdescribed by the generalizations. Here, as we saw in chapter 4, the concern is not about the use of spurious generalizations. Even the most ardent opponents of age discrimination accept that age is a statistically relevant (though, to those opponents, often overused) predictor of characteristics that are themselves frequently material to job performance. But these statistically relevant predictors do not predict for every individual, as even the most ardent proponents of age discrimination acknowledge, and thus the debate about age discrimination, a debate that culminated in the ADEA, was a debate about the wisdom and justice of allowing the use of a statistically relevant but sometimes mistaken predictor of job performance.

The ADEA is the consequence of victory by the opponents of using age even though it is a statistically nonspurious predictor, and the ADEA thus appears to be a victory against generalization. Yet we need to look more closely at what the ADEA does, and how it does it. The premise of the ADEA is that age-based generalizations are sometimes or often mistaken with respect to particular individuals. Consequently, the ADEA prohibits their use. In prohibiting the use of this generalization, however, the ADEA takes a predictor—age—that is sometimes or often, but certainly not always, mistaken and mandates that it may *never* be used. Because age discrimination sometimes (but only sometimes) produces the wrong result (in the sense of forcing the retirement or nonhiring of someone with no fewer skills than a younger person), the ADEA says, the law will treat it as *always* unlawful. The ADEA thus takes a factor that is usually but not universally irrelevant and mandates its nonuse in both the irrelevant and the relevant cases.[18] In other words, the ADEA generalizes about irrelevance in much the same way that age discrimination itself generalizes about the effects of aging. The structure of the ADEA, therefore, is strikingly similar to the structure of the phenomenon to which it is opposed, the imperfect generalizing of the practice of discrimination on the basis of age. With respect to age and also with respect to those other contexts in which a legal or moral principle is directed against a trait that is not totally spurious—in which case the irrelevance would be universal—therefore, the structure of an antidiscrimination law or an antidiscrimination moral or political principle turns out to have an intriguing similarity to the structure of the evil that it is aimed at eradicating.

There is nothing wrong with this. The use of generalizations to combat discrimination by generalization does not indicate that anything is amiss. Recall from chapters 5, 6, and 7 the possibility that under some circumstances—distinctions drawn on the basis of gender or ethnicity, for example—the mandated underuse of a nonspurious generalization may serve as a necessary corrective for a likely overuse of that generalization. In much the same fashion, the ADEA attempts to combat a particular form of generalization with a generalization of its own about the irrelevance of age (although the possibility that age-based generalizations might be overused is not necessarily the actual or only possible reason for compelling their underuse). Like most generalizations, the ADEA's generalization about the irrelevance of age to job performance is inaccurate in some cases, here the cases in which the age-based prediction of job performance would be accurate. But although there is no problem with combatting a generalization with a different type of generalization, the presence of a generalization in both the remedy and the disease does show that the problem is, once again, not with the idea of generalizing itself. If the remedy for what society believes to be an inappropriate use of a nonspurious generalization is another generalization, the lesson is simply that generalizations are all around us, and are as capable of being used for good as for ill.

The implications of this kind of corrective generalization become even clearer once we see how the ADEA operates in actual practice. One consequence of the ADEA, and indeed the ADEA's intended result, is that fewer capable senior citizens are compelled to retire. But another consequence, and the corollary of the previous consequence in a world in which individualized assessment is not without actual costs, is that there are a larger number of incapable senior citizens who are still on the job. Perhaps in an ideal and cost-free world, replacing age-based generalizations with individual assessment would still exclude all of those who are incapable of performing; but in practice the costs of individualized assessment, combined with actual or perceived risks of litigation, produce a world in which at least some older people who ideally should no longer still be on the job are allowed to remain. This is partly the consequence of one of the costs' being the cost of error in an imperfect world, and the other is the cost of litigation. When employers are risk averse and individualized assessment is costly, we remedy the overexclusion of the elderly with an underexclusion. And this is because the ADEA offers employers two alternatives, both more costly than pre-ADEA practice. One alternative is individualized testing of all employees to determine if they have the skills that most, say, under-sixty-fives have, and that many over-sixty-fives do not. If the original proxy had been reliable, as at least in the case of age it often had been, then eliminating the reliable proxy and substituting individualized assessment can be quite expensive.

Some employers have in fact gone to individualized testing, but it is well known that the individualized testing builds in a margin for error in order to guard against age discrimination litigation.[19] This margin for error helps to forestall litigation, but at the price of keeping on the job at least some people who would otherwise have been forced to retire.[20] And even employing a margin for error is still less inaccurate than the common alternative of essentially letting people work as long as they wish. This alternative involves fewer testing costs than individualized assessment for everyone, but at the cost of having even more people still on the job who in a world of perfect information would have been compelled to retire.

It is of course also true that there have been fewer erroneous exclusions under the ADEA than there were under pre-ADEA mandatory retirement. Using the same measure of whether someone should have been allowed to keep his or her job in a world of perfect information and maximally individualized assessment, there can be no doubt that the ADEA has, while keeping on the job some people who should correctly have been retired, also kept on the job many people who would previously have been incorrectly forced to retire. Recognizing that the ADEA has traded the decrease in one type of error for an increase in another type of error highlights the way in which the ADEA operates just like any other generalization, and just like the generalization it is attempting to combat. By preventing age discrimination in all cases, even in those individual cases in which age accurately reflects diminished capacity, the ADEA keeps on the job some people who should not be there, just as its predecessor practice kept off the job some people who should still be on it. Like its predecessor practice, the ADEA creates a universal practice out of a nonuniversal class, and in so doing operates just like any other generalization.

The same phenomenon of remedying discrimination by a compensatory generalization arises in the context of recent initiatives and discussion about the issue of older drivers.[21] Like people who operate passenger airplanes, those who operate automobiles also experience less-acute hearing, slower reflexes, and worse eyesight, especially in low light, as they get older. In addition, older drivers, like older pilots, have an increased risk of sudden incapacitation from stroke, heart attack, and similar afflictions. Not much less for operating a Buick Riviera than for operating a Boeing 747, these age-correlated impairments and risks are plainly material to the ability to drive safely.

One age-independent solution to the problem of aging drivers is periodic testing of everyone, but the cost of that is widely thought to be prohibitive. Accordingly, a commonly offered (and, recently, frequently enacted) alternative is a less draconian form of age discrimination, one in which there is periodic testing of drivers after they have reached a specified age, often seventy or seventy-five, but not before (except for initial licensing, of course). In the various proposals and legislative responses, the age-triggered test is sometimes a road test, sometimes a vision test, and sometimes just the visual inspection of the driver that comes from requiring older drivers (but not younger ones) to appear in person to renew their licenses, rather than permitting renewal by mail or on-line.

Without such age-triggered testing, there would be three alternatives: periodic testing for everyone, no periodic testing for anyone, and mandatory license revocation at a certain age, such as eighty. The third alternative would be a prototypical exclusionary generalization, excluding all because of the deficiencies of some (or many). But if periodic testing for everyone is implausible, then the remedy for the exclusionary generalization of license revocation for everyone over eighty is the inclusionary generalization of continued driving for everyone, a remedy in which more elderly drivers are allowed to keep driving even though some of them ought not to be, the ones who would have been excluded were everyone to have been looked at individually. Because the inclusionary generalization—not excluding anyone because of age—is thought to involve so many erroneous inclusions, and because universal testing is thought to be so expensive, the modified form of age discrimination now commonly proposed is best understood as an exclusionary generalization in which the costs to those mistakenly excluded are dramatically minimized.

The irony of discriminatory generalization's being cured by another generalization is a function of just how we go about making judgments. "Discrimination," after all, is not necessarily a pejorative, and to have discriminating taste is a virtue and not a vice. Yet as we have seen before, the ability to discriminate even in individual cases is a function of the careful use of all the available evidence, and the available evidence itself takes the form of a series of generalizations.

Imagine a driving test for two different sixteen-year-olds. One is quite nervous about the test itself, and makes a small but potentially dangerous mistake, for which he immediately apologizes. The other is confident to the point of arrogance, makes the same mistake, and proceeds on. Were the inspector to pass the first and fail the second, in the plausible belief that the mistake of the first is a function of the nervousness that comes from testing, but that the mistake of the second is more likely to be repeated under actual driving conditions, it is likely that the inspector would be relying on a generalization, presumably gleaned from experience, about the future behavior of people based on how they behave during testing. As with the inspector here, and as we have seen again and again, judgment without generalization is impossible, and even individualized assessments are the products of multiple generalizations by the assessor.

When law, policy, or practice excludes a nonspurious generalization, therefore, what is excluded is one of the factors on which even good judgment rests. To exclude age from the array of relevant factors that might go into determining whether this particular eighty-five-year-old should be licensed to drive is to exclude a relevant factor that may be determinative in some cases. Antidiscrimination, therefore, is not a restatement of a principle of rationality whereby irrelevant characteristics should be ignored. Antidiscrimination principles, policies, or laws do serve this purpose in some instances, especially in response to people who persist in making decisions on the basis of characteristics that are actually irrelevant. Just as commonly, however, a principle of antidiscrimination, itself operating as a generalization, mandates the exclusion of even relevant characteristics, treating different cases similarly precisely because of the generalization on which the antidiscrimination principle is based.

The point is a recurrent one. If soccer stadiums are not permitted to employ nationality in determining which potential hooligans to exclude, their exclusions will be less accurate, and less particularistic, than would otherwise be the case. If airport safety personnel are not permitted to employ nationality or ethnicity in determining whom to screen more closely, the screening process will again be less accurate, at least if we hold constant the time and cost of the screening. So too with the use of race or gender in medical diagnoses, and of course age as well. A physician's diagnosis is based on a series of generalizations, and were we to exclude one or more of those generalizations—African Americans are at greater risk of hypertension and sickle-cell anemia than the population at large; Jews are more likely than members of other ethnic groups to have Tay-Sachs disease; there is a much higher incidence of colon cancer in older than in younger people—we would make the process of medical diagnosis less accurate.[22] When for good or not-so-good reasons we prohibit the use of a nonspurious generalization, we combat one generalization with another, and may produce a decisionmaking process less accurate (or more costly for an equivalent degree of accuracy) than it would otherwise have been.

But this is not necessarily or always to condemn the process by which we generalize in order to compensate for the use of what are thought to be socially inappropriate uses of nonspurious generalizations. Rather, framing the issue in this way highlights the fact that the demands of equality themselves both rest on and operate by the use of generalizations. If the demands of treating all citizens equally prohibit singling out people for airport screening on the basis of even relevant characteristics such as national origin or ethnicity, it turns out that the demands of equality operate as a generalization. These demands often require us to treat all citizens or all people the same, but the important point is that these demands often require us to treat all citizens or all people the same *even if they are not.* Ignoring real differences, which is what most generalizations do, is often desirable; but even when ignoring real differences is desirable it is not without costs. As a generalization, the principle of treating all equally is a principle that ignores real differences, and consequently comes at a price.

## The Generality of Equality

At the conclusion of the previous section we slid from considering specific antidiscrimination laws and principles such as the Age Discrimination in Employment Act to considering equality more generally. Accordingly, it is now appropriate to return to the larger themes of equality that opened this chapter. And in doing so, it will be illuminating to take up one of the more venerable statements of the principle of equality. "All men are created equal," announced the Declaration of Independence in 1776, and the world has never been the same. For even apart from its role in launching American independence, the Declaration of Independence, along with the French Declaration of the Rights of Man, established equality as a central goal of political, legal, and moral aspiration.

"All men are created equal," however, is a curious claim, and not only because its limitation to "men" was not simply a linguistic quirk, and not only because women were hardly the only group excluded from the aspirations of the Declaration's authors. Even were we to remedy the exclusion of women, the acceptance of slavery, and some of the other glaring inconsistencies between the Declaration's announcement of equality and its society's entrenchment of inequality, there remains a startling anomaly. That anomaly, put starkly, is that the claim "All men are created equal" is false. Some of us are bright and others of us dim; some of us are physically strong and others weak; some are coordinated and others clumsy; some have the gifts of creativity while others see things only as they have been seen before; and some are born healthy while others come into the world with illness or disability. In a very real and very important sense, therefore, the claim that all are created equal is a claim that, descriptively, is simply untrue.

Yet although it is false that all men are created equal, it is not false that it is possible to treat all men as being created equal even if they are not. Equality, as has often been recognized, has both descriptive and prescriptive dimensions.[23] Equality is descriptive when the things that are said to be equal really are equal, as when we say that five plus five equals ten, or that two people are equally qualified for a job. But equality takes on a prescriptive dimension when the claims of equality are offered as reasons for treating people in the same way. Yet although descriptive and prescriptive equality are different, it is important to see that claims of prescriptive equality coexist with and at times are even built on the fact of descriptive equality.

The relationship between descriptive and prescriptive equality stems from the extent to which claims of prescriptive equality are commonly (but not necessarily) built on the fact of descriptive equality,[24] and here we can distinguish two different relationships that might exist between descriptive and prescriptive equality. First, a good reason for treating people the same is that they really are the same. As we saw in the previous section of this chapter, one possible meaning for the principle that like cases should be treated alike is that irrelevant characteristics should not be the basis for distinguishing among people or events. Justice is blind to the difference between those with Type A blood and those with Type B because that distinction can make no possible difference to virtually any of the goals of a system of justice. In such cases, treating like cases alike is not only a principle of rationality, but is also a different way of saying that descriptive equality is, typically, a sufficient condition for prescriptive equality.

As we have noted, the problem with this first relationship between descriptive and prescriptive equality is not that it is unsound. The problem is that it is uninteresting. Even when the principle of treating like cases and like people alike appears to make an actual difference, it makes that difference precisely because those to whom the prescription is directed typically do not believe that the cases are actually the same. We can explain the rejection of the apartheid laws in South Africa or the Jim Crow laws in the United States by saying that the color of one's skin is irrelevant to, say, which water fountain one drinks at or where in a bus or train one sits; and we can further support this conclusion by saying that it is just a matter of treating likes alike. But of course the proponents of Jim Crow or apartheid laws did not believe that these were like cases. They believed, however wrongly, that skin color makes a difference; and thus to them the laws they favored were simply a matter, for them, of treating unalikes unalike. They were (and still are) wrong in so believing, and the fact that people believe it makes it neither right nor plausible. But the fact that the proponents of apartheid and Jim Crow laws did not believe that they were dealing with like cases explains again why the principle that like cases must be treated alike is of little assistance. Those who believe that people with different skin color are still alike do not need the principle of treating like cases alike, because they would not draw a distinction, except irrationally, even in the absence of the principle. And those who believe that skin color does make a difference are people for whom the principle would be unpersuasive. The principle that like cases must be treated alike turns out, therefore, to be either superfluous or irrelevant—superfluous where the cases really are alike, and irrelevant where the cases are not.

There is a second type of relationship between descriptive and prescriptive equality, however, that does not rest on the tautology that like cases must be treated alike. Here *some* aspect of descriptive equality, ordinarily, is what justifies equal treatment of people or events that are otherwise unequal.[25] Treating all people equally, as the Declaration of Independence urges, is based on the idea that a dimension of descriptive equality—we are all human beings—justifies equal treatment even as to unequal dimensions. Because we are all the same in some respects—we are all Americans; we are all adults; we are all sentient creatures; we are all human beings—we should be treated the same in some other respects, even if we are not the same in those other respects.

This second relationship between descriptive and prescriptive equality is thus one in which the real bite of prescriptive equality becomes apparent, for now it is clear that prescriptive equality requires that, like Procrustes, we treat as alike those people and events that are in some, many, or even all respects (other than the ex-post respect in which they are forced together by the equality principle itself) unalike. At times we will do so because we are, as discussed in chapters 5, 6, and 7, afraid that people will overuse even relevant differences. Accordingly, we mandate the underuse of those differences, and prescriptive equality can be the consequence of this mandated disregard of genuine distinctions.

More importantly, however, the underuse of real differences is what gives the very idea of equality its bite. When the drafters of the Declaration of Independence declared that all men were created equal, and when animal-rights activists declare that porpoises are in many moral and decisional contexts equal to humans, they mean to make the claim that some common characteristic mandates common treatment even in the face of other characteristics not held in common, and even in the face of differences of degree of the common characteristic.

Obviously the choice of the common and equalizing

characteristic must come from somewhere, and it may come from ideas of citizenship, as we will explore in chapter 11. The controversial question is whether it comes from the idea of equality itself, but examining this question would take us too far afield from the central themes of this book. For purposes of those themes, the important issue is not where a norm of equality comes from but what it does. And what it does, centrally and importantly, is, like the Declaration of Independence itself, to force together particular people, places, and events that are not merely irrelevantly different, but *relevantly* different. The consequence of the operation of the norm of equality, like the consequence of any generalization, will be to make the relevant differences irrelevant; but that is not to say that they were antecedently irrelevant. By virtue of the demands of equality, they become irrelevant.

Even when formal equality seems perverse, as with maintaining that the demands of equality are satisfied when neither pregnant men nor pregnant women receive medical benefits, the basic point remains.[26] If equality demands treating women differently from men because on the matter of pregnancy they are differently situated, then the demands of equality are producing an outcome in which different cases are still being treated similarly, for here the dissimilar cases of men and women are being treated similarly in likely financial outcome. In other words, seeing the issue as one of equality of need rather than equality of entitlement does not alter the deep structure of the equality principle. As with other debates about the conflict among formal equality, equality of opportunity, and equality of outcome, recognition of the basic structural property of equality will not resolve the debate. It will, however, reemphasize that at its core equality is, in Procrustean fashion, equalizing. What we equalize and what we do not equalize is not determined by this logical point, but the logical point makes clear the continuity between issues of equality and issues of generality.

Having seen that equality is at its core about treating unlike cases alike, we can return to Procrustes. The condemnation of Procrustes, as with other condemnations we have encountered, is ultimately a particularistic one, urging that all real differences be accommodated. But if, rather than stretching or removing body parts, Procrustes had simply said that all guests would be fed the same amount, regardless of size, age, or appetite, or if he had mandated that all guests would have to sleep in the same bed regardless of height or heft, we could more directly replay many of the traditional debates about equality. On the one side would be those who would argue, often with much force, that norms of formal quality are often insufficient in light of background differences, a point most famously captured by Anatole France's facetious observation that the law in its "majestic equality" forbids rich and poor alike to beg in the streets, to steal bread, and to sleep under the bridges of Paris.[27]

But Anatole France occupied only one side of the debate. On the other side are those who maintain that formal equality even in the face of background differences may serve important moral goals. At times the goals of equality in the face of relevant differences may be trivial, as when the municipal golf course assigns starting times by lottery rather than by golfing skill; and at times the goals may be more consequential, as when we grant the same one vote to the informed and the ignorant, the kind and the wicked. But the goal here is not to resolve or even to rehearse these debates. It is only to make the case for Procrustes, whose aims were equality and whose methods were the methods of generalization. Procrustes was evil and rapacious, but those who pursue equality for more noble reasons will also find that generalization is both their instrument and their outcome.

# CHAPTER 9

# Ships with Altered Names

### Presumed Offenses

One of the less well-known parts of Jeremy Bentham's *Principles of the Penal Code* is a discussion of what Bentham calls *presumed offenses*.[1] Presumed offenses, according to Bentham, are to be distinguished from ordinary criminal offenses, which punish people for doing something wrong. By contrast, presumed offenses, said Bentham, punish people not for doing something wrong, at least not directly. Instead, presumed offenses punish people for doing something not itself wrong or "injurious," but the doing of which creates a presumption that the people doing it are doing something else as well. This "something else" is the actual wrong, explained Bentham, and the likely presence of this genuine wrong justifies punishing people for doing something not necessarily wrong in itself. Presumed offenses, which Ben-

tham also called *evidentiary offenses,* embody in the penal
code the maxim "Where there's smoke, there's fire."

As an example of a presumed offense, Bentham offered the case of the crime of possessing a ship (or other
shipwrecked property) with an altered or obliterated
name. In seventeenth- and eighteenth-century England,
it appears, it was an offense to be found in possession of
any ship or shipwrecked property whose original or officially registered name had been painted over or otherwise altered. Making illegal the possession of a ship with
an altered name was not, Bentham tells us, based on anyone's having thought that there was anything intrinsically or necessarily wrong about having a ship whose
name had been changed. After all, people might paint
over and then change the name of a ship named for a
former spouse or lover after a domestic spat, or might
change a name similar to the name of a ship that had just
been lost at sea, or might just believe that a previous
name was unlucky. Any of these could lead a perfectly
innocent ship owner to scrape off the previous name and
paint on the new one.

Such completely innocent justifications for having a
ship with a changed name (and whose change of name
might through inadvertence remain unregistered) would
have been extremely rare, however. Possessing a ship
with an altered name was made an offense because in almost all such cases people knew that the name had been
altered for far less benign reasons. Typically, the name
and markings would have been changed in order to dis-
guise the fact that a ship or shipwrecked property had
been stolen from its rightful owner. Changing or obliter-
ating the markings would make it more difficult for the
authorities or the legitimate shipowner to locate the stolen

ship or stolen property. So although it was remotely possible for there to be ships or shipwrecked property with innocently altered markings, such a high percentage of altered markings were illicit, said Bentham, that any particular ship or property with altered markings could be *presumed* to have been stolen. Making possession of a ship with an altered name an offense in itself would thus be an effective way of apprehending and prosecuting, especially in long-past days of crude communications and cruder ship's registries, those whose ships had been obtained illicitly.

Neither the problem of stolen ships nor the offense of possession of a ship with an altered name survives into the twenty-first century.[2] Yet presumed offenses are still with us. Consider the requirement of U.S. federal law that anyone entering or leaving the United States with more than $10,000 in currency or other monetary instruments must report to customs authorities the amount transported, the origin and destination and route of the money, the identity of the owner of the money, and the relationship between the transporter and the owner.[3] Anyone traveling in or out of the country with this amount of currency without disclosing the required information is guilty of a felony and liable for a fine up to $250,000 and imprisonment for a period of up to five years. Yet this currency reporting requirement is not, as might be the case in some other countries, related in any way to currency or monetary controls. You can enter or leave the United States with millions of dollars in currency and not be guilty of anything so long as the transaction is reported to the authorities.

At first glance the reporting requirement looks foolish. Given that it is not a crime to enter or leave the United States with large amounts of currency, the reporting requirement appears to be bureaucratic overkill. Yet things become clearer once we understand that although most people would not dream of carrying that much cash onto an airplane, there are some people who do so routinely. A high percentage of these people, not surprisingly, are engaged in illegal transactions, and most of these illegal transactions have something to do with narcotics or money laundering. The reporting requirement, it turns out, has nothing to do with financial control and everything to do with apprehending drug dealers, money launderers, and various other species of international criminals.

Because innocent people so rarely carry this much cash with them when traveling internationally, the law presumes that anyone doing so is doing so for illegitimate reasons and would thus have good reason not to report the transaction to the customs authorities. Consequently, it is presumed that anyone not reporting the transaction is attempting to hide the existence of otherwise illegal activity. The vast majority of those found guilty of the presumed offense, therefore, will be those who have done something else illegal, even if the actual illegality cannot be directly proved. And if on occasion people who fail to report are guilty of nothing else—perhaps they both distrust credit cards and simply forgot to report the cash transaction—the fact that anyone entering or leaving the country is put on clear notice of the criminality of nonreporting is thought sufficient to prevent what some might think of as a major injustice.[4]

A similar presumed offense is the crime of possessing more than a specified quantity of illegal drugs. Although possession of any quantity of heroin, cocaine, marijuana, and other narcotics is a crime in most countries, possession of more than a statutorily designated amount is often treated differently. In such cases, the law presumes that the possession is not solely for personal use, but rather that the possessor is someone who is trafficking in narcotics.[5] In other words, a person possessing more than the specified quantity is presumed to be a drug dealer. Although this example is not nearly so clean as the previous ones—people possessing large quantities of illegal narcotics for purely personal use are not quite as innocent (so long as simple possession remains a crime) as people who innocently carry large amounts of cash or innocently change the name of their ships—once again the offense is based on the idea that it can be a crime to do something not itself wrong (or *as* wrong), but which indicates that the person doing it is almost but not quite certainly doing something itself wrong. Similar principles, though perhaps not as well known, support the criminalization of possession of drug paraphernalia,[6] the crime of possession of burglar tools,[7] and the fact that even where possession of a shotgun is legal it is often unlawful to possess a shotgun with a shortened barrel (a "sawed-off" shotgun),[8] here again on the theory that possession of such a weapon is almost but not quite always in aid of planned illegal activity. None of these examples is as pure as the examples of ships with altered names and of leaving the country with a large amount of unreported currency, because in all of these the offense could be considered not as evidence of a crime that has already taken place, but instead as an offense of *preparation* for a primary offense that has yet to take place. Still, both preparatory offenses, as Bentham called this latter class, and presumed offenses, as Bentham called the offenses that provided evidence of a crime that had already taken place, share the trait of being generalizations probabilistically but not certainly indicating a primary offense.

Although numerous examples demonstrate that presumed offenses remain quite common, many people still find the idea of a presumed offense to be, shall we say, offensive. For such people, there is something unjust about the idea of finding people guilty of a crime because they have done something that only *indicates* that they have done something wrong, rather than finding them guilty by suitable proof of having actually done something wrong. The presumed offense, to many people, reeks of something close to guilt by association. Bentham, after all, also referred to presumed offenses as *evidentiary offences,* and we like to think that we convict people for committing crimes and not simply for committing evidence.

Consider the crime of selling a magazine or book without a cover. Although it may not be immediately apparent that there is anything wrong with selling a coverless book or magazine, a glance at the top of the copyright page of any mass-market paperback exposes the nature of the problem. Here, on the copyright page, one typically finds the following message: "If you purchased this book without a cover you should be aware that this book is stolen property. It was reported as 'unsold and destroyed' to the publisher and neither the author nor the publisher has received any payment for this 'stripped book.'" Behind this message is the practice in the paperback book and magazine industries for publishers and distributors to give retailers full return credit for any unsold book or magazine. But because it would be very costly for a retailer like Manny's Newsstand to ship back to the distributor every unsold (and by now virtually worthless) copy of last week's edition of *Time* magazine, Manny is required to return only the cover to the distributor or publisher. When he sends back the covers of the unsold copies, Manny warrants that the contents of the magazine have been destroyed. The publisher or distributor then gives Manny full credit for each cover he sends back, but both Manny and the publisher save the cost of packing and shipping a large volume of virtually worthless paper. If Manny is of a mind to steal, however, he sends back the cover but does not destroy the rest of the magazine. Rather, he sells the now-coverless magazine (albeit at a discount), receiving full credit from the distributor and (discounted) payment from the purchaser of the coverless magazine. The notice on the inside cover of paperback books (where the practice is even more prevalent than it is in the magazine industry, largely because year-old paperback books have more use and thus retain more of their value than year-old or even week-old magazines) is designed to warn the purchaser of a coverless book about the true nature of the transaction in which he is participating.

Because the practice of selling books and magazines reported as unsold amounts to stealing from the publisher or distributor, and because identifying the culprits is difficult, the state of New York once attempted to make illegal the practice of selling a coverless magazine or other periodical. Under the New York law, a person selling a magazine without a cover was guilty of a crime, without the necessity of further proof that the seller was engaged in any kind of fraudulent transaction. New York thus treated selling a coverless magazine as a presumed offense, presuming any seller of a coverless magazine to be engaged in a fraudulent transaction, even though it is (remotely) possible to imagine an innocent sale of a coverless magazine. If you sold a coverless magazine, you were guilty of a crime, and the prosecutor did not need to allege or prove that the sale was part of a fraudulent transaction.

The New York Court of Appeals, New York's highest court, would have none of it.[9] In 1961 that court declared the coverless-magazine law unconstitutional, concluding that the statute presumed "corruption or impropriety" on the part of anyone selling a coverless magazine, rather than requiring proof of such corruption or impropriety in each individual case. To the New York Court of Appeals, the statute represented the worst kind of generalization, presuming that *all* sellers of coverless magazines were crooks even though it was actually the case that only most of them were. By refusing to recognize the possibility of a noncrooked seller of a coverless magazine, the court held, the law engaged in just the kind of "arbitrary" generalization that neither the Constitution nor the concept of justice could countenance.

In reaching this conclusion, the New York court plainly sided with Plato's Stranger, with Aristotle, with the older airline pilots, with the indignant pit bull owners, and with many of the others we have encountered throughout this book. In one or another form, all have believed that justice, ideally, demands an individualized determination of culpability (as well as capability), and the New York Court of Appeals eagerly aligned itself with this tradition. Only if the innocent sellers of coverless books were exempt from prosecution, the court reasoned, could the law permit the inference that the seller of a coverless book was engaged in a fraudulent transaction.[10]

The conclusion of the Court of Appeals tracks the reasoning we have seen again and again. Like the Massachusetts Supreme Judicial Court's refusal to allow probabilistic evidence in the case of Betty Smith, like the pit bull owners' unwillingness to accept breed profiles, and like the claims of the older but quick-reflexed airline pilot, the law-abiding English soccer fan, the conscientious but younger voter, the fit and aggressive woman wanting to attend the Virginia Military Institute, and the innocent airline passenger whose sunglasses, destination, and cash purchase fit the profile of a drug courier, the New York Court of Appeals appears to have believed that justice requires, to put it most starkly, that only the wicked people be punished. When phrased this way, of course, it seems hard to disagree with the court. Yet as we have seen, this conclusion may be too quick and often wrong. With the assistance of a larger look at presumptions in the law, we will be able to see why this is so. And once we see that the error of the New York Court of Appeals is similar to the error of many others, we can see as well that there may be less that is offensive about the idea of a presumed offense than appears at first glance.

## On Irrebuttable Presumptions

The same particularistic instincts that led the New York Court of Appeals to invalidate the presumption that sales of coverless magazines were fraudulent led the Supreme Court of the United States, a bit more than a decade later, to start down a very similar path. Consider one of the Supreme Court's first steps down that path, a 1973 decision that arose out of a challenge to a rule at the University of Connecticut that presumed that a person who had an address outside the state of Connecticut for any part of the year prior to enrolling for admission was not a resident of Connecticut at the time of admission, and could not be a resident for his or her entire student career.[11]

Connecticut's rule drew its significance from the fact that the University of Connecticut, like all other state colleges and universities, charges lower tuition for residents than for nonresidents. Indeed, in 1972, when the case first arose, the annual tuition for nonresidents was more than three times the annual tuition for Connecticut residents. Especially where the differential is as great as this, state universities are constantly on the lookout for students who attempt to claim that they are residents when they are not, or who attempt to change their residency solely in order to obtain the benefits of lower tuition. Granting lower tuition rates to such students would have frustrated Connecticut's desire to ensure that only "real" or "bona fide" Connecticut residents were charged at the lower rate, consistent with Connecticut's understanding of the primary mission and primary constituency of its state-run institutions of higher education. Because of the widespread practice of changing one's residence for purposes of obtaining lower tuition rates, however, the state of Connecticut suspected, not unreasonably, that almost all students with addresses outside Connecticut for part of the year prior to matriculation were not in fact the kind of "real" Connecticut residents that Connecticut desired to assist.

The catch, of course, is in the "almost." Quite a few people actually *do* move to Connecticut from out of state, and many of these people genuinely do so with every intention that the move be permanent. And it is reasonable to suppose that at least a few of these genuine residence-changers change their residence just before enrolling at the University of Connecticut, or change their residence during the years in which they are students. In other words, some people change their residency from out-of-state to in-state just prior to matriculation or while they are students not to obtain lower tuition rates, but for the same completely legitimate reasons that might lead anyone else to change residency: family connections, employment opportunities, weather, scenic beauty, cultural attractions, or just a desire for change. Under the Connecticut rule, however, none of these bona fide residence-changers could obtain the benefit of lower in-state tuition. Like the opportunistic ("fraudulent" might be a bit too strong here) residence-changers, the bona fide residence-changers must pay higher tuition for their entire student careers just because they had had an address outside Connecticut at some time during the year prior to their entrance or just because the legitimate reasons for changing their residence arose while they were enrolled as students at the University of Connecticut.

Because the Connecticut rule allowed no exceptions from the presumption that anyone with an out-of-state address at any time within one year prior to matriculation was a nonresident, the Supreme Court ruled that Connecticut's "irrebuttable presumption" of nonresidency violated the Constitution, and in particular violated the requirement in the Fifth (as to the federal government) and Fourteenth (as to the states) Amendments that no one be deprived of "life, liberty, or property without due process of law." Because neither the bona fide residence-changers nor any of the others who were or became bona fide Connecticut residents even though they had had an out-of-state address during the relevant period were provided any opportunity to present evidence that their situation was different from that of the vast majority at whom the rule was directed, the Connecticut rule, said Justice Potter Stewart for the Supreme Court, could not be upheld. As with Aristotle's argument that justice demanded—through the vehicle of equity—an escape valve for those incorrectly encompassed within the reach of a general rule, so too did Justice Stewart conclude that procedural justice demanded a similar escape valve—the opportunity to rebut the presumption—for those incorrectly encompassed within the boundaries of an irrebuttable presumption.

The story of the Supreme Court's irrebuttable-presumption doctrine is not a long one. Nor is it the story of the expansion of the idea that all laws must provide opportunities for those they reach to demonstrate that they do not fall within the purpose of the law. Indeed, it is not even the story of increasing judicial skepticism about laws that were based on nonuniversal generalizations. On the contrary, the Supreme Court itself, a mere two years after deciding the University of Connecticut nonresident tuition case, declared dead the very doctrine of the unconstitutionality of irrebuttable presumptions that it had so recently created.[12] Although the Court in the intervening years had struck down a few other laws that did not allow individuals to show that they were within the area overencompassed by exceptionless general rules, it finally recognized that the irrebuttable presumption doctrine was untenable.[13]

The Supreme Court's quick turnaround on irrebuttable presumptions was based on its belated realization that virtually all legislation classifies imprecisely. The Court finally understood that it would be implausible to strike down, or even consider challenges to, any legislative category whose reach was broader than the evil it was intended to address. The Connecticut approach to residency, after all, is little different from the minimum voting age, which sets a precise event—one's eighteenth birthday, at least in the United States—to encompass all of those deemed insufficiently mature, civic-minded, invested in the community, or whatever, to cast a ballot. And, as we have seen in chapter 4, few would object to the irrebuttable presumption contained in this voting restriction. No matter how persuasively some seventeen-year-old might argue that she has none of the negative attributes that the minimum voting age was designed to screen out, no one is interesting in listening to her. The minimum voting age is thus an irrebuttable presumption, just as is the typical speed limit, which makes driving in excess of that speed a crime without giving the safe driver under ideal driving conditions the opportunity to demonstrate that the reasons for the rule do not apply in this instance. What the Connecticut law did was simply to establish a rule for residency, and like all rules it was actually or potentially overinclusive, applying its strictures to at least some people who would have fallen outside the justification for creating the rule in the first place.

The genuine residence-changer who happened to have lived outside Connecticut at some point in the year prior to matriculation is thus no different from the mature seventeen-year-old wishing to vote, the responsible fifteen-year-old who wants a driver's license, the safe driver wishing to drive at seventy-five under ideal road conditions, the law-abiding English soccer fan, the docile pit bull, and the alert pilot who has passed the age of sixty. In all these cases the law scoops up some of the innocent along with many of the guilty, and it was the Supreme Court's belated recognition of the inevitability and ubiquity of this phenomenon that led it, finally but properly, to abandon the idea that all legislative classifications not allowing for exceptions were for that reason unconstitutional. For a brief period, the Supreme Court appeared to believe that law must always be particularistic, and that exceptionless generalizations had no place in a just legal system. The Court quickly recognized the error of its ways, and in doing so reinforced the inevitable conclusion that probabilistically sound but nonuniversal generalizations are a common, an unavoidable, and a frequently desirable feature of any workable legal system.[14]

## Presumed Offenses and the Ubiquity of Error

Although the University of Connecticut's in-state residence rules were regulatory criteria and not actually "offenses," there remains a strong similarity between the University of Connecticut's irrebuttable presumption of nonresidence and eighteenth-century England's irrebuttable presumption that a ship with an altered name was a stolen ship. In both cases the legal rule is blind to the cases in which the rule's generalization does not hold, whether it be the genuine residence-changer or the innocent name-changer. It turns out, therefore, that Bentham's idea of a presumed offense may be more ubiquitous than we think, and more ubiquitous than Bentham thought. Vast segments of regulatory law—perhaps most of it—involve the attempt to address some problem or evil with a prohibition not itself directly framed in terms of that problem or evil. We prohibit driving in excess of sixty-five miles per hour and not driving unsafely. A portion of American securities law prohibits insiders from buying and selling (or selling and buying) within a six-month period in order to address the problem of trading on inside information, even though some "short-swing" sales are not based on inside information at all.[15] People below a certain age cannot vote, or marry, or drive, or drink, even though the problem is irresponsible voting, marrying, driving, or drinking rather than juvenile voting, marrying, driving, or drinking. As discussed in chapter 3, recently enacted laws would prohibit people who operate automobiles from talking on their cellular telephones while driving, even though the problem is dangerous driving and not holding a conversation on the telephone. And we make it an offense to drive with a blood alcohol level higher than, say, .10, although the problem is driving while intoxicated and not driving with a certain amount of alcohol in one's blood, and although at least some people who are over the legal limit are not actually intoxicated.[16] As these and countless other examples demonstrate, we often—indeed, usually—regulate indirectly, basing regulation on probabilistic generalizations rather than training the legal and regulatory arsenal directly on the primary concern.[17]

So is there any difference between these omnipresent probabilistic regulations and Bentham's presumed offenses? One of the differences might be the difference between the criminal law and other forms of regulation. Perhaps it is acceptable to have various privileges and entitlements turn on generalizations, but is it not something else again for such generalizations to provide the basis for possibly imprisoning people who might be wholly innocent? Surely this was what bothered the New York Court of Appeals in refusing to allow the criminal conviction of *everyone* who sold a magazine without a cover. And although the Supreme Court might have misfired in applying this instinct to qualifications for in-state tuition at the University of Connecticut, would we be so quick to criticize the Supreme Court if it applied the same rule to prohibit irrebuttable presumptions in Connecticut's criminal law?[18] What if, for example, all of those claiming in-state tuition who had had an out-of-state residence at any time during the year prior to matriculation were not just subject to higher tuition rates, but were prosecuted for criminal fraud as well? For the person who is the exception to the generalization about the class in which she is placed, is this not a simple case of criminal liability for innocent conduct, and an instance elevating the "Where there's smoke, there's fire" maxim to morally unacceptable dimensions?

Yet although the specter of imprisoning people because of the behavior of others or because of the aggregate behavior of a class in which they are placed is indeed frightening, it is hardly clear that this is what is happening in the case of a presumed offense. Perhaps most importantly, there is no doubt that in the typical instance the person committing the presumed offense knows that the activity in which he is engaged is unlawful, even if in his case it is not intrinsically wrong. Even if Mr. Bunis, our dealer in coverless magazines, was engaged in an entirely innocent transaction (what that would be is somewhat hard to grasp, but let us give him the benefit of the doubt), he nevertheless was engaged in what he knew or should have known was an illegal transaction. Mr. Bunis may not have been doing anything wrong in the larger sense, but we can say the same thing about people who run red lights in the middle of the night, who keep harmless pit bulls in municipalities that outlaw all pit bulls, who possess narcotics that they (and many others) think harmless, or who as corporate officers in the United States engage in uninformed (by insider knowledge) open-market short-swing transactions in the shares of their own companies. In these and countless other instances, we do not believe that prosecution of people whose own individual behavior is morally blameless violates any principle of procedural justice, because we understand that fair notice of what is illegal is sufficient to justify any of the vast range of laws that are drafted with sufficient breadth that they catch some people who know they are breaking the law but have otherwise done nothing inherently and fundamentally wicked.

Indeed, the reporting requirement for carrying more than $10,000 in cash into or out of the United States provides an ideal example. This is so in part because the nature of the notice—for people entering or leaving by plane the reporting requirement is contained on the customs form 4790 required for entry, and is further emphasized in the written, oral, and televised instructions for the form's use—makes it virtually inconceivable that anyone violating the law is ignorant of the requirements, and in part because the actual activity—transporting the money—is not itself illegal as long as the act is reported. The requirement of reporting large cash transactions is thus a perfect example of the way in which ample notice appears to cure much or all of the objection to punishing people who themselves have done nothing fundamentally wrong. If, knowing that I am neither a drug dealer or money launderer, I intentionally fail to report, believing—correctly—that I am not within the class of people at whom the law is aimed and believing—also correctly—that I am doing nothing wrong other than failing to report, I will engender little sympathy. Under conditions of adequate notice, the individual overincluded by a presumed offense has little cause for complaint. Should I intentionally fail to report the cash I am otherwise innocently carrying, I am properly punished, just as Mr. Bunis should have been for selling coverless magazines,[19] at least on the assumption that he well knew or should have known that such sales violated the law.[20] Similarly, if Connecticut were to have prohibited anyone with an out-of-state address at any time within the year prior to matriculation from claiming residency or applying for in-state tuition, we ought to be far less sympathetic to objections to even criminal prosecution of those who would knowingly and thus misleadingly have made the very claim that the law explicitly prohibited.

In addition to the fact that ample notice appears to cure almost all the claims of injustice for even the over-included criminal defendant, there is no indication that the risks of punishing the "innocent" in cases of pre-sumed offenses are greater than such risks would be for any kind of offense. Recall from chapter 3 our discussion of the Blue Bus Problem and related conundrums sur-rounding the use of probabilities and statistics in the law of evidence. Although some people think it unjust to impose liability under circumstances in which there is a possibility that liability is being imposed on those who have done nothing wrong, one of our conclusions was that allowing liability on the basis of probabilistic evi-dence was no different from the routine application of standards of proof short of absolute certainty or the rou-tine admission of nonstatistical evidence despite some likelihood of its inaccuracy. This lesson is directly appli-cable to the case of presumed offenses. Suppose that 99 percent of the ships with altered names are stolen, that 99 percent of the people entering or exiting the United States with unreported large amounts of cash are drug dealers or money launderers, and that 99 percent of all sales of magazines without covers are directly or indi-rectly part of a fraudulent scheme to deprive publishers or distributors of their rightful revenues. Although in each of these cases there is then a one percent chance that someone not truly evil is being punished, there is also a one percent chance that someone not evil at all is being punished whenever we convict someone of a crime under circumstances in which we say—by virtue of the distinction between proof by absolute certainty and proof beyond a reasonable doubt—that he or she can be convicted by evidence that falls short of absolute certainty.[21] Indeed, the fact that there is full notice makes the injustice even greater in the routine case. The likelihood that Mr. Bunis, knowing that sales of coverless magazines were unlawful, was in fact innocent would strike most people as being smaller than the chances that Mr. Bunis was innocent under circumstances in which he was convicted under a beyond-a-reasonable-doubt standard of being engaged in a fraudulent sale of coverless magazines.

The point becomes even clearer when we compare two different approaches to drug trafficking. In Florida, as noted above, anyone knowingly possessing more than 28 grams of cocaine is guilty of drug "trafficking," without the necessity of any proof of actual selling, distributing, or otherwise transferring or trading in cocaine. Even if they are just stocking up for a rainy day (quite a few rainy days, actually), the very definition of the crime, and the penalty that attaches to it, *presumes* from the quantity of cocaine that they possess that they are trafficking in cocaine. By contrast, in Illinois it is a crime to possess cocaine with an intent to sell, but the law requires proof in each case of that intent to sell. In practice, however, evidence of possession of a large quantity of cocaine— more than 28 grams, say—is sufficient to justify the jury's inference of an intent to sell.[22] So although the Florida approach takes the form of a presumed offense while the Illinois approach does not, there is no reason to believe that the Illinois approach, which allows the jury to rely on exactly the same presumption that motivated the Florida legislature, is any less likely to trap the "innocent." Indeed, because the Florida approach enshrines its presumption in a statute publicly accessible to all, while the Illinois approach allows the presumptions to exist less transparently in the hearts and minds of judges and jurors, there is a more than plausible argument that the Florida approach is superior. As the Florida cocaine law and many of the other foregoing examples show, there is little reason to believe that presumed offenses are rare, and even less reason to believe—again assuming adequate notice—that criminally prosecuting people for committing them is unjust.

## From Presumed to Indicative Offenses

Bentham's label of presumed offenses captures the idea that such offenses are based on a presumption, and thus on the way in which we frequently draw an inference from something we know "directly" to something we can know only indirectly.[23] Yet as we saw in exploring the issues of probability and evidence, and revisited in the previous section, the distinction between direct and indirect knowledge is, at best, misleading. When I look out of my office window and see people walking along the street with open umbrellas, I *presume* that it is raining. In doing so, I engage in a process that Bentham and millions since would have described as indirect. After all, I have not seen any raindrops. I have seen only open umbrellas, but I know from experience that open umbrellas almost always indicate rain, so I presume rain from the presence of the open umbrellas.[24]

Yet although the inferential process is obvious when I infer rain from the presence of open umbrellas, there is also an inferential process when I see the rain itself. When I see what I perceive to be actual raindrops and thus "infer" that it is raining, I am again making inferences, most significantly the inference from the fact that this appears to me to be rain to the fact that it *is* rain. And although describing this process as an "inference" may look strange from my own perspective—when I am "inferring" the accuracy of my own observation—it makes much more sense, in light of what we know about the hardly perfect accuracy of sensory perception, to think of the process as involving an inference when we are moving from Jack's perception of what looks like rain to Jack's perception that it is rain to Jill's conclusion, based on Jack's perceptions, that it is raining. Like the distinction between direct and circumstantial evidence, the distinction between direct and indirect observation typically overstates the reliability of allegedly direct evidence, and equally typically understates the inferential nature of its use.

The inferential process in presuming that it is raining from my seeing umbrellas is thus not significantly different from the inferential process in my presuming that it is raining from Jack's account, to me, that he saw raindrops. Recognizing the presumptions involved in both of these inferential processes thus significantly weakens the distinction between direct and indirect accounts, and also, therefore, much of the distinction between presumed and nonpresumed offenses. The presence of inferences in virtually all observations undercuts some of the distinction between presumed and nonpresumed offenses, and the uncertainty and inaccuracy surrounding both presumed and nonpresumed offenses undercuts more of the distinction.

Yet even after we have weakened the distinction between the direct and the indirect and the presumed and the nonpresumed, there still seems a worry. Surely there is a difference between making murder a crime and making possession of a smoking gun a crime (and not simply evidence of some other crime), and it still seems important to develop a principle that will recognize this difference.

What seems to be a large difference between the crime of murder and the crime of possession of a smoking gun turns out to dissolve, however, for all of those offenses that are formulated in terms other than intrinsic wrongness. Whenever the offense is formulated instrumentally, to reflect rather than simply to restate some background justification, the distinction between the offense and the evidence for it is weakened substantially. The difference between the offense of driving at greater than sixty-five miles per hour and the offense of causing a radar speed detector to indicate a speed in excess of sixty-five miles per hour may appear, as with murder and possession of a smoking gun, to be the distinction between the evidence and the offense, but once we recognize that both the evidence and the offense are but imperfect indicators for our deeper concern (unsafe driving), it is hardly clear that the category of presumed offenses is either small or problematic. Much the same applies to the offense of driving with a blood alcohol level higher than .10. A presumed offense is one in which the offense is described in ways that probabilistically but imperfectly predict our deeper concern, but the universe of such offenses is quite large. Traffic offenses predict unsafe driving, possession offenses (child pornography, burglar tools, sawed-off shotguns, and many others) predict unlawful use, corporate reporting offenses predict illicit transactions, and numerous other offenses are described in ways that are instrumental to, rather than descriptive of, our ultimate concern.

Yet although presumed offenses are more common than we or Bentham may have thought, there remains an important distinction between two types of presumed offense. In one type we have the potential for a causal relationship between the offense itself and the evidence that we then choose to define as the offense. Many murders do cause smoking guns, and our inference from the smoking gun to a murder, even if imperfect, is still based on the fact that many or perhaps most murders do cause there to be smoking guns, just as many or most cases of raining do cause there to be open umbrellas on the street. And when this kind of causal relationship exists, the case for presumed offenses appears to be the strongest.

But now let us consider another type of presumed offense, one that we can label an *indicative* offense. Here some observable form of behavior still indicates the likelihood of an offense, but in most or even all of the cases there will be no causal connection between the primary offense and the observable behavior. Take, for example, the relationship between broken factory windows (or, perhaps, nonfunctioning monitoring gauges) and unsafe working conditions for workers, such as inadequate sound control, insufficient protective devices on dangerous machines, or a failure to furnish protective clothing.[25] Because broken factory windows and insufficient attention to worker safety often have a common cause—employer negligence or inattention—there is a correlation between the two phenomena, even though the unsafe working conditions do not cause the broken windows nor do the broken windows cause the unsafe working conditions. But because the incidence of the two phenomena is correlated, the presence of broken windows *indicates* an increased likelihood of unsafe working conditions.

Because the presence of broken windows indicates the presence of something that is our genuine concern, could we not just treat the broken windows the same way we treat the unreported $10,000 and make having broken factory windows an offense in itself, not because we care about broken windows but because punishing those with broken factory windows might turn out to be an efficient way of punishing those maintaining unsafe conditions for their workers? The offense of having a factory with broken windows would thus be an indicative offense, in contrast to the direct offense of having a factory with unsafe working conditions, and also in contrast to the (causally connected) presumed offense, such as making it an offense to have more than a designated number of reported injuries per month.[26]

The absence of a causal relationship between the offense and the indicator appears to make this type of offense different from the ones in which such a causal relationship does exist. Most cases of unreported cash carrying, possession of ships with altered names, and selling coverless books are *caused* by the very illegal activity with which we are primarily concerned, and the presence of this causal relationship might at first appear to distinguish most of the examples in this chapter from the examples in which the relationship between the offense and the indicator is entirely noncausal. Perhaps there is nothing unjust about prosecuting Mr. Bunis for selling coverless magazines, for it is highly likely that he is being prosecuted for an activity that almost certainly was caused by his illegal activities, but is there not something different about prosecuting someone for doing something that appears to have no relationship with a genuine concern except the presence of a common cause?

Yet does the presence or absence of a causal relationship really make a difference? Let us consider the case in which a causal relationship is absent, the case in which the argument against indicative offenses ought to be the strongest. Returning, for example, to the occupational safety scenario described above, we know it is likely that certain features of a workplace indicate unsafe worker conditions even if those features were not caused by unsafe conditions. The presence of broken windows is one instance. A very high level of production might be another. Under these circumstances, would there be something untoward about punishing people for having, say, broken windows, or sloppy trash disposal, even if those indicators were not thought intrinsically harmful? Initially, we bridle at the prospect. Should totally innocent behavior be punished just because it happens, imperfectly, to indicate the presence of guilty behavior for most but certainly not all people or, in this case, companies?

Yet again we must ask whether there is any difference between punishing a safe driver on clear dry roads for driving in excess of the speed limit and punishing a business for having broken factory windows. In both cases the behavior itself is harmless. And in both cases the costs of locating only the harmful behavior are seen to be excessive. In the broken-window case it might be thought too costly (or too intrusive) to search the factory for safety violations, just as in the speed-limit case it might be thought too costly or too intrusive to require police officers to determine whether each driver is or is not driving safely. So the rule operates as a heuristic to produce the right result in most cases. Punishing people on the basis of the heuristics appears initially unfair, but having seen that punishing people for breaking rules rather than for breaking the justifications behind them is a form of punishment on the basis of heuristics, it is hard to accept the basis of the objection. And having seen as well that in an imperfect world any punishment risks punishing the totally innocent, any objection to the overinclusiveness of indicative offenses is further weakened. As long as there is adequate notice of what activity will be punished, a concern about innocence in the case of indicative offenses that is not reflected in an equivalent concern about innocence in most cases of rule application, and most prosecutions based on so-called direct evidence, is exposed as misplaced.

Criminalizing purely indicative activity will rarely be a wise strategy, because the absence of the causal relationship will usually make it too easy for a potential miscreant to manipulate the system by fixing the indicator but not fixing the problem. We do not, after all, want people with unsafe factories to deflect the law's attention just by replacing the broken windows. And in most cases the possibility of gaming the system will undercut the utility of criminalizing indicative behavior that is not the causal consequence of our primary concern. Still, understanding that punishing even indicative offenses may be less different from normal practice than it first appears helps us to recognize as well that in the more normal case—in which the causal relationship is likely to exist—having a criminal or civil penalty rest on an imperfect generalization is less unusual than we suppose, less abhorrent to justice than the New York Court of Appeals and briefly the U.S. Supreme Court thought, and more properly part of the regulatory arsenal than we may have appreciated. Presumed offenses create some risk of punishing the innocent, but so does virtually every other aspect of our system of punishment.[27] In an imperfect world this outcome is inescapable, and although it would plainly be desirable to reduce the possibility of wrongful punishment within the constraints of satisfying the other goals that we need any system of regulation or punishment to serve, there is little reason to believe that serving this goal requires that criminal or civil offenses not be defined in terms of imperfect generalizations.[28] It could hardly be otherwise, and Bentham's mistake may only have been in thinking that presumed offenses are the exception rather than the rule.

# CHAPTER 10

# The Generality of Law

## Let the Punishment Fit the Crime— but How Closely?

"Let the punishment fit the crime!" announced the Mikado in the Gilbert and Sullivan operetta of that name, parroting one of the venerable maxims of the common law. Indeed, the adage that the punishment should fit the crime comes to mind not only when we are considering whether a punishment is excessively severe or excessively lenient, but also when we encounter especially creative forms of sentencing. When judges sentence graffiti artists to building-cleaning duty, car thieves to service as chauffeurs, or drunk drivers to service as hospital emergency room orderlies, they seek to devise a punishment uniquely tailored to the nature of the crime. Similarly, when judges offer convicted youthful petty criminals the choice of serving a sentence or joining the military, they are attempting to mold a sentence to the current and future rehabilitative needs of the particular defendant as well as the deterrence and retributive needs of the society. And when judges suspend a sentence for first offenders or those whose crimes were inspired by financial desperation but mete out the maximum to career criminals or to those whose only motive was greed, again we think of the judge imposing a sentence as someone performing the maximally particularistic task of letting the punishment fit not only the crime, but the criminal as well.[1]

The exercise of judicial discretion in imposing sentences carefully tailored to individual defendants and individual crimes has a long and distinguished history. But the abuse of that discretion has a long history as well, even if that history is not nearly so distinguished. Anecdotal evidence and systematic studies have demonstrated that judicial discretion has produced sentences not only that often fit the crime, but also that much too often are determined less by the nature of the crime and more by the defendant's race, religion, class, or appearance.[2] Even when such factors are properly ignored, moreover, judges remain subject to the same human foibles as the rest of us, and sentences have been shown to vary dramatically for the same crimes and the same types of defendants depending on the moods and ideologies of individual judges.[3] All too often, it has seemed, the punishment was found to have fitted the judge's peculiarities and proclivities even more than it fitted the defendant's particular crime and the defendant's particular history.

One prominent manifestation of the consequences of misplaced sentencing discretion has been the treatment of so-called white-collar criminals. Don Corleone in Mario Puzo's *Godfather* observed wryly that "a lawyer with a briefcase can steal more than a thousand men with guns," yet those who have stolen with briefcases have historically fared better when sentenced for their crimes than have those who have stolen in cruder fashion.[4] Concerned with the systematic underpunishment of white-collar criminals relative to those no more evil but less well dressed, concerned also with the perceived underpunishment of narcotics offenses,[5] and concerned finally with the overwhelming evidence of bias or randomness in criminal sentencing in the federal courts of the United States,[6] Congress in 1984 passed the Sentencing Reform Act of 1984.[7] This act established the U.S. Sentencing Commission and gave the commission the initial mandate of examining the entire issue of disparity in sentencing and, if necessary, setting forth guidelines for judges to use in imposing criminal sentences. Three years later, the commission proposed the Federal Sentencing Guidelines. After approval by Congress, the guidelines took effect on November 1, 1987, and things have not been the same since.

The Federal Sentencing Guidelines do not remove all discretion from judges in imposing sentences after conviction, but they remove much of it.[8] In place of the particularized and personal process that formerly prevailed—"individualized sentencing" is the common label—the Sentencing Guidelines create an elaborate grid, formally called the Sentencing Table, that judges are required to use in determining sentences. The vertical axis of the grid contains forty-three offense levels, from the least to the most serious, with the offense level being determined not only by the nature of the offense itself—murder is more serious than insider trading, and insider trading is more serious than the failure of a truck driver to keep a proper logbook—but also by the magnitude of the specific offense—theft of a small amount is not as serious as theft of a large amount, and theft from a person is worse than theft from a locker at the bus station—the degree of the defendant's involvement in the crime—accessories are different from principals, and foot soldiers are different from organizers—the extent of the defendant's cooperation with the authorities, the presence or absence of acceptance of responsibility and statements of remorse, and a number of other factors bearing on the severity of the particular offense. All these factors are used to "customize" the crime beyond the basic offense as set forth in the United States Code.

The horizontal axis of the grid is focused not on the crime but on the criminal. Here there are six different levels representing different "Criminal History Categories," with the level determined by the number and nature of the defendant's previous offenses. Felonies are worse than misdemeanors, and longer sentences are worse than shorter ones. The defendant accumulates points for his previous transgressions, and the higher the number of points, the more serious the criminal history.

Making the determinations required by the categories in the vertical and horizontal axes is not totally mechanical, but it is far more so than the system it replaced. Certain factors are simply excluded, such as education, socioeconomic status, age, employment history, mental and emotional condition, and family background. And most of the factors that are permissibly used are capable of a relatively objective assessment. It is usually easy to determine, for example, how much the defendant stole, or whether or not he cooperated with the authorities. And so by making these relatively objective determinations, the judge can place the defendant and his conduct within one of the 258 boxes that make up the grid. The placement on the grid produces a score, and the score indicates the narrow range of months within which the judge may impose sentence. The judge still has some discretion, but the area of judicial discretion is limited for each of the 258 boxes on the grid to 25 percent of the total sentence. Moreover, the law allows the judge to go outside the range indicated by the grid only on the basis of documented and appealable reasons for departing from the guidelines in a particular case. Even though such departures amount to close to 25 percent of all federal sentences—almost all a result of the defendant's having provided substantial assistance to the prosecution—the fact that departures are limited in size and limited in the reasons on which they may be based has changed the process of sentencing in federal criminal cases from one characterized by judicial discretion and flexibility to one in which the role of the judge in imposing sentence is substantially more mechanical. If this is the defendant's second offense for embezzlement, and the amount of the embezzlement the first time was $10,000 and this time is $100,000, and if the defendant has cooperated with the authorities in order to help them apprehend an accomplice, for example, then the defendant's sentence must be between, hypothetically, thirty-two and thirty-six months' incarceration. Period. The sentencing judge determines whether it is to be thirty-two or thirty-six, but, except in very rare circumstances, the sentence must be within the range indicated by the grid.

As might have been expected, the federal judges whose sentencing discretion was to be so dramatically curtailed reacted angrily to this restriction on their discretion, and remain angry to this day. In the early days of the guidelines, 200 federal district judges expressed their hostility to the Sentencing Guidelines by declaring them to be an unconstitutional infringement of the separation of powers between the judicial and legislative branches of government.[9] The Supreme Court ultimately overturned all 200 of these rulings and upheld the constitutionality of the guidelines, but the vast number of decisions the Supreme Court was required to overturn demonstrates the deep hostility the guidelines have provoked among the federal judges who before the guidelines had an enormous amount of sentencing discretion and after the guidelines have very little.[10]

There remains some doubt about the extent to which the Federal Sentencing Guidelines have in fact achieved their goal of reducing case-to-case or judge-to-judge sentencing disparity.[11] To some extent the discretion formerly resting with the judge has moved to the prosecuting attorney, who can influence the sentence by determining the offense with which the defendant will be charged, and whose discretion in the plea-bargaining process is far less constrained than judicial discretion is constrained by the guidelines. Insofar as discretion has been relocated more than it has been restricted, the Sentencing Guidelines may have helped to create a system in which, rather than having the punishment fit the crime, the crime that is charged is tailored to fit a prosecutor's (or, on occasion, a judge's) view of the appropriate punishment.[12] And it is also possible that the current system, perversely, magnifies the effects of what discretion is left to judges, thus occasionally producing more rather than less disparity in sentencing. Still, there is little doubt that the guidelines have produced at least some more consistency and predictability in the sentencing process, even if they have produced less than some of their most ardent proponents had hoped.[13]

Yet even if the results of the Sentencing Guidelines are at best mixed,[14] the anger that almost all the affected judges harbor toward the Sentencing Guidelines reflects a deeper view about law itself. Occasionally implicit but usually quite explicit in the judicial fulminations against the Sentencing Guidelines is not only the widespread phenomenon by which discretion is typically highly valued by those who have it and often suspected by those who would grant it. Equally important in explaining judicial resentment of the Sentencing Guidelines is the view that discretion in sentencing is the quintessential embodiment of the most particularistic side of the law. Sentencing, many judges believe, lies at the heart of the judicial function, and judging, many of those same judges believe as well, lies at the heart of law itself.

The Sentencing Guidelines stand as a repudiation of this particularistic understanding of the nature of law, for the guidelines are an exercise in generalization and not in particularized assessment. More than before, the individual judge is less a sentencer and more an implementer of sentencing decisions made by others, largely the U.S. Sentencing Commission or its state counterparts. Because the Sentencing Commission could not have evaluated the individual defendant and individual crime involved in a particular case, the Sentencing Guidelines represent a triumph of generalization over individuation. The grid that produces the sentences is premised on the idea that uniformity in sentencing is desirable, and that generalizations are typically the keys to uniformity.

In the context of criminal sentencing, however, uniformity turns out to be a highly complex matter. First, the Sentencing Guidelines, like all generalizations, do not on their face, and certainly do not to their critics, treat like cases alike. The judge who feels constrained by the Sentencing Guidelines believes, often correctly, that the individual case and individual defendant before her are ones to which the guidelines' generalizations do not apply, or, if they apply, do not produce the correct outcome, frequently because *this* case involves a mercy-producing or (less often)[15] a punishment-increasing factor that the guidelines simply do not recognize or do not permit.[16] In one case, for example, a young Alabama man named Ephraim Bristow had pawned as collateral for a loan his father's lawfully owned and unloaded gun, and had done so with his father's permission, and in order to be able to afford his child support payments. Ephraim had the gun in his possession only for the time it took to carry the weapon from his family home to the pawnshop, and he did not possess any ammunition for the gun. But because he had some years earlier pleaded guilty to a narcotics possession offense, for which he was given probation and served no time in prison, he was someone with a felony conviction, and was thus a felon in possession of a firearm.[17] Under the Sentencing Guidelines the judge was compelled to impose a sentence of at least twelve months' incarceration, a sentence that the appellate court reluctantly felt equally compelled to uphold.[18]

All the judges who confronted Ephraim Bristow's case strained to find a way of reducing the sentence, but the Sentencing Guidelines foreclosed any such option. By reducing all the possible aspects and dimensions of sentencing to at most forty-nine objective factors (the total number of factors on the vertical and horizontal axes of the grid), the guidelines have eliminated many of the factors that might turn out to be important in a case like Ephraim Barstow's.[19] Like the factors that might make a particular pit bull docile or a particular over-sixty pilot highly qualified, the guidelines, as with all generalizations, ignore features of the particular case that might actually make a difference. And once we understand this, we can see that the guidelines, as with any equalizing (Procrustean) generalization, do not treat like cases alike, but rather treat unlike cases alike by intentionally ignoring various factors that may produce the unlikeness.

There are two reasons for treating unlike cases alike in this context. First, and consistent with what the authors of the guidelines thought they were doing, the guidelines might produce in the aggregate fewer mistakes in sentencing than would be produced by less-constrained judicial discretion. Following simple guidelines for a complex process will, to be sure, produce mistakes, but we know that discretion produces mistakes as well.[20] Consequently, one argument for the guidelines is that, although they produce mistakes, they produce fewer mistakes than the alternative. Now it is not surprising that this argument carries little weight with the judges, for the judges, like the rest of us, are systematically unlikely to recognize the full extent of their own capacity for mistakes. What the complaining judge sees is the case in which her own judgment about what the best individualized sentence would be is put aside in the service of the generalization. Yet the complaining judge is rarely able fully to appreciate the extent to which her own judgment about the best sentence would actually be worse than the judgment reflected in the guidelines' generalizations.[21] And only slightly less likely is the possibility that judges would believe that the class of judges is likely to make more mistakes than would be made in the application of some anonymously produced formula.

It is possible, of course, that the judges are right, and that the judgment of judges as a whole (itself a generalization) will produce fewer mistakes than would be produced by the systematic application of the guidelines.[22] But in determining whether this is true, it may not be the best strategy to listen only to the judges, for it should come as no surprise that judges, just like carpenters, police officers, customs officials, and university professors, are hardly the best judges of the frequency and magnitude of their own errors. One argument for the guidelines, therefore, is that although they systematically and inevitably produce more mistakes than the mistakes that would be produced by perfect judges making perfect individualized judgments, in the world we inhabit of imperfect judges making imperfect individualized judgments, it may well be that there will be fewer mistakes made by applying the crude guidelines than will be made by imperfect judges relying on their own best but often mistaken judgment. This argument tracks Plato's argument from the second-best, and it is an argument that is as applicable here as it was when Plato first used it to explain why the arguments he made in the *Statesman* might not be the best arguments to use in designing an actual legal system.

In addition to these familiar arguments about the value of imperfect generalizations in an imperfect world, there is another argument that is quite different. It may well be, especially in the case of sentencing, that uniformity for its own sake is a valuable goal, and that uniformity is valuable precisely for the way in which it ignores real differences.[23] Here the argument is not about the second-best. Indeed, we can even assume for purposes of this argument that the guidelines produce more errors than would be produced by actual judges given the discretion to use their best and most sensitive judgment in tailoring individual sentences to individual crimes and to individual defendants. Yet even if this is so, uniformity for its own sake might be valuable. One reason for this is that there are limits to the number of factors that can plausibly be explained to a larger public. So if it is important not only that the law be just but also that it be seen to be just, it may be desirable for the law to operate in such a way that it is widely understood as treating large numbers of people in the same way even if in fact there might be relevant differences. As long as those relevant differences cannot fully be explained to a larger public, it may be preferable to ignore them than to rely on factors whose importance cannot publicly be explained and understood.

Moreover, there may be an even stronger value in uniformity for its own sake, a uniformity that produces an artificial—"Procrustean" is the common pejorative—similarity or uniformity in the face of genuine differences. And this is the value of understanding our common situation and our common plight as one in which there are limits to how much difference our own personal individual situations ought to make. It is no accident that Justice wears a blindfold. And she wears a blindfold not because she needs to steel herself against her own biases, prejudices, and mistakes, but because it is central to one conception of justice that equal treatment for its own sake—treating unlikes alike—serves important functions beyond the possibility that such a decision procedure might produce fewer errors. As we saw when discussing equality in chapter 8, equality is in large part about ignoring real differences. When we treat people equally we treat them in some respects the same even in the face of good reasons for treating them differently. Ignoring real differences in sentencing—sentencing socially beneficial heart surgeons to the same period of imprisonment for murder as socially parasitic career criminals—may well serve the larger purpose of explaining that at a moment of enormous significance—determining how much of the state's power will be brought to bear against those who transgress its laws—we are all in this together.

## The Wisdom of Solomon and the Reality of Judging

There may be a culprit behind the unwillingness of judges (and many others) to accept strong constraints on judicial discretion. That culprit is King Solomon, or, in fairness to Solomon, perhaps the blame lies not with him but with how history has understood his most famous legacy.

Recall the story of King Solomon and the baby.[24] Two women both claim to be the mother of the same baby, a consequence of the baby of one of them's having died during the night in a house in which both resided. Solomon at first does not know how to decide between the two, but he then devises an ingenious solution. He offers to divide the baby in half, not because he actually plans to do so, but because he believes that the threat of such cruelty will expose who the real mother is. As expected, one woman is willing to divide the baby, but the other woman is appalled at the prospect of dividing the baby, and so offers to give up the baby and let the other woman have him. This willingness to sacrifice, Solomon perceives, shows that the one willing to give up the baby is the actual mother, for no one willing to see the baby cut in half could possibly be that baby's real mother.

Solomon is celebrated for this act of wisdom, an act that has secured his place in history as the quintessential wise judge, and thus as the paragon of exactly what it is to be a judge. Judging, our judges constantly remind us, is about judgment. Yet before we too quickly encourage our judges to act like Solomon or bridle at restrictions that would prevent them from doing so, let us look a bit more closely at Solomon and the case of the contested baby.

Although King Solomon is often thought of as the quintessential judge, Solomonic wisdom is not understood to be a function of obeying rules, following precedent, or fitting the dilemma of contested parentage into a preexisting rule for the general category of cases of this type. Rather, Solomon is revered for having come up with the perfect solution to *this* case as he then perceived it personally and closely. Yet Solomon was forced into making the decision he did because, we can safely assume, there was no legal rule for him to interpret or to apply. As far as we know, there was no statute providing that in cases of disputed parentage the decision should be in favor of the older, or the younger, or the richer, or the poorer, or even the one who was better able to persuade a jury of twelve by a preponderance of the evidence that she was the biological mother. As the story is told in the Bible, and as it has been understood down through the ages, it appears that none of these dispute-resolving rules existed. As a result, Solomon was compelled not to apply law but to make it. Solomonic judging and even Solomonic wisdom turns out not to be an example of applying the law, but instead an example of the fact that when no law is available to resolve a dispute it then becomes incumbent upon a judge to make some.

This understanding of Solomonic wisdom reminds us that a quite plausible conception of judicial wisdom and discretion is that it is interstitial and not universal. When the law runs out we want our judges to act like Solomon, but it is far less clear that we want our judges to act like Solomon even if in doing so they violate the law, and also far less clear that we want to set up a system to give Solomonic wisdom as free a hand as possible. If the law of biblical Israel had provided a precise mechanism for deciding cases of this type and Solomon had ignored it, would we be as ready to praise Solomon as we now are, and would we be as ready to take Solomon's behavior as judging at its highest? That it is better to exercise discretion wisely than foolishly is obvious, but it is far less obvious that discretion is necessarily better than constraint, or that discretion should be seized even when it is not lawfully granted.

This is not to say that we should never create systems in which judges are unconstrained by generalizations like the Federal Sentencing Guidelines, and in which they are consequently empowered to make their decisions in as particular a way as possible. But whether and when to constrain our judges and their discretion is a difficult question. Judges need to have a voice in helping their society address this difficult question, but there is little reason to believe that judges, more of whom have Solomonic aspirations than have Solomonic wisdom, ought to be the only or the most important voice that is heard.

Even if a society does desire its judges to be Solomonic, however, it is hardly clear that judging is the largest part of what law is all about. Solomon may be the ideal judge, but Solomon himself probably existed at the edges and not at the center of law.[25] Indeed, perhaps the most interesting aspect of the story of Solomon is that it arose in the context of such an unusual event. Although what we now call dispute resolution became necessary when it turned out that two women claimed natural motherhood of the same child, it is noteworthy that neither King Solomon nor any other judge was probably called upon to decide those cases in which a childless woman desired another woman's child because the childless woman thought she would be a better mother, or desired a child more than did some child's natural mother, or because of class and wealth could provide the child with a better upbringing than the natural mother. Although Solomon's decision was part of the law broadly conceived, so too, we can assume, was the prevailing practice in which the overwhelming majority of natural mothers were allowed to keep their children even when others desired them or could better care for them. In almost all cases, child custody, then as now, was determined by the generalization that children should remain with their natural mothers, a generalization that, then and now, controls even when there appear to be pretty good reasons for abandoning it. The case of Solomon was one in which it was not clear who was entitled to the benefit of the generalization, and so Solomon was compelled to make a wise and particularistic judgment. But the story of Solomon turns out to tell us very little about whether the law should be understood as particularistic, and very little about whether Solomon accurately represents what is most important about the law.

What the story of Solomon does tell us, however, is that the image of the wise judge is not the same as the image of the law. The debate about the Federal Sentencing Guidelines is a debate framed, at least on one side, by an ideology of judicial discretion and judicial wisdom and thus by an ideology of particularity. Yet the other side of the debate, the one that recognizes the dangers as well as the virtues of discretion, and recognizes that regularity for its own sake has its uses, is one that needs to be appreciated. This side of the debate is also an ideology, and here it is an ideology of distrust and an ideology of generality. The debate about the Sentencing Guidelines is but one manifestation of this debate between dueling ideologies, both of which have much to recommend them. But is the law as such the home more to one than to the other? We can all recognize that discretion and particularity have their place, and we can all recognize as well that limitations on discretion, and thus generality, have their places as well. But is the place of one of these more within the law than the other? In other words, is law itself the repository of particularity, or is law instead a practice and an institution in which the virtues of generalization are most at home?

## Thinking like a Lawyer

The role of generality and particularity in legal thinking is part of a larger question about whether there is a characteristic mode of legal thinking at all. Lawyers, of course, typically believe that there is, and this belief is inculcated from the first day of law school. At most law schools, at least in the United States, the new crop of incoming law students receives its welcoming address from the dean. This welcoming address includes the familiar paeans to justice and to the role of lawyers in protecting the rights of the downtrodden; it recalls famous events and epic figures in the glorious history of law and lawyers; and it reminds the new law students that, unlike the carefree experience of their undergraduate years, law school will be very hard work.

At this point in the welcoming address, the dean typically shifts course, and foreshadows what the students will actually learn during their three years of law school. Law school is not about learning a battery of legal rules, the dean cautions, thereby attempting to alleviate the expected anxieties of first-year students who, come November, grow increasingly anxious about the small number of legal rules they have actually been taught. Nor is law school about learning where to stand in the courtroom or how to write a will, the dean continues, hoping to inoculate the school and its administration from the complaints of those who worry that law school is insufficiently practical. Rather, the dean concludes, law school is about learning how to think like a lawyer, and about mastering a skill sometimes called *legal reasoning*.

In holding out the promise that students will learn how to think like lawyers, the dean reinforces the view that legal reasoning is a concrete and learnable skill, sort of like long division or French. And in the hands of the skillful practitioner of the art of decanal oratory, the dean's welcoming address serves its intended goal. Students commence their studies with a sense of purpose and mission, confident that at the end they will have a discrete and important skill, and will have had unlocked for them the mysteries of law itself.

It is often tempting to think of these mysteries, and of legal reasoning, as being in important ways particularistic. The story of King Solomon emphasizes the particularity of legal decisionmaking, and the anger of judges at the Sentencing Guidelines underscores the pervasiveness of this view. Yet although excellence in particularistic and individual judgment *is* important for judges and lawyers, there is no reason to believe that it is *more* important for lawyers and judges than it is for physicians, psychologists, detectives, social workers, architects, and schoolteachers. In all these professions we laud, and properly so, the exercise of keen individual judgment. Physicians are expected to find the right diagnosis and treatment for *this* patient; detectives are expected to solve *this* crime; social workers are expected to understand and manage *this* family or community problem; architects are expected to produce unique buildings; and teachers are expected to understand the educational needs of individual students. We can and do praise lawyers and judges when they make the right argument for this particular situation or reach the right decision in this particular case, but that praise does not take us very far in identifying those characteristics—if any—that distinguish legal reasoning from any other form of reasoning. Lawyers and judges, after all, are praised not only when they are particularistic and context sensitive, but also when they are compassionate, empathetic, eloquent, intelligent, trustworthy, loyal, helpful, friendly, and brave. But no one would suggest that any of these traits, however admirable they are and however important it is that lawyers possess them, captures the idea of thinking like a lawyer; and that is because few would suggest that these traits, praiseworthy as they are when they appear in lawyers, are in any way unique to lawyers or even disproportionately represented in lawyers or in what lawyers do.

If we look not at particularity but at generality, however, the picture is different. For when we focus on generality, and look at those aspects of legal decisionmaking that embody generality rather than particularity, it turns out that some of the characteristic devices of legal argument and legal thinking appear to be less present in other domains than they are in law. It would be too strong a claim to maintain that legal reasoning consists of modes of thought found in the legal system and nowhere else, but if generality looms larger in law than elsewhere it may explain much of what it is to think like a lawyer.

We have already seen that rules are essentially general, and that understanding rule-based decisionmaking entails understanding the way in which rules are prescriptive generalizations. Take as an example the U.S.

federal law prohibiting possession of an unregistered shotgun with a barrel shorter than eighteen inches.[26] Lurking behind this legal rule is the reliable but nonuniversal generalization that shotguns with short barrels—sawed-off shotguns—do not have legitimate sporting or other legitimate uses and are almost always used in the pursuit of robbery or other unlawful activities. But "almost always" is not the same as "always." So when a Vietnamese immigrant named Hoa Cam Lam innocently purchased a shotgun with a 16.5-inch barrel in order to protect his small family business and found himself the subject of a criminal prosecution for possessing an unregistered sawed-off shotgun, his plea that his was not within the class of activities that inspired the law was to no avail.[27] Like speed limits aimed at average drivers that constrain the good ones, the sawed-off-shotgun law was overinclusive vis-à-vis its background justification, encompassing those whose activities would not have been encompassed by precise and direct application of their background justification—in this case restricting the use of weapons in the commission of violent crimes. Mr. Lam was convicted by a generalization, and the fact that the generalization did not apply to him was of no consequence. Mr. Lam was not only a victim of this rule, but he was also a victim of the point of having rules, which is to tolerate some inaccurate applications as an alternative preferable to the greater inaccuracies that would come from direct application of the rule's background justifications.

Although rules are all over the law, they are less of a presence in numerous other human endeavors. Physicians may rely on rules and generalizations in diagnosing and treating their patients, but when a physician is certain that the rule would generate the wrong result in this particular case she does not follow it, treating the rule as a rule of thumb indicating the right result in most cases, but having to claim to force when it would produce the wrong result. The rule that snared Mr. Lam, however, is of a different type, and Lam's argument that the rule had produced the wrong result in this case helped him not at all. In law, it seems, but much less elsewhere, the prescriptive generalizations that are rules have importance as generalizations, and have a prominence and a weight not nearly as significant outside the law. For reasons that are persuasive to some and absurd to others—a best-selling book a few years ago titled *The Death of Common Sense* lamented the legal system's reliance on exceptionless rules[28]—there are more rules in law than elsewhere, they matter more in law than elsewhere, and they matter even when it is plain that they have produced the wrong result.

Yet rules are not the only part of legal thinking in which generalizations loom large. Consider also the importance of precedent in the legal system.[29] Most people know that precedent means a great deal in law, but they may not fully appreciate just how much that is. Consider the House of Lords case with which generations of English law students have wrestled with the idea of precedent, *Donoghue v. Stevenson*.[30] Miss Donoghue was having lunch at a café one day with a friend and ordered a bottle of ginger beer. Her friend poured the ginger beer into Miss Donoghue's glass, and in the process it became apparent that the bottle contained not only ginger beer, but also the carcass of a decomposed snail. This incident caused Miss Donoghue much distress, and she sued the manufacturer and bottler of the ginger beer. Because her claim was against the manufacturer and not against the party (the café) from whom she herself had purchased the product, the case went all the way to the House of

Lords, England's highest court, which ruled in Miss Donoghue's favor and in the process changed an important common-law rule.

After the case was concluded, other courts were expected to follow the *Donoghue v. Stevenson* precedent, but what exactly was it that they were expected to follow? Were they expected to reach the same result only in cases involving decomposed snails found in opaque ginger-beer bottles sold in cafés in Paisley, Scotland? Clearly, the case stands for something more than that as a precedent, and with the assistance of the court's explanation in *Donoghue v. Stevenson* the case is understood to stand as a precedent for *all* cases involving defective consumer products in which negligence existed on the part of the manufacturer and not on the part of the immediate vendor. Yet whether the case is a precedent for all such cases, or for all of the narrower class including only food products, or for the still narrower class including only food products in opaque containers, the precedent that other courts are expected to follow is still a class, and the idea of precedent, like the idea of a rule, is centrally about imposing an outcome not just in one case, but in a class of cases. Perhaps if subsequent judges felt free to look at each subsequent case in its full particularity the idea of precedent would not matter, but in law more than in other activities precedent does matter, and thus, once again, generalizations matter in ways in which they may matter less elsewhere.

Consider also the understanding of law by which legal decisionmakers are expected to provide *reasons* for their decisions.[31] In some areas of law, as with the decisions of juries, reason-giving is not required; but the normal expectation of the law is that judges and administrative decisionmakers are under an obligation to give rea-

sons for their decisions.[32] Yet the logical form of a reason
is that it is more general than the result that the reasons
support—as when, to continue the same example, the
House of Lords says that Miss Donoghue's case is to be
decided in the way it was because a manufacturer of consumer products "owes a duty to the consumer to take . . .
reasonable care."[33] The outcome is about Miss Donoghue
and ginger beer and snails, but the reason for that outcome is expressed, as it must be, in more general terms,
encompassing other consumers, other products, and other
forms of negligence. As with rule-based and precedent-
based decisionmaking, therefore, the requirement of
reason-giving is, at bottom, a mandate to generalize.[34]

This lesson about the generality of law is typically reinforced in the training of law students, especially but
not only in the Socratic examination characteristic of
American law schools. After having been forced to recite
the facts of a case in which some penniless widow has
been unable to recover against a wealthy but nonnegligent corporation, the student is asked whether the
court's conclusion was correct. "No," the student announces, making clear that he thinks that *this* widow
ought to be able to recover against *this* corporation under
*these* circumstances. But then the professor, assisted more
by having conducted the same interrogation for the past
forty-seven years than by any great insight, offers a series
of hypotheticals, all designed to demonstrate to the rest
of the class at this student's expense that any legal rule
allowing this widow to recover against this corporation
would entail much worse results in other cases and
would thus be bad policy. The goal, therefore, is to get
the students to understand that morally relevant features
are not necessarily legally relevant, and thus that legal
reasoning involves grouping together morally, politically,

socially, and possibly economically different events under the same legal heading. At least in its traditional guise, the Socratic examination is designed to involve training in generalization.

Some of the good features of Socratic examination have fallen by the wayside as its numerous bad features—professorial bullying, most notably—have become largely and deservedly unacceptable. But it is important not to lose the sense of the goal of the Socratic examination, and, in an important way, the goal of legal training. The Socratic examination was located and to some extent is still located at the intersection of thinking about rules, thinking about precedent, and thinking about reason-giving. At this intersection lies the idea of generality and generalization, and if we think that rules, precedent, and reason-giving are important to law then we have to think that generality is important to law as well.

Unlike particularity, however, generality is not important to law in just the same way that it is important to medicine, psychology, social work, architecture, and criminal investigation. All these endeavors use rules, but they use them less, they use them less strongly, and they do not train their practitioners in using rules, even if they may at times train their practitioners to use particular rules. So too with reason-giving. All sorts of professions and human activities require the giving of reasons, but none obsesses about it the way law does, and few—philosophy may be an exception—consider reason-giving a central feature of the enterprise.

The point is even more extreme in the case of precedent. In the case of precedent, what the law often lauds is scorned in other areas. Philosophers treat an argument from precedent as essentially a fallacy, and in the world of public policy the idea of precedent drops out almost

entirely. That George W. Bush should do something because Bill Clinton did it is, except in very rare circumstances, simply not a credible argument at all. In the
world of policy and politics the practitioners are expected to make the correct decision on *this* occasion, and
the idea that one would make an incorrect decision on
this occasion because a similar incorrect decision was
made in the past is not an idea that has much purchase
in the world of public affairs, let alone in the world of
medicine, social work, architecture, psychology, or criminal investigation.

In law, it thus seems, generality has a disproportionate presence, but particularity has only a proportionate
presence. If this is right, we may in the idea of generality
have located what is, though hardly unique to law and
though hardly absent outside law, a form of thinking
that would undergird law's claim to be different, and our
hypothetical law school dean's claim that there is something to the idea of legal reasoning, and something to the
idea of thinking like a lawyer.

## The Stability of Law

Like the other aspects of generality we have considered,
generality in the law is not initially appealing, in large
part because the errors wrought by generality are often
painfully apparent. Consider again Mr. Lam, the owner
of the slightly-too-short shotgun, snared not only by a
federal statute not aimed at all at him or those like him,
but also by the Federal Sentencing Guidelines, which
prevented the trial judge from giving Mr. Lam the individualized mercy his own case so richly deserved. It turns
out, we learn from the appellate opinion, that Mr. Lam
had several years earlier been found guilty of the misde-

meanor of driving with a suspended license. Because he
was no longer a first offender, therefore, he could not be
given probation, and the Sentencing Guidelines sentenced him to eighteen months in prison, a sentence the
Court of Appeals found itself legally obliged to affirm.
Law's generality trapped poor Mr. Lam twice, in ways
that could have been avoided were law more willing to
set aside the errors that its generalizations produced.

We lament the plight of Mr. Lam, but the generality
that is the characteristic feature of law has its purposes,
purposes that track those we have repeatedly encountered. First, generality may be the vehicle of stability. By
treating unlike cases alike, law, and not just in the area of
precedent, embodies Justice Brandeis's conclusion that
"sometimes it is better that things be settled than that
they be settled correctly."[35] In reaching this conclusion,
Justice Brandeis recognized that the particular mission
of law may be that of achieving certainty for certainty's
sake, consistency for consistency's sake, and stability for
stability's sake. These are hardly the only goals of any
system of social organization, and often it is more important to be right than to be consistent, more important
to be flexible than to be stable, and more important to be
wise than to be certain. Yet any complex social structure
will engage in substantial separation of powers, in the
nontechnical sense of that term, and will recognize the
virtues of functional division of responsibilities. When
this is so, it may well be that some institutions are more
likely to be the vehicles of change and others more likely
the vehicles of stability, and thus it may well be that law
is best understood as having the particular vocation of
stability while it leaves to other institutions the vocation
of change.

This idea relates closely to the second argument for

seeing law, normatively as well as descriptively, through the lens of generality. When the "rule of law" is contrasted with the "rule of men," the core idea is that individual power, creativity, initiative, and discretion have their dark side. The rule of men would be fine if all men were good, but when many men are not so, and when a degree of risk aversion is justified, we may often prefer to lose the most positive efforts of the best of men in order to guard against the most negative efforts of the worst of them. When such a view of official power prevails, and it certainly prevailed when the Federal Sentencing Guidelines were being generated, law looms large, and law may be the institution charged with checking the worst of abuses even if in doing so it becomes less able to make the best of changes. Once again, therefore, the idea of generality, putting official action in larger categories rather than relying on the individual discretion of individual officials, links closely with that understanding of law that generations of rule of law rhetoric have attempted to capture.

Finally, generality relates closely to the idea of authority. Authority, also the characteristic mode of the law, is once again about generalization, because authority is about treating the emanations from certain sources—certain courts, certain books, certain institutions—as being important just because of their source.[36] And if the source and not the content is to be important, then it must be that the source itself is a generalization, and that the idea of authority is at the very least a close cousin to the idea of generality.[37]

As with precedent, authority is hardly a universal good. In many domains it is best to do what is right rather than what someone else thinks is right. But if again in a complex world there is room for authority and

authorities, then the fact that authority is more important in law than elsewhere says a great deal about the distinctiveness of legal reasoning, and the distinctiveness of
the idea of generality that undergirds authority itself.

Much of this may be depressing to those who see law
in more idealistic ways. If law is a vehicle of stability and
not of change, of pessimism about human nature and not
of optimism, of restraint and not of progress, and of the
past rather than of the future, law may not be at all times
and at all places the instrument of social change. If law is
a shield and not a sword, its power may be limited even
though its necessity is no less. Yet of course we know that
law is often the latter element of each of these pairs, and
that it is often a force for change, for progress, and a way
of breaking down the encrustations of existing thought.
When law does this, however, it may do so not because it
is being lawlike, but precisely because it is not. Law as a
system may be an agent for particularistic creativity, but
law as a mode of thinking may even more be an agent for
the stability and consistency that only generality can
bring.

# CHAPTER 11

# Generality, Community, and the Wars of the Roqueforts

### The Pasteurization of Cheese and the Homogenization of Europe

"How can you be expected to govern a country that has 246 varieties of cheese?" Charles de Gaulle lamented in 1962.[1] De Gaulle's wry critique of the fragmentation of his own country reminds us that the idea of a nation presupposes at least some unity of purpose, a unity that de Gaulle found sorely lacking in his fellow citizens. Indeed, de Gaulle's cheese count was on the low side when he made it, and would be even more so today, with the number of French cheeses now approaching 600.

For de Gaulle cheese was only a metaphor for the national characteristics of a country in which regions, cities, and even villages frequently insist on going their own way. But de Gaulle's commentary on *les Français et leur fromage* provides a valuable lesson in the inevitable tensions between the goals of individual or regional variety, on the one hand, and the goals of nationhood, on the other. The very idea of a nation, as de Gaulle well understood, presupposes some uniformity, some commonality of purpose, and, most importantly, at least some willingness to suppress small-scale diversity in the service of large-scale homogeneity.

Yet what in the context of cheese appears to be a conflict between national uniformity and local variation is in broader context an example of the conflict between community and particularity. The idea of community itself, as we shall see, is an intriguing variation on the theme of generality, and on closer inspection generality turns out to be both a precondition of community and a promoter of it. In order to appreciate a relationship between generality and community that may not be immediately or intuitively obvious, therefore, let us linger a bit longer over the politics and policy of cheese.

Among de Gaulle's 246 kinds of cheese are Camembert, Epoisses, Mont d'Or, St.-Marcellin, Brie de Meaux, and Roquefort, each well known for its taste and texture but each increasingly controversial for its method of production. For these cheeses, as well as about 80 others, are manufactured not with pasteurized but with raw milk. Although the cheesemakers and the dairy farmers who supply them with the milk maintain that using raw milk in cheese production is perfectly safe, others think differently. And although the others who think differently include the food safety authorities of countries such as Australia and the United States, most relevant here is the fact that the list of raw-milk doubters (the cheesemakers

would call them alarmists) include the food safety officials of the European Union (EU).[2] These officials,
thought by the French cheesemakers disproportionately
to represent northern European countries such as Den-
mark and Germany which insist on pasteurization of all
milk used for cheese, have been for more than a decade
concerned about cheesemaking methods prevalent in
France, Italy, Spain, Portugal, and Greece but rare or
nonexistent in northern Europe. In an effort to minimize the incidence of listeria (as well as salmonella and
*E. coli*), a disease caused by unpasteurized milk (and a
few other things), the EU has since 1992 closely regulated the sale of raw-milk products, including, most importantly, cheeses—primarily French and frequently
Italian. Raw milk may still be used in cheese production,
say the regulators from Brussels, at least for now, but
only under conditions requiring processes, machinery,
and expenditures beyond the means of the typical small
village *fromager*.[3] Persuaded that the financial burdens of
transforming from traditional to modern methods were
substantial, the EU did grant a six-year delay in the enforcement of the raw-milk regulations against the small
producers; but that delay has expired, and subsequent
delays and dispensations are in jeopardy as well. For the
cheesemakers of Roquefort, Camembert, and quite a few
other communities, fear is growing that their products,
their livelihoods, and their whole way of life will be lost
to the unifying forces of the bureaucrats in Brussels.
Barely beneath the surface is a worry that before too long
de Gaulle's 246 varieties of cheese will be reduced to a
single cheese conforming to a single European standard
of what cheese should be. In the place of Camembert
and Roquefort and Epoisses there will be only—cheese.[4]

The bureaucrats in Brussels, of course, do not see it

this way, and insist on pointing out embarrassing facts such as the death of twenty-three people from listeria in France in 1999, far more than in any other EU country. For the EU, the French cheesemakers' insistence on the use of unpasteurized milk is a dangerous refusal to give up old ways, and a barely rational obsession with the frequently trumpeted virtues of the *terroir*.[5] Moreover, maintain the EU authorities, the willingness to be less stubborn about regional variations based on historical anomalies in the service of Europe-wide standards is what the European Union is all about. In clinging to the glories of raw-milk Roquefort, the cheesemakers of Roquefort represent, say the Brussels authorities, an unwillingness to accept the idea of an increasingly unified and therefore uniform Europe. In the eyes of the EU, the French cheesemakers have committed the sin of being unwilling to accept Europe as an idea as opposed to a continent, a charge to which most of the French cheesemakers would quickly plead guilty.

It is not irrelevant in this context to note that the European Union was until recently called the European *Community*. What the EU officials are trying to create, the officials say, is not only a healthy and safe environment, but also a community in which the special pleading of boutique industries will go properly unheeded. And what the cheesemakers are trying to preserve, the cheesemakers counter, is a regional and historical diversity that the faceless and soulless forces of community will inevitably suppress. It should come as little surprise, therefore, that the advocacy group representing the cheesemakers originally called itself the International Coalition to Preserve the Right to Choose Your Cheese, recently shortened to the Cheese of Choice Coalition.

The alleged dangers of raw-milk cheese give the debate an added bite, but the debate is not dissimilar to the debate that preceded the introduction of the Euro, the currency that displaced francs, lira, pesetas, drachmas, marks, and (Irish) pounds in thirteen European countries. No one has died from francs and pesetas in the way that people have died from listeria and salmonella, and there does not appear to have been a Currency of Choice Coalition, but in both the currency and the cheese cases the debates were not only about food safety or international trade, but also about the extent to which the growing importance of Europe was coming at the expense of variation among the formerly more discrete countries that make up the European Union.

What makes the grievances of the Roquefort cheesemakers important to the topic of generality is the way in which the cheesemakers' pleas are couched not only in the language of regional variation, but also in the language of special circumstances. The Roquefort cheesemakers are unlike the purveyors of lionfish in Tokyo, or even the oyster farmers of France, who urge that fully informed people should be allowed to take health risks in the pursuit of culinary pleasures. Such arguments are not about special circumstances at all, but reflect basic disagreements about the balance between regulation and individual choice. The Roquefort cheesemakers, however, are less concerned with challenging the basic premises of regulation and more with maintaining that the EU's implementation of those basic premises is too coarse, ignoring the degree of variation in how those basic premises might be effectuated. The Roquefort cheesemakers claim that their own methods make the use of raw milk every bit as safe as pasteurized, and that the insistence on a uniform standard, if it comes to that, will be a victory not for safety, but only for an insistence on achieving safety through an imposed uniformity.

These debates about the virtues and vices of European hegemony parallel other debates about the uses and misuses of generality and generalizations. Once we recognize that the often-maligned Brussels bureaucrats believe they are creating something new—a unified and more uniform Europe—we can begin to appreciate that their primary goal is not so much to stamp out Camembert as it is to create a new community.[6] And once we appreciate as well that the creation of a community may entail—perhaps must entail—the suppression of local variation, we can understand the way in which communities are not only fostered by generality, but perhaps are also defined by it. Ultimately what the French cheesemakers desire most is the ability to preserve and protect the particular virtues of their particular situation, and what the Brussels bureaucrats desire most is the ability to create a single community with common norms, common values, and common goals. That these two sets of desires are in conflict should come as no surprise, and the two sets of desires show us not only the ways in which the goals of locality conflict with the goals of centrality, but also the ways in which the goals of centrality, by pressing against particularistic variation, are goals that are at home with generality. In terms of the conflicts between generality and particularity that inform this book, it is only a slight oversimplification to see the Roquefort cheesemakers as the party of particularity, and the Brussels bureaucrats as the party of generality. But as the name European *Community* reminds us, the party of generality is also the party of community, and so the relationship between generality and community is now directly before us.

### Generality and Community

The contentions of the raw-milk cheesemakers have been replicated in numerous controversies throughout the world. The eleven official languages in South Africa, for example, represent a victory for more particularity and a loss for the form of community that generality may at times promote.[7] Those who decry specialization in academic study or in the professions or in the shift from broadcasting to so-called narrowcasting worry about the loss of a community of scholars, or a community of lawyers, or a community of informed citizens, or any of the other communities whose hallmark is common knowledge and common method.[8] And policy debates about federalism and devolution center on the way in which too much centralization stifles local initiative and variation, and conversely the way in which too much freedom for local initiative and variation produces excess fragmentation and too little national unity.[9]

In inquiring more closely into the relationship between generality and community, we need to be especially careful about terminology. Although we are considering a cluster of claims in which the values of the community, the collective, or the group are taken as important, this cluster of ideas should by no means be taken as represented by the movement or movements going by the label "communitarianism." Our concern here is with themes rather than movements with manifestos to which one can affix one's name and become a member. Nor is our concern even with communitarianism as representing a cluster of academic perspectives sharing, if nothing else, a willingness to challenge other perspectives as excessively concerned with the individual and individual choice. These debates between the communitarians and the so-called liberal individualists have been useful at times, but all too often the debates seem much like the kinds of conflicts best represented on *Monday Night Football.*

This caveat out of the way, the concern here is still with the theme of community. At times the community may be a nation, at times a group, at times a city, at times a village, at times an orchestra, and at times a team, but the key feature is that all of these are collections of people connected by some common goal, purpose, or even identity.[10] These communities need not be exclusive, in the sense that their members cannot be members of other overlapping communities. Still, when the tympanist of the Boston Symphony Orchestra is occupying that role, rather than his role as soloist, citizen, or spouse, for example, the orchestra represents a kind of community, making claims that are necessarily inconsistent with the maximum pursuit of individuality, at least in that role.

What is interesting and important about communities, and what the politics of cheese may illuminate even better than the responsibilities of the tympanist, is that communities exist precisely insofar as their constituent members have relinquished their separate identities, their separate characteristics, and their separate sovereignty. An orchestra is something other than ninety people on the same stage at the same time playing whatever they wish to play however they wish to play it. Thus, the move from Europe as simply a multicolored geographic region on the map to the European *Community* as something with more coherence and more singularity as an entity is a move that has been fostered by the extent to which individual nations have given up some or much of their individual power, their individual laws, their individual sovereignty, and some of their individual characteristics. Indeed, to think of these diminutions of individual autonomy as "fostering" the community may be inaccurate. Rather, these diminutions have defined and created the community, which exists just insofar as its powers and characteristics are held collectively (in this case by nations and not individuals) and not individually.[11]

When the Roquefort makers fear the extinction of their individual cheeses in the service of a European generic cheese, they engender much sympathy. When South Africa establishes eleven official languages, however, the sympathies are not so clear, because we see shared tongues as being more central to the making of a community (as, ironically, the French recognize better than anyone) than we see shared cheeses. And when members of a sports team or military unit or even a business wear a common uniform (and so too when the uniform is not unique to that organization, as with the gowns at dinner at Oxbridge colleges or with the white tie and tails of the male members of a symphony orchestra), we understand even better the suppressions that are an inevitable part of any community.

The debates between individuality and community are hoary ones, and there is no need to rehearse them here.[12] Nor is there any need to take sides in these debates, for few sensible people could fail to acknowledge that there are virtues in both individuality and in community, nor fail to recognize that the pull in one or the other of these directions varies with time, with place, and with circumstances.

Yet although little more need be said here about the circumstances under which a stronger community will be desirable, it is important to appreciate the frequency with which generality is the instrument of community. Indeed, this is as much a logical and formal point as it is a political one. Each of us is a collection of attributes, but we become members of communities when some of those attributes are shared and others suppressed. Even the thinnest communities we can imagine, for example a community whose members are grouped entirely by geographic accident and by nothing else, becomes a community precisely because the attribute of geographic location excludes other attributes in some contexts. The fact of the European Community's being a *community* means that being European is more important and being French less important than was the case before Europe became both a community and an idea in addition to being a place. At the heart of the complaints of the cheesemakers of Roquefort is that something they share with large numbers of others—their Europeanness—has become more important, and that something they share with fewer—their Frenchness, or their Roquefortness—has become less important. So too with issues of language. If English (the most likely candidate among the eleven) were to become the single national and official language of South Africa, the *special* claims of those whose primary language has been one of the other ten will become less pressing. The larger category of South African identity will again become comparatively more important than the smaller category exemplified by the linguistic communities of each of the other ten languages.[13]

It is these dimensions of larger and smaller that create the relationship between generality and community. Generality and particularity are relative terms, and any larger group that encompasses a smaller one is for that reason more general, just as the smaller group is more particular. The category of American is more general than the category of Texan, the category of European is more general than the category of German, and the category of pitcher for the New York Yankees (of which there are about ten at any given time) is smaller than the category of New York Yankee (of which there are about twenty-five at any given time). As a result, whenever it is thought important to create a community around the larger grouping, that grouping will serve as a generalization excluding otherwise germane variations among individuals or subgroups. Recognizing the category of Germans will thus have much the same effect on the importance of the category of Bavarians that actuarial recognition of the category of teenage drivers has on the category of responsible teenage drivers. Once we make the larger category salient, the legitimate distinctions between the smaller category and the larger become less important, just as do the distinctions among the smaller categories that make up the larger.

The importance of this point is partly a function of the importance of community in general, or of the importance of particular communities. But once we see the relationship between generality and community, we can see that the arguments for generality are not all negative. That is, most of the arguments for generality that we have seen to this point have been arguments that generality is, in general, not unjust. The argument running throughout this book, at times explicit and at times implicit, is that it is not unjust to generalize about pit bulls, bus companies, English soccer fans, younger drivers, and possibly older pilots because justice does not necessarily lie in the particulars. Particularity itself is not justice, even though in some contexts justice may demand particularity.

But even if justice does not lie in the particulars, this conclusion has a negative or damn-with-faint-praise feeling. Perhaps saying that generalization is not unjust is the best we can do, but most of us know what would happen were we to tell our loved ones that they were not ugly or our students that they were not stupid. At times this is possibly as far as we can honestly go, but the negative praise seems often unsatisfying.

Recognizing the connection between generality and community, however, shows that at times, though certainly not at all times, generality and generalization may bring positive virtues. Generality, by excluding local variation (and not just in the geographic sense of "local"), can serve important binding and community-creating functions, just as it has done in Europe. For most Europeans, even if not for very many of the Europeans who make cheese in Roquefort, the rise of Europe as a power, a force, an idea, and a community has been a positive development, even if that positive development has come at the cost of some loss of some local identity and national autonomy. By imposing uniformity in the face of diversity, harmonization in the face of difference, and consistency in the face of variance, generality flattens or dampens the variations among people, places, groups, and events, often to the discomfort of those whose particular claims and situations are flattened, but often, as in Europe, to the benefit of the larger group. Think of what de Gaulle would have said had he tried to imagine governing a community with as many kinds of cheese as exist throughout Europe and not just within France.

Recall again the typical speed limit, which requires all drivers to drive below, say, sixty-five miles per hour, even if some particular driver believes (correctly) her particular car to be safer, her driving record better, her reflexes faster, and the conditions more favorable than the average around which the single speed limit was designed.

The speed limit is designed for the herd, as Plato so felicitously put it, but half the members of the herd are above average. Or consider the minimum age for drinking, which prohibits even the mature and responsible seventeen-year-old from drinking beer. The existence of these generalizations in the form of generalization-based rules makes individual claims and other varieties of "special pleading" more difficult. No longer is it as easy to argue that *my* case is different, or *my* situation is special, or *my* needs are more important, because the generalization excludes, whether absolutely or presumptively, arguments based on the actual and relevant differences that the generalization suppresses.

Indeed, the suppressions of individual claims have an additional benefit in drawing the sting from some of life's inevitable hardships, hardships that appear more palatable when they are imposed on the group than when they are imposed on individuals. Consider a common example in these days after the end of mandatory retirement. In many workplaces there are people who are actively and productively working after the age of sixty-five, or seventy, or whatever the mandatory retirement age was in that workplace before mandatory retirement came to an end. Some of those people will voluntarily retire at an appropriate time in light of their physical and mental abilities, their health, their energy, and the way in which they want to spend what formerly were referred to quaintly as their "golden years." Others, however, will wait until the boss, the supervisor, the dean, the director, or the senior partner comes to see them and suggests that the time has come to depart. Even when this devastating visit is fully justified on the basis of declining abilities, the effect is crushing.

When mandatory retirement prevails, however, the

indignity of the "visit" is avoided. Even for those individuals for whom the generalization that produced the age of mandatory retirement is off the mark, there is still no one telling them, individually, that they are no longer up to the job. The elderly victim of an age-based profile may be affronted, but not nearly so much as the elderly victim of the individualized judgment that he or she, in particular, will have to go. In an important way, being "punished" for being a member of a group is considerably more palatable than being punished because of something negative about who you, individually, are or what you, individually, have done.

## The Generality of Rights

This relationship between generality and community becomes more concrete as we look at it in the context of the idea of *rights*. Rights do many things, but one of the things they do is to provide reasons, justifications, and arguments. Rights are not just there, but are things we appeal to in moral, political, and legal argument.

Yet rights can serve this function of supporting moral, political, and legal argument only if the rights themselves precede the particular argument or the particular case in which they are urged. A right functions by providing a reason for some conclusion, as in "I have a right to exclude you from my property." In order for a right to be able to provide a reason for a decision, however, the right must, as with virtually any other reason, be broader and more general than the outcome it supports.[14] So when I say that I have a right to exclude you from my property I am relying on the existence of something—the right—that includes rightholders other than me, property other than mine, and trespassers other than you. The right, functioning here like a reason, is logically and necessarily more general than the particular outcome it is supporting. When we appeal to or argue from a moral, political, or legal right, we appeal to or argue from something general under which particular outcomes at particular times are claimed to be encompassed.

The upshot of this is that an essential feature of rights is their generality. And although rights may differ in their degree of generality—my right to exclude hunters from my property if I have posted the requisite signs is less general than my right to exclude everyone from my property regardless of whether I have warned them or not—rights must be at least somewhat general in order to serve the reason-providing and conclusion-justifying function central to all rights. It follows from the logical structure of a right that it is a species of rule, and it follows from the way in which rights are rules that a right must have more than one rightholder, or at least more than one right-exercising event.[15] Putting aside the latter as rare even if not logically impossible, let us focus on the implications of rights' having numerous rightholders. If the right of members of the Ku Klux Klan to march with hoods and concealed identities in New York City is justified by the right in the United States to engage in anonymous political speech, then the category of holders of that right includes all of those encompassed by the right as it has been created, articulated, and understood.[16] Thus, the category of holders of the right to engage in anonymous political speech includes not only hooded Klansmen in New York but also hooded Klansmen anywhere else and, more importantly, includes not only hooded Klansmen but also masked political demonstrators with different agendas and different political views from those of the Klan, distributors of unsigned political pamphlets, anonymous telephone pollsters and solicitors for political causes, and a host of others engaging in anonymous political activity.

Most of us would doubt that the pamphleteers urging lower taxes, the civil rights demonstrators of the 1960s, and the Klansmen marching in New York have much in common. Even had all three of these groups been active at the same time, their members would be unlikely to have belonged to the same clubs, unlikely to have frequented the same establishments, and unlikely to have been invited to the same parties. Yet despite this degree of social and political differentiation among the diverse beneficiaries and active claimants of the same right to engage in anonymous political speech, the three groups have something important in common, and that is that they are all protected by and actively wish to exercise the same right. When a right to engage in anonymous political activity exists, the existence of the right not only protects the people who wish to exercise that right, but also constructs a category of people who would not otherwise have been grouped nearly as closely.

An important feature of rights is thus the way in which rights have the potential for constructing affinities among those who would otherwise be unconnected or less connected. Rights create similarities across more obvious differences. This feature of rights has both a logical and an empirical dimension. In terms of the logical dimension, we start with the way in which logical affinities are a function of shared attributes. Logically I am connected not only with members of my own species but also with all other two-legged animals (and thus with birds), all others with brown hair (and thus with donkeys), all other residents of Cambridge, Massachusetts (and thus with raccoons), all other cyclists, all other lawyers, all other aficionados of French cooking, and so on. Similarly, and more relevantly, I am also connected with all other possessors of the American legal right to free speech, and with all other humans in possessing the human right to be free from torture. And insofar as many of the categories of our conceptual apparatus are socially constructed,[17] it is a modest observation to note that rights with their necessary generality can be the vehicle for the creation of formal affinities that otherwise would not have existed.

The logical claim has limited importance in itself, for little of my consciousness is devoted to the logical affinities I share with two-legged birds, brown-haired donkeys, and Cambridge-resident raccoons. My membership in these "communities" is just not salient for me. But things are different concerning my affinities with other academics, other cyclists, and other aficionados of French cooking; for these are affinities, logically equivalent to the previous ones, that are as an empirical but not as a logical matter much more a part of my identity. The question of which of our logical affinities are culturally, politically, and socially salient is an empirical question of great importance.

Viewed in this light, general rights may be important precisely because of their ability to create not only formal but also empirically salient social, cultural, and political affinities. Insofar as racist Klansmen and civil rights demonstrators are both encompassed by and actively rely on their rights to free speech, the affinity of being grouped under the same right may turn out to be quite important. So too with the minority language claims of both the Afrikaaners and the Vendans in South Africa, two groups with little in common other than their shared and now constitutionally protected right to resist the encroachment of the English language. Being protected by the same right may turn out, therefore, to be something that creates a certain form of community, that creates a certain form of political alliance, that creates a shared goal in the face of otherwise-divergent ones, and that creates a group that can under some circumstances bridge otherwise divisive social cleavages.

The phenomenon is a common one. We often see otherwise-divergent religious groups joined by the claims of freedom of religious observance. Shared claims of equality or tolerance may join otherwise-different racial or ethnic groups. In these and other cases, the affinities created, the associations compelled, and the claimants grouped are more than simple logical affinities; they may be affinities that have important social and cultural consequences for the people who are part of the rights-generated groupings. Indeed, it is possible that the culture of rights that some bemoan precisely because of its perceived excess focus on the individual has a less well-noticed but possibly equally important nonindividualistic dimension just because of the community of rightholders that a culture of rights creates.[18] Those who lament a culture of rights might wish to contemplate the possibility that a culture of rights is, for all its perceived failings, still a culture, and thus nevertheless still a community.

It is undoubtedly true that community is sometimes or often overvalued, and that there are times when we need not more grouping and more affinities, but less. But the arguments that this is more often true than not are not ones we need engage here. The immediate point is only one about the group-creating, affinity-creating, and community-building capacities of rights themselves. These capacities, however, are less a function of the idea of rights than they are of the generality of rights, a necessary feature of rights but of course not unique to rights. What the generality of rights illustrates, however, is the way in which generality itself can be the vehicle of logical as well as empirical grouping, and thus the formal as well as the practical vehicle of community.

### Equality and Community

In chapter 8 we explored the relationship between generality and equality, and it is now time to complete the circle. Having first explored the relationship between generality and equality, and then between generality and community, we can now see that community, in the broadest sense, can provide one of the stronger arguments for equality. If we are not a community of equals, perhaps we are equals because we are a community.

The affinity between community and equality stems from our recognition of the real bite of the idea of equality. That bite emerges not from the fact of descriptive equality but, as we have seen, from the fact that most of the interesting exemplars of equality exist against the background of important inequalities. Rather than being important because it treats like cases alike, equality becomes important precisely because it treats unlike cases alike.

Even once we have recognized this fact, it remains puzzling for many people why we would want to treat unlike cases alike. Indeed, most of the skeptical writing about equality has maintained that equality for equality's sake has little to be said for it, and that typically what masquerades as equality is something else entirely. But perhaps there is something to be said for equality for equality's sake, and perhaps that something is closely related to the idea of community.[19] That is, perhaps equality for equality's sake is important precisely because the leveling or Procrustean effect of equality for equality's sake is just what creates communities. To abstract away from our differences is to bring us closer together and to generate a focus on our similarities. When we ignore or abstract away from our differences, we necessarily increase our emphasis on shared standards and equal treatment.

As modern debates about affirmative action, diversity, and tolerance have emphasized, formal equality has its limitations, especially when formal equality is imposed upon a domain of background inequalities. Yet when formal equality has its uses, and to those for whom it frequently has its uses, formal equality may be justified precisely for the way in which it cuts off claims of special circumstances. And when claims of special circumstances are extinguished, it is community more than anything else that is promoted. Consider, for example, the idea of group responsibility. By treating all members of a group as equally culpable and equally responsible, and by resisting claims of individual innocence by members of the group, what emerges, perhaps more than anything, is the importance of the group itself. Conversely, by treating all members of a group as equally deserving, and by resisting claims of individual nonworthiness on the part of members of a group, what emerges once again is the idea of the group itself.

Confronting the fundamental questions of community is not the goal of this book, any more than its goal is confronting the fundamental questions of equality. Nevertheless, it is important to recognize the extent to which ideas of generality are central to both. When community is pursued, one important way of pursuing it, and one consequence of its pursuit, is the emergence of a generality whose effect, in turn, is to treat unlike cases alike in the service of community. As we saw in chapter 8, treating unlike cases alike is also, formally, a large part of the idea of equality, and it may well turn out that at the deepest level of moral reasoning we will discover that the foundations of that large branch of the idea of equality that equalizes across real differences lie largely in the idea of community.

# From the Justice of Generality to the Generality of Justice

The links among equality, community, and generality serve to punctuate the way in which the argument throughout this book has progressed. Although the morality, the politics, the history, and the psychology of race and gender, among others, provide strong reasons for rejecting the use of even those racial and gender generalizations that may have a statistical basis, this rejection stands as an exception to the central message: justice does not itself, Aristotle to the contrary, lie in the particulars. Not only is the total avoidance of generalization impossible, but even the comparative avoidance of generalization is often unwise. And when, exceptions aside, we choose to rely on larger rather than smaller generalizations, we do not in the process violate any principle of justice. In this sense, to prefer the larger generalization to the smaller—and this is really the only choice confronting us—does not produce or constitute injustice.

Yet not only is generality not, in general, unjust, but justice itself may involve considerable components of generality. To the extent that justice is centrally about fairness,[1] and to the extent that fairness itself is closely related to equality, then fairness, and therefore justice, can now be seen as themselves resting on the idea of generality. Part of being fair is treating people equally, and part of treating people equally, we can now appreciate, is treating people the same even in the face of relevant differences. The just society is not necessarily one in which each individual is treated as an isolated collection of uniquely arrayed attributes demanding individualized attention. Rather, in some even if not in all respects the just society is one in which differences among individuals are often and desirably suppressed in the service of both equality and community. As such, the good society is one in which generality is not only inescapable, but is also necessary for justice itself.

## Introduction

1. The following letter to the editor in the Melbourne (Australia) *Age* aptly portrays the issue: "So the 'hapless car salesman is again languishing last in the perceived honesty and ethical rating. Surprise, surprise. Be careful, though, not to stereotype the salesman next time you buy a car as a fast-talking, untrustworthy character only after your money. In my so-far-brief time as a car salesman, I'm constantly amused and frustrated at how wrong people are in their perception of many car salespeople. I have two university degrees and have spent the past four years as a Christian youth pastor. I used to be treated as intelligent and unquestionably trustworthy—however, now people perceive me as an unenlightened scam artist all because of how I occupy my days from nine to five. Matthew Thomas, Hawthorn." With typical (but perhaps inappropriate for an editor) skepticism, the editors titled the letter "Trust me, I'm a car salesman." *The Age,* December 12, 2001, p. 12. Also interesting is Mr. Thomas's eagerness to rely on the positive stereotypes of youth pastors and holders of university degrees while he condemns the negative stereotypes of car salesmen, a contrast that will reappear throughout this book.

2. See Gregory D. Squires, ed., *Insurance Redlining: Divestment, Reinvestment, and the Evolving Role of Financial Institutions* (Washington, D.C.: Urban Institute Press, 1997); Geoffrey M. B. Tootell, "Discrimination, Redlining, and Private Mortgage Insurance," Federal Reserve Bank of Boston Working Paper 95-10 (1995). The proposed federal Anti-Redlining Insurance Act of 1999, H.R. 1429, was not enacted, but there are some state laws in force, such as Massachusetts General Laws Annotated, chap. 175 §4A (West 1996).

3. See Katy Chi-Wen Li, "The Private Insurance Industry's Tactics against Suspected Homosexuals: Redlining Based on Occupation,

Residence and Marital Status," *American Journal of Law and Medicine*, 22 (1996): 477–502; and Deborah A. Stone, "Beyond Moral Hazard: Insurance as Moral Opportunity," *Connecticut Insurance Law Journal*, 6 (1999): 12–46.

4. "'Calling all skinheads Nazis is like a Klansman calling all black people muggers,' said a 25-year-old nonracist skinhead from Washington who gave his name as Wingnut"; Serge F. Kovaleski, "Swastikas and Hate Music: Skinhead Subculture Steps Up Racist Violence," *International Herald Tribune*, January 17, 1996, p. 3.

5. See Joseph Tussman and Jacobus tenBroek, "The Equal Protection of the Laws," *California Law Review*, 37 (1949): 341–381, discussing various possible relationships between a "trait" and some "mischief" that the trait is thought to indicate.

6. Generalizations that appear universal but are not logically so are sometimes referred to by philosophers as "unrestricted generalizations," and the classes they encompass as "open classes." See P. F. Strawson, *Introduction to Logical Theory* (London: Methuen, 1952), pp. 198–199.

7. As my colleague Susan Dynarski has pointed out to me, there is evidence that in some contexts date of birth may not be totally spurious. When date of birth determines the beginning of schooling, for example, it turns out to be slightly correlated with some aspects of educational achievement. See Joshua Angrist and Alan Krueger, "Does Compulsory Schooling Attendance Affect Schooling and Earnings?" *Quarterly Journal of Economics*, 106 (1991): 979–1014. And because extremes of heat or cold during a child's early months have potentially deleterious health effects, the month of one's birth may be correlated with certain aspects of health and indirectly with education and wages; John Bound, David A. Jaeger, and Regina M. Baker, "Problems with Instrumental Variables Estimation When the Correlation between the Instruments and the Endogenous Explanatory Variable Is Weak," *Journal of the American Statistical Association*, 90 (1995): 443–450. A similar result has been identified in Canada for junior hockey players. "In Canada, male birthdays are evenly distributed over the year. However, the same is not true for elite minor-hockey players," this being a function of "using the calendar year to determine who plays with whom"; William Hurley, Dan Lior, and Steven Tracze, "A Proposal to Reduce the Age Discrimination in Canadian Minor Hockey," *Canadian Public Policy*, 27 (2000): 65–75.

8. The rise and fall of phrenology is recounted in Roger Cooter, *The Cultural Meaning of Popular Science: Phrenology and the Organization of Consent in Nineteenth-Century Britain* (Cambridge: Cambridge University Press, 1984); Thomas Hardy Leahey and Grace Evans Leahey, *Psychology's Occult Doubles: Psychology and the Problem of Pseudoscience* (Chicago: Nelson-Hall, 1983); Madeleine B. Stern, *Heads and Headlines* (Norman: University of Oklahoma Press, 1971).

9. See "Sorry, but We Don't Want Your Type in This Job," *Sydney Morning Herald*, December 19, 2001, p. 10.

10. See Patrick J. Langan and David J. Levin, *Recidivism of Prisoners Released in 1994*, Bureau of Justice Statistics Special Paper NCJ193447 (Washington, D.C.: U.S. Department of Justice, 2002); Michael D. Maltz, *Recidivism* (Orlando: Academic Press, 1984); Mark A. Peterson, Harriet B. Braiker, and Suzanne M. Polich, *Who Commits Crimes: A Survey of Prison Inmates* (Cambridge, Mass.: Oelgeschlager, Gunn and Hain, 1981).

11. Enron and other financial fiascos in the contemporary United States may even cast doubt on the "Accountants are cautious" generalization, but it has never been suggested that the generalization was ever universal.

12. "Profile" is more complex, as we shall see in chapter 6.

13. See Lee Jussim, Clark R. McCauley, and Yueh-Ting Lee, "Why Study Stereotype Accuracy and Inaccuracy?" in *Stereotype Accuracy: Toward Appreciating Group Differences*, ed. Yueh-Ting Lee, Lee J. Jussim, and Clark R. McCauley (Washington, D.C.: American Psychological Association, 1995), pp. 4–6. Indeed, the definitional complexities explored in the text are well illustrated by the controversy within social psychology about whether it is appropriate to do research on stereotype accuracy at all. See Susan T. Fiske, "Stereotyping, Prejudice, and Discrimination," in *The Handbook of Social Psychology*, ed. Daniel Todd Gilbert, Susan T. Fiske, and Gardner Lindzey, 3d ed., vol. 2 (New York: McGraw-Hill, 1998), pp. 381–385; Charles Stangor, "Content and Application Inaccuracy in Social Stereotyping," in Lee, Jussim, and McCauley, *Stereotype Accuracy*, pp. 275–292.

14. Onora O'Neill, "Theories of Justice, Traditions of Virtue," in *Jurisprudence: Cambridge Essays*, ed. Hyman Gross and Ross Harrison (Oxford: Clarendon Press, 1992), p. 61; Thomas Hardy, *Tess of the D'Urbervilles* (New York: Signet Classics, 1999), chap. 49, p. 361. (I

am grateful to Terry Sandalow for this reference.) Similarly, William James claimed that "the highest ethical life of the mind consists at all times in the breaking of rules which have grown too narrow for the actual case"; *Principles of Psychology* (Boston, 1890), p. 209, quoted in Cass R. Sunstein, "Problems with Rules," *California Law Review*, 83 (1995): 956.

15. William Blake, *Annotations to Sir Joshua Reynolds's Discourses* (London, 1808).

16. Cass R. Sunstein, *One Case at a Time: Judicial Minimalism on the Supreme Court* (Cambridge, Mass.: Harvard University Press, 1999); Philip K. Howard, *The Death of Common Sense: How Law Is Suffocating America* (New York: Random House, 1994).

17. Jonathan Dancy, *Moral Reasons* (Oxford: Blackwell, 1993); Brad Hooker and Margaret Olivia Little, eds., *Moral Particularism* (Oxford: Clarendon Press, 2000).

18. See Mary Field Belenky, Blythe Clinchy, Nancy Goldberger, and Jill Tarule, *Women's Ways of Knowing: The Development of Self, Voice, and Mind* (1987; reprint, New York: Basic Books, 1997); Carol Gilligan, *In a Different Voice: Psychological Theory and Women's Development* (Cambridge, Mass.: Harvard University Press, 1993); Martha Nussbaum, *The Fragility of Goodness: Luck and Ethics in Greek Tragedy and Philosophy* (Cambridge, Mass.: Harvard University Press, 1986), pp. 298–306; Katharine T. Bartlett, "Feminist Legal Methods," *Harvard Law Review*, 103 (1990): 849–856.

19. Stangor, "Content and Application Inaccuracy," p. 286.

20. On rule-utilitarianism in particular, see Michael D. Bayles, ed., *Contemporary Utilitarianism* (Garden City, N.Y.: Doubleday, 1968); R. M. Hare, *Moral Thinking: Its Levels, Method and Point* (Oxford: Clarendon Press, 1981); Brad Hooker, *Ideal Code, Real World: A Rule-Consequentialist Theory of Morality* (Oxford: Clarendon Press, 2000); Conrad D. Johnson, *Moral Legislation: A Legal-Political Model for Indirect Consequentialist Reasoning* (Cambridge: Cambridge University Press, 1991). On rules in general, see Frederick Schauer, *Playing by the Rules: A Philosophical Examination of Rule-Based Decision-Making in Law and in Life* (Oxford: Clarendon Press, 1991). See also Larry Alexander and Emily Sherwin, *The Rule of Rules: Morality, Rules, and the Dilemmas of Law* (Durham, N.C.: Duke University Press, 2001).

21. See Louis Kaplow, "The Value of Accuracy in Adjudication: An Economic Analysis," *Journal of Legal Studies*, 23 (1994): 307–401.

## 1. In Training with the Greeks

1. For Plato, and later for Aristotle, "law" was necessarily general, and I follow this usage in this chapter. But whether law as we now understand that term is properly thought of as necessarily general is a topic to which we shall return in chapter 10.

2. Charles H. Kahn, "The Place of the *Statesman* in Plato's Later Work," in *Reading the Statesman,* ed. Christopher J. Rowe (Sankt Augustin, Germany: Academia Verlag, 1995), p. 51.

3. Plato, *Statesman* 294a–b. This is the translation in J. B. Skemp, *Plato's Statesman: A Translation of the Politicus of Plato with Introductory Essays and Footnotes* (Bristol, England: Bristol Classical Press, 1952), p. 196. All subsequent quotations of the *Statesman* are taken from this translation.

4. Aristotle, *Nicomachean Ethics* 5.1131a25, 1131a–b. On understanding this idea and the complications surrounding it, see Kenneth Winston, "On Treating Like Cases Alike," *California Law Review,* 62 (1974): 1–39. We will take up a thorough analysis of this principle in chapter 8.

5. Plato, *Statesman* 294a–b.

6. Plato, *Statesman* 297a.

7. Plato, *Statesman* 295d–e.

8. This is a familiar point in the American literature on interpreting legislation, although the claim that judges or other interpreters (as opposed to the original legislature or rulemaker) should have the authority to do the updating is not without controversy. See, for example, Guido Calabresi, *A Common Law for the Age of Statutes* (Cambridge, Mass.: Harvard University Press, 1982); William N. Eskridge Jr., *Dynamic Statutory Interpretation* (Cambridge, Mass.: Harvard University Press, 1994); T. Alexander Aleinikoff, "Updating Statutory Interpretation," *Michigan Law Review,* 87 (1988): 20–66; Cass Sunstein, "Interpreting Statutes in the Regulatory State," *Harvard Law Review,* 103 (1989): 405–508. For skeptical views on the authority of judges to update statutes or the desirability or legitimacy of allowing them to do so, see John C. Nagle, "Newt Gingrich, Dynamic Statutory Interpreter," *University of Pennsylvania Law Review,* 143 (1995): 2209–50; Frederick Schauer, "The Principles and Practice of Plain Meaning," *Vanderbilt Law Review,* 45 (1992): 715–741.

9. "A change of instructions is not the same as the overthrow of the laws; furthermore, most such changes, especially in the case of

medicine, will be on an individual basis, not with respect to a large group"; Stanley Rosen, *Plato's Statesman: The Web of Politics* (New Haven: Yale University Press, 1995), p. 163.

10. See Terence Irwin, *Plato's Ethics* (New York: Oxford University Press, 1995), ¶¶ 30, 172–176.

11. See Melissa S. Lane, *Method and Politics in Plato's Statesman* (Cambridge: Cambridge University Press, 1998), pp. 148–155; and John M. Cooper, "Plato's *Statesman* and Politics," in *Reason and Emotion: Essays on Ancient Moral Psychology and Ethical Theory* (Princeton: Princeton University Press, 1999), pp. 165–191.

12. If it is morally wrong but pragmatically necessary to make generalized rather than particularized decisions in some contexts, then in those contexts the particular individuals who are mischaracterized are moral victims, plausibly entitled to something by way of apology, compensation, or feelings of regret on the part of the decision-maker. Though not normally applied to the problem of generality, this is a familiar point in the literature on moral dilemmas. See Walter Sinnott-Armstrong, *Moral Dilemmas* (Oxford: Basil Blackwell, 1988); Philippa Foot, "Moral Realism and Moral Dilemmas," *Journal of Philosophy*, 80 (1983): 379–398; Ruth Barcan Marcus, "Moral Dilemmas and Consistency," *Journal of Philosophy*, 77 (1980): 121–136; Patricia Marino, "Moral Dilemmas, Collective Responsibility, and Moral Progress," *Philosophical Studies*, 104 (2001): 203–225; Bernard Williams, "Ethical Consistency," in *Moral Dilemmas*, ed. Christopher W. Gowans (Oxford: Oxford University Press, 1987), pp. 115–137. Of course if there is no moral obligation to make particularized decisions, then a failure to do so would produce no moral residue and thus occasion no cause for regret, apology, or compensation. The existence of a moral residue, therefore, would be a consequence of there being a moral obligation to particularize but tells us nothing about whether such an obligation exists.

13. See Lawrence C. Brody and Barbara Bowles Biesacker, "Breast Cancer Susceptibility Genes," *Medicine*, 77 (1998): 208–245; Donna Shattuck-Eidens et al., "BRCA1 Sequence Analysis in Women at High Risk for Susceptibility Mutations," *Journal of the American Medical Association*, 278 (1997): 1242–50; Barbara L. Weber, "Update on Breast Cancer Susceptibility Genes," *Recent Results in Cancer Research*, 152 (1998): 49–59. See also Judy Siegel, "New Risk of Breast Cancer Found," *Jerusalem Post*, September 2, 1998, p. 5; Eeta Prince-Gibson, "Put to the Test," ibid., September 4, 1998, p. 8.

14. See Trudo Lemmens, "Selective Justice, Genetic Discrimination, and Insurance: Should We Single Out Genes in Our Laws?" *McGill Law Journal,* 45 (2000): 347–412; Per Sandberg, "Genetic Information and Life Insurance: A Proposal for an Ethical European Policy," *Social Science and Medicine,* 40 (1995): 1549–59.

15. This suggests the possibility that there might be an issue even when the category is universal. Consider an insurance company that excluded from coverage or charged higher rates for those with missing limbs at the time of initiation of coverage. In such a case the cost of necessary prosthetic devices would be one that applied to all members of the class, and not just to some of them or a majority of them. Yet even though the policy would turn out to have universal and not selective application for the class, there could well still be an objection to the insurance company's policy. That objection, however, would be a consequence of the social loss-spreading dimension of insurance, and not a function of the use of a statistically justifiable but nonuniversal class characteristic. This is an important problem, but it is not the problem that is the concern of this book.

16. For related concerns, see Deborah Hellman, "Is Actuarially Fair Insurance Pricing Actually Fair?: A Case Study in Insuring Battered Women," *Harvard Civil Rights—Civil Liberties Law Review,* 32 (1997): 355–411.

17. See Ian Hawkey, "English Fans Face Ban from Europe," *Sunday Times,* August 27, 2000, p. 16; James Lyons, "New Laws to Halt Shame of Soccer Rowdies Abroad," *Birmingham Post,* July 8, 2000, p. 7.

18. Let us ignore for the time being the possibility that discriminating against the English is but an instantiation of the larger and less benign category of discriminating on the basis of ethnicity or national origin. We will address this question directly in chapter 7, but the assumption here is that social, cultural, and historical factors make discriminating against the English different in kind from discriminating against Africans.

19. For a collection of modern views on "moral particularism," views that often claim a lineage with Plato and, even more, Aristotle, see Brad Hooker and Margaret Olivia Little, *Moral Particularism* (London: Oxford University Press, 2001). See also Jonathan Dancy, *Moral Reasons* (Oxford: Basil Blackwell, 1993); David McNaughton, *Moral Vision* (Oxford: Basil Blackwell, 1988); Jonathan Dancy, "Ethical Particularism and Morally Relevant Properties," *Mind,* 92

(1983): 530–597; John McDowell, "Virtue and Reason," *Monist*, 62 (1979): 331–350.

20. Aristotle, *Nicomachean Ethics*, trans. J. A. K. Thomson (Harmondsworth: Penguin, 1977), 1137b. All subsequent translations are from this edition.

21. Aristotle, *Nicomachean Ethics* 1137a–b. For useful discussions, see Georgios Anagnostopoulos, *Aristotle on the Goals and Exactness of Ethics* (Berkeley: University of California Press, 1994), pp. 363–382; Bernard Yack, *The Problems of a Political Animal: Community, Justice, and Conflict in Aristotelian Political Thought* (Berkeley: University of California Press, 1993), pp. 193–194.

22. Aristotle, *The "Art" of Rhetoric*, trans. John Henry Freese (Cambridge, Mass.: Harvard University Press, 1947), 1374a. All subsequent quotations are from this translation.

23. C. D. C. Reeve, *Practices of Reason: Aristotle's Nicomachean Ethics* (Oxford: Clarendon Press, 1992), p. 76.

24. See Martha C. Nussbaum, "Equity and Mercy," *Philosophy and Public Affairs*, 22 (1993): 83–125, especially 92–94.

25. For my own extended analysis of rules and rule-based decisionmaking, see Frederick Schauer, *Playing by the Rules: A Philosophical Analysis of Rule-Based Decision-Making in Law and in Life* (Oxford: Clarendon Press, 1991).

26. See Frederick Schauer, "Constitutional Invocations," *Fordham Law Review*, 65 (1997): 1295–1312; idem, "The Jurisprudence of Reasons," *Michigan Law Review*, 85 (1987): 847–868.

27. This is recognized and well argued in Roger Shiner, "Aristotle's Theory of Equity," *Loyola of Los Angeles Law Review*, 27 (1994): 1245–64.

28. Aristotle, *Rhetoric* 1374a. For a modern version of this claim, see Ronald Dworkin, *Law's Empire* (Cambridge, Mass.: Harvard University Press, 1987), pp. 16–20, arguing that the official written versions of statutes and other legal rules are to be distinguished from the "real" rules that the written versions only indicate.

29. Aristotle, *Rhetoric* 1374b.

30. Cicero, *De Oratore* 1.57. Cicero's importance more broadly in the institutionalization of equity is one of the running themes in Bruce W. Frier, *The Rise of the Roman Jurists: Studies in Cicero's Pro Caecina* (Princeton: Princeton University Press, 1985).

31. "The over-subtlety of the ancient jurists made the slightest error fatal"; Gaius, *Institutes* 4.30, in *Pomeroy's Equity Jurisprudence*, trans.

Spencer W. Symons, 5th ed. (San Francisco: Bancroft-Whitney, 1941), p. 4.

32. Jill E. Martin, *Hanbury & Martin, Modern Equity*, 16th ed. (London: Sweet & Maxwell, 2001), p. 6.

33. Hecht v. Bowles, 321 U.S. 321, 329 (1944).

34. Christopher St. German, *Doctor and Student*, ed. T. F. T. Plucknett and J. L. Barton (London: Selden Society, 1974), dialogue 1, chap. 16. For useful explication of the point, see J. A. Guy, *Christopher St. German on Chancery and Statute* (London: Selden Society, 1985).

35. *Pomeroy's Equity Jurisprudence*, pp. 61–62. See also Lawrence B. Solum, "Equity and the Rule of Law," in *The Rule of Law*, ed. Ian Shapiro (*NOMOS* XXXVI) (New York: New York University Press, 1994), p. 123.

36. This appears to be Justice Story's interpretation; Joseph Story, *Commentaries on Equity Jurisprudence as Administered in England and America*, 13th ed., ed. Melville M. Bigelow (Boston: Little, Brown, 1886), pp. 2–23.

37. This theme is documented and celebrated in Calabresi, *A Common Law for the Age of Statutes*. The restriction in the text to American judges is intentional, for it is hardly clear that judges outside the United States have as capacious an understanding of their own authority. See P. S. Atiyah and R. S. Summers, *Form and Substance in Anglo-American Law: A Comparative Study in Legal Reasoning, Legal Theory and Legal Institutions* (Oxford: Clarendon Press, 1987).

38. See Sheena S. Iyengar and Mark R. Lepper, "Rethinking the Value of Choice: Considering Cultural, Individual and Situational Mediators of Intrinsic Motivation," *Journal of Personality and Social Psychology*, 76 (2000): 349–366.

39. On the tendency of vague rules to become more specific in application and the converse tendency of specific rules to become more flexible in application, see Frederick Schauer, "The Convergence of Rules and Standards," University of Toronto Legal Theory Workshop Paper LTW-2000–2001 (8) (January 2001) and Regulatory Policy Program Working Paper RPP-2001–07, Center for Business and Government, John F. Kennedy School of Government, Harvard University, June 2001.

40. *Table Talk of John Selden*, ed. Frederick Pollock (1927), p. 43, quoted in William Holdsworth, *History of English Law*, vol. 1, (London: Methuen, 1903), pp. 467–468.

41. *Pomeroy's Equity Jurisprudence*, p. 57. More recently, see Steven J.

Burton, "Particularism, Discretion, and the Rule of Law," in Shapiro, *The Rule of Law,* pp. 179–201.

## 2. Pit Bulls, Golden Retrievers, and Other Dangerous Dogs

1. Alessandra Stanley, "New York Acts to Lift Pit Bull Controls," *New York Times,* May 5, 1992, p. B1.

2. Cincinnati Ordinance 43-1987 (January 28, 1987), codified in Cincinnati Municipal Code, §701-24; Tijeras, N.M., ordinance (May 14, 1984); Maumelle, Ark., ordinance (June 16, 1986); City of North Miami, Fla., Ordinance no. 422.5 (1988); Sallyanne K. Sullivan, "Banning the Pit Bull: Why Breed-Specific Legislation Is Constitutional," *University of Dayton Law Review,* 13 (1988): 279–295.

3. See Scott Armstrong, "Attacks by Pit Bulls Prompt Vicious-Dog Laws," *Christian Science Monitor,* July 3, 1987, p. 1; Vicki Hearne, "Stop Intimidating Pit Bulls and Owners," *New York Times,* August 10, 1987, p. 19.

4. See, for example, Lawrence, Kansas, Ordinance no. 5683 (April 22, 1986), placing controls on "vicious dogs" and defining a vicious dog as "any dog which by virtue of its breeding, training, characteristics, behavior or other factors the owner or custodian thereof knows or has reason to know how [*sic*] a propensity, tendency, or disposition to attack unprovoked, to cause injury or to otherwise endanger the safety of human beings."

5. Some of the dangerous-dog ordinances listed various factors that would support a finding of dangerousness, and included the factor of being a pit bull as conclusive evidence of dangerousness. See Cleveland Codified Ordinances, §604.01(k)(3). But the inclusion of a breed-specific per se conclusion of dangerousness does nothing to vitiate the concerns of those who object to breed stereotyping, and in fact converts the dangerous-dog restriction back into a breed-specific restriction.

6. Stanley, "New York Acts."

7. Studies on breed and other dangerousness factors include Randall Lockwood and Kate Rindy, "Are 'Pit Bulls' Different? An Analysis of the Pit Bull Terrier Controversy," *Anthrozoos,* 1 (1987): 2–8; Jeffrey J. Sacks, Randall Lockwood, Janet Hornreich, and Richard W. Sattin, "Fatal Dog Attacks, 1989–1994," *Pediatrics,* 97 (1996): 891–895;

Jeffrey J. Sacks et al., "Breeds of Dogs Involved in Fatal Human Attacks in the United States between 1979 and 1998," *Journal of the
American Veterinary Association,* 217 (2000): 836–840.

8. See Chris Olson, "Some Dogs Cost Homeowners Breeds of Questions," *Omaha World-Herald,* July 9, 1995, p. F1.

9. Peter Applebone, "Series of Pit Bull Attacks Stirs a Clamor for
Laws," *New York Times,* July 12, 1987, p. A24. For judicial recogni-
tion of pit bull dangerousness, see Gucalli v. Bright, 584 So.2d 187
(Fla. App. 1991); Starkey v. Township of Chester, 628 F. Supp. 196
(E.D. Pa. 1986).

10. See Lynn Marmer, "The New Breed of Municipal Dog Control
Laws: Are They Constitutional?" *University of Cincinnati Law Review,* 53 (1984): 1076–77.

11. See Larry Alexander, "What Makes Wrongful Discrimination
Wrong? Biases, Preferences, Stereotypes, and Proxies," *University of
Pennsylvania Law Review,* 141 (1992): 149–219. Although pit bull restrictions do entail both under- and overinclusiveness, it is worthwhile pointing out that underinclusiveness does not logically entail
overinclusiveness, nor does overinclusiveness logically entail underinclusiveness. A good example of the former comes from the relatively
recent outbreak in Europe of bovine spongiform encephalopathy,
commonly known as "mad cow disease." As the common name of the
disease indicates, it is carried only by cows, but not by all cows. As a
result, a remedy of killing all cows would be overinclusive in that it
would kill many cows not carrying the disease, but would not be underinclusive because it would not miss any carriers of the disease.
Conversely, if, counterfactually, all cows and some sheep carried the
disease, then killing all and only cows would be underinclusive in not
killing some carriers of the disease, but would not be overinclusive,
because all the killed animals would have been carriers.

12. As long as the incidence of the trait is higher among pit bulls than
it is among dogs as a whole, then the percentage of nondangerous
pit bulls within the class of pit bulls will be smaller than the percentage of nondangerous dogs within the class of dogs as a whole.
So although regulating all dogs will subject a larger number of
problem dogs to regulation, the degree of overinclusiveness will
necessarily be higher.

13. *Newsweek,* September 14, 1970, p. 123, quoted in Joel Feinberg,
*Social Philosophy* (Englewood Cliffs, N.J.: Prentice-Hall, 1973),
p. 98, n. 1.

14. The city of Lafayette, Colorado, has repealed its "Fierce Dogs" regulation and substituted one regulating "Vicious Animals," the replacement ordinance being explicitly intended to include dangerous animals that might not be dogs; Ordinance no. 33, City of Lafayette, Colorado, October 11, 2000, repealing and replacing Code of Ordinances, sec. 25-34.

15. The U.S. Supreme Court more than a century ago dealt with just this issue, upholding a general dog-control regulation against the charge that it unconstitutionally regulated "harmless" as well as harmful dogs; Sentell v. New Orleans & Carrollton R.R., 166 U.S. 698 (1897). The Court held that such overinclusiveness was justified as a public safety measure and that the overinclusiveness did not constitute a deprivation of the equal protection of the laws.

16. In the psychological literature there is a debate, paralleling the debate foreshadowed here, about the comparative accuracy of actuarial and clinical determinations of the likely dangerousness of people. For an example of the view that actuarial assessments are superior to individualized clinical ones, see Vernon L. Quinsey, Grant T. Harris, Marnie E. Rice, and Catherine A. Cormier, *Violent Offenders: Appraising and Managing Risk* (Washington, D.C.: American Psychological Association, 1999). For the opposing view, see, for example, Thomas R. Litwack, "Actuarial versus Clinical Assessments of Dangerousness," *Psychology, Public Policy, and Law,* 7 (2001): 409–443.

    Note the close parallels between this issue and the debates between proponents of machine as opposed to hand recounts in the contested Florida component of the 2000 American presidential election. Although intelligent and nonpartisan argument was sorely lacking at the time, there is a plausible claim that machine recounts are crude devices that will inevitably make mistakes by being unable to look at the characteristics of individual ballots, and that hand recounts correct these errors but at the possible risk of allowing an even larger number of errors because of the biases and other human foibles of the hand recounters.

17. The same controversy persists in Germany, however, where breed-specific attempts to regulate *Kampfhunde* (attack dogs) have generated similar reactions, including a subsequently and wisely abandoned proposal by the attack-dog owners that attack dogs, defined to include pit bulls and some mastiffs, be outfitted with Stars of David to demonstrate the similarity between singling out Jews

for persecution and singling out certain breeds of dogs for special restrictions. See Roger Cohen, "A Dog's Best Friend, It Seems, May Be a German," *New York Times,* June 20, 2000, p. A4.

18. See Glenn Collins, "Kennel Club Recalls Its Dog Bible after Outcry on Profiles," *New York Times,* April 10, 1998, p. A17.

19. "All Dogs Are Good," *CNN Saturday Morning News,* April 11, 1998, interviewing Dr. Michael Fox (LEXIS transcript 98041103V28).

20. Collins, "Kennel Club Recalls Dog Bible."

21. See Jonah Goldberg, "Mau-Mauing the Dogcatcher," *Slate,* March 10, 1999.

22. Collins, "Kennel Club Recalls Dog Bible."

23. The clearest suspect classification under the equal protection clause of the Fourteenth Amendment is race; Korematsu v. United States, 323 U.S. 214 (1944); Loving v. Virginia, 388 U.S. (1967). Classifications based on gender are treated as presumptively invalid, but the presumption of invalidity is not so strong as it is in the case of race; Craig v. Boren, 429 U.S. 190 (1976); Mississippi University for Women v. Hogan, 458 U.S. 718 (1980). Classifications based on sexual orientation and age have yet to be considered by the Supreme Court as of the same variety, although in the case of sexual orientation there is movement in that direction (Romer v. Evans, 517 U.S. 620 [1996]), while in the case of age the unwillingness to treat age discrimination as suspect, at least as a matter of constitutional law, appears firmly entrenched; Massachusetts Board of Retirement v. Murgia, 427 U.S. 307 (1976).

## 3.　A Ride on the Blue Bus

1. Smith v. Rapid Transit, 317 Mass. 469, 470, 58 N.E.2d 754, 755 (1945).

2. See *McCormick's Handbook of the Law of Evidence,* 2d ed. (St. Paul: West, 1972), §339, p. 794; Ronald J. Allen, "Burdens of Proof, Uncertainty, and Ambiguity in Modern Legal Discourse," *Harvard Journal of Law and Public Policy,* 17 (1994): 627–646; James Brook, "Inevitable Errors: The Preponderance of the Evidence Standard in Civil Litigation," *Tulsa Law Journal,* 18 (1982): 79–109; Bruce Hay and Kathryn Spier, "Burdens of Proof in Civil Litigation: An Economic Perspective," *Journal of Legal Studies,* 26 (1997): 413–431; Frederick Schauer and Richard Zeckhauser, "On the Degree of Confidence for Adverse Decisions," *Journal of Legal Studies,* 25 (1996): 27–52.

3. James Brook argues that the *Smith* case actually stands for less than this, maintaining that because Smith presented no evidence whatsoever as to the likelihood (or lack thereof) of buses other than Rapid Transit's buses this was essentially a case in which the plaintiff offered no proof at all on an essential element of the case. James Brook, "The Use of Statistical Evidence of Identification in Civil Litigation: Well-Worn Hypotheticals, Real Cases, and Controversy," *St. Louis University Law Journal,* 29 (1985): 301–303. But the entire tenor of the court's opinion makes clear that statistical evidence on this score would have availed Smith not at all, and the case seems more plausibly supportive, as generations of scholars of the law of evidence have taken it to be, of the proposition that statistical evidence of identification is insufficient as a matter of law.

4. See Guenther v. Armstrong Rubber Company, 406 F.2d 1315 (3d Cir. 1969); Sawyer v. United States, 148 F. Supp. 877 (M.D. Georgia 1956); Curtis v. United States, 117 F. Supp. 912 (N.D. New York, 1953); Sargent v. Massachusetts Accident Company, 307 Mass. 246, 29 N.E.2d 825 (1940); Lampe v. Franklin American Trust Company, 339 Mo. 361, 96 S.W.2d 710 (1936); Day v. Boston & Maine Railroad, 96 Me. 207, 52 A. 771 (1902).

5. One exception is Kaminsky v. Hertz Corporation, 94 Mich. App. 356, 288 N.W.2d 426 (1979), in which the court allowed a jury to conclude that a vehicle with Hertz markings was owned by the Hertz Corporation on the basis of proof that, although some so-marked vehicles were owned by licensees, approximately 90 percent of the so-marked vehicles were directly owned by Hertz.

6. David Kaye, "The Limits of the Preponderance of the Evidence Standard: Justifiably Naked Statistical Evidence and Multiple Causation," *American Bar Foundation Research Journal,* 1982, pp. 487–516.

7. See, for example, Ronald J. Allen, "On the Significance of Batting Averages and Strikeout Totals: A Clarification of the 'Naked Statistical Evidence' Debate, the Meaning of 'Evidence,' and the Requirement of Proof beyond a Reasonable Doubt," *Tulane Law Review,* 65 (1991): 1093–1110; Craig Callen, "Adjudication and the Appearance of Statistical Evidence," ibid., pp. 457–498; Neil B. Cohen, "Confidence in Probability: Burdens of Persuasion in a World of Imperfect Information," *New York University Law Review,* 60 (1985): 385–422; Charles Nesson, "The Evidence or the Event?: On Judicial Proof and the Acceptability of Verdicts," *Harvard Law Review,* 98 (1985), 1378–85; Michael J. Saks and Robert F. Kidd, "Human Information Processing and Adjudication: Trial by

Heuristics," *Law and Society Review*, 15 (1980): 140–160; Daniel Shaviro, "Statistical-Probability Evidence and the Appearance of Justice," *Harvard Law Review*, 103 (1989): 530–554; Judith Jarvis Thomson, "Liability and Individualized Evidence," in *Rights, Restitution, and Risk: Essays in Moral Theory* (Cambridge, Mass.: Harvard University Press, 1986), pp. 225–250; Laurence H. Tribe, "Trial by Mathematics: Precision and Ritual in the Legal Process," *Harvard Law Review*, 84 (1971): 1340–41 (Tribe's article is the original source for the Blue Bus hypothetical).

8. L. Jonathan Cohen, *The Probable and the Provable* (Oxford: Clarendon Press, 1977), pp. 74–81. For a sampling of the debates spawned by Cohen's hypothetical example, see idem, "The Logic of Proof," *Criminal Law Review*, 1980, pp. 91–103; Richard Eggleston, "The Probability Debate," ibid., pp. 678–688; David Kaye, "The Paradox of the Gatecrasher and Other Stories," *Arizona State Law Journal*, 1979, pp. 101–109; David Kaye, "Paradoxes, Gedanken Experiments and the Burden of Proof: A Response to Dr. Cohen's Reply," ibid., 1981, pp. 635–645; Glanville Ll. Williams, "The Mathematics of Proof—I," *Criminal Law Review*, 1979, pp. 297–312; idem, "The Mathematics of Proof—II," ibid., pp. 340–354; idem, "A Short Rejoinder," ibid., 1980, pp. 103–107.

9. One of the earliest court cases to address the problem distinguished between probabilistic and "real" evidence: "Quantitative probability, however, is only the greater chance. It is not proof, nor even probative evidence, of the proposition to be proved. That in one throw of dice there is a quantitative probability, or greater chance, that a less number of spots than six will fall is no evidence whatever that in a given throw such was the actual result. Without something more, the actual result of the throw would still be utterly unknown. The slightest real evidence that sixes did in fact fall uppermost would outweigh all the probability otherwise"; Day v. Boston & Maine Railroad, 96 Me. at 207, 52 A. at 774, quoted in Thomson, "Liability and Individualized Evidence," p. 234, n. 13.

10. Among the exceptions is the occasional case that distributes liability in "mass tort" according to the market share of various possible defendants. Most noteworthy is the widely discussed Sindell v. Abbott Laboratories, 26 Cal. 3d 588, 163 Cal. Rptr. 132, 607 P.2d 924 (1980), distributing liability among eleven manufacturers of the pharmaceutical diethylstillbesterol (DES), a drug designed to prevent miscarriages but which, though relatively ineffective at lessening the risk of miscarriage, did increase the risk of cancer for the daughters of

women who took the drug. The case is helpfully discussed in, inter alia, Glen O. Robinson, "Multiple Causation in Tort Law: Reflections on the DES Cases," *Virginia Law Review,* 68 (1982): 713–769; Judith Jarvis Thomson, "Remarks on Causation and Liability," in *Rights, Restitution, and Risk,* pp. 192–224. Yet although many people find some intuitive appeal in allocating 80 percent of the damages to defendant A, who has 80 percent of the market, and 20 percent of the damages to defendant B, who has 20 percent of the market, at least in a case brought by 1,000 identically situated plaintiffs, the intuitions seem to change, perhaps irrationally and perhaps not, when a single plaintiff in a single case against defendant A alone is allowed to collect 80 percent of her damages against defendant A.

There are some who advocate moving the legal system more into line with expected-value principles. See Michael Abramowicz, "A Compromise Approach to Compromise Verdicts," *California Law Review,* 89 (2001): 231–314; John E. Coons, "Approaches to Court Imposed Compromise—The Uses of Doubt and Reason," *Northwestern University Law Review,* 58 (1964): 750–793; idem, "Compromise as Precise Justice," *California Law Review,* 68 (1980): 250–273; David Rosenberg, "The Causal Connection in Mass Exposure Cases: A 'Public Law' Vision of the Tort System," *Harvard Law Review,* 97 (1984): 849–929; idem, "Mass Tort Class Actions: What Defendants Have and Plaintiffs Don't," *Harvard Journal on Legislation,* 37 (2000): 393–432; Steven Shavell, "Uncertainty over Causation and the Determination of Civil Liability," *Journal of Law and Economics,* 28 (1985): 587–609. There are others, however, who continue to demur.

11. The all-or-nothing idea pervades contract law, for example, since the law operates such that if all the formalities of making a contract are satisfied, both parties are bound to all the terms, but if there is anything less than a full "meeting of the minds" as to all the terms, then there is no contract whatsoever, and no one is bound to anything. See Omri Ben-Shahar, "Against the 'Meeting of the Minds': Exploring a New Basis for Contractual Liability," Harvard Law School Faculty Workshop Paper, September 27, 2002.

12. William Blackstone, *Commentaries on the Laws of England,* vol. 4 (London, 1769), p. 358.

13. See Richard O. Lempert, "Modeling Relevance," *Michigan Law Review,* 75 (1977): 1021–57.

14. Indeed, that would explain why we have come to refer to those who testify in court, many of whom (like expert witnesses) have not witnessed anything, as "witnesses."

15. For an excellent survey of the literature, see Daniel Schachter, *Searching for Memory* (New York: Basic Books, 1996). See also Elizabeth F. Loftus, *Eyewitness Identification* (Cambridge, Mass.: Harvard University Press, 1996); Elizabeth F. Loftus and James M. Doyle, *Eyewitness Testimony: Civil and Criminal* (Charlottesville, Va.: Lexis Law, 1997); Gary L. Wells and Elizabeth F. Loftus, eds., *Eyewitness Testimony: Psychological Perspectives* (Cambridge: Cambridge University Press, 1984); Deborah Davis and William C. Follette, "Foibles of Witness Memory for Traumatic/High Profile Events," *Journal of Air Law and Commerce,* 66 (2001): 1421–1548. Good examples of the studies include Elizabeth Loftus, Julie Feldman, and Richard Dashiell, "The Reality of Illusory Memories," in *Memory Distortion: How Minds, Brains, and Societies Reconstruct the Past,* ed. Daniel Schachter (Cambridge, Mass.: Harvard University Press, 1995); Elizabeth Loftus, David Miller, and Helen Burns, "Semantic Integration of Verbal Information into a Visual Memory," *Journal of Experimental Psychology: Human Learning and Memory,* 4 (1978): 19–31; Gary L. Wells and Amy L. Bradford, "'Good, You Identified the Suspect': Feedback to Eyewitnesses Distorts Their Reports of the Witnessing Experience," *Journal of Applied Psychology,* 83 (1998): 360–372.

    Though not to the same extent as eyewitness testimony, fingerprint evidence is increasingly understood as being less reliable than the conventional wisdom assumes. See Jennifer L. Mnookin, "Fingerprint Evidence in an Age of DNA Profiling," *Brooklyn Law Review,* 67 (2001): 13–70.

16. See David L. Faigman and A. J. Baglioni Jr., "Bayes' Theorem in the Trial Process," *Law and Human Behavior,* 12 (1988): 1–17; Malvin Manis, Ismael Dovalina, Nancy Avis, and Steven Cardoze, "Base Rates Can Affect Individual Predictions," *Journal of Personality and Social Psychology,* 38 (1980): 231–248. The phenomenon exists among professionals as well as among ordinary people. See John I. Balla, Robert Iansek, and Arthur Elstein, "Bayesian Diagnosis in Presence of Pre-Existing Disease," *The Lancet,* February 9, 1985, pp. 326–329. On the base-rate issue as applied to law and the statistical evidence problem, see Jonathan J. Koehler and Daniel N. Shaviro, "Veridical Verdicts: Increasing Verdict Accuracy through the Use of Probabilistic Evidence and Methods," *Cornell Law Review,* 75 (1990): 247–279.

17. Amos Tversky and Daniel Kahneman, "Judgment under Uncertainty: Heuristics and Biases," *Science,* 185 (1974): 1124–31.

18. These numbers can be worked out by the application of Bayes' Rule, such that the probability of the guilty cab's being a blue cab given a witness testifying that it was a blue cab is .41, while the probability of the cab's being a green cab given that the witness testified it was a blue cab is .59. For the calculations, see Ian Hacking, *An Introduction to Probability and Inductive Logic* (Cambridge: Cambridge University Press, 2001), pp. 72–73.

19. See, for example, John Monahan, *Predicting Violent Behavior: An Assessment of Clinical Techniques* (Beverly Hills: Sage, 1981), p. 97; Vernon L. Quinsey, Grant T. Harris, Marnie E. Rice, and Catherine A. Cormier, *Violent Offenders: Appraising and Managing Risk* (Washington, D.C.: American Psychological Association, 1998); Kevin S. Douglas, David N. Cox, and Christopher D. Webster, "Empirically Validated Violence Risk Assessment," *Legal and Criminological Psychology,* 4 (1999): 149–184; Stephen D. Gottfredson, "Statistical and Actuarial Considerations," in *The Prediction of Criminal Violence,* ed. Fernaud N. Dutile and Clem H. Foust (Springfield, Ill.: Charles C. Thomas, 1987), pp. 71–81; N. Zoe Hilton and Janet L. Simmons, "The Influence of Actuarial Risk Assessment in Clinical Judgments and Tribunal Decisions about Mentally Disordered Offenses in Maximum Security," *Law and Human Behavior,* 25 (2001): 393–408; Ann Ward and John Dockerill, "The Predictive Accuracy of the Violent Offender Treatment Program Assessment Scale," *Criminal Justice and Behavior,* 26 (1999): 125–140. There are occasional dissenting voices. See Gary B. Melton, John Petrila, Norman G. Poythress, and Christopher Slobogin, *Psychological Evaluations for the Courts: A Handbook for Mental Health Professionals and Lawyers,* 2d ed. (New York: Guilford, 1997); Thomas R. Litwack, "Actuarial versus Clinical Assessments of Dangerousness," *Psychology, Public Policy, and Law,* 7 (2001): 409–443.

20. On the phenomenon of professional overconfidence, including its relationship to base-rate issues, see Leilani Greening and Carla C. Chandler, "Why It Can't Happen to Me: The Base Rate Matters, but Overestimating Skill Leads to Underestimating Risk," *Journal of Applied Social Psychology,* 27 (1997): 760–780; Colin Camerer and Dan Lovallo, "Overconfidence and Excess Entry: An Experimental Approach," *American Economic Review,* 89 (1999): 306–318.

21. Judith Thomson, "Liability and Individualized Evidence," appears to come close to this view in resting her support for requiring individualized evidence on the way in which a person who claims to *know*

something is offering a guarantee of its truth, even when the guarantee is as likely to be unfounded as a warrant coming solely from aggregate probabilities. Yet insofar as her argument is grounded on there being an important difference between "I know $x$" and "I believe to a high probability that $x$," then her argument may only be a highly sophisticated version of the view that probabilistic evidence is for mysterious reasons inferior to other sorts of evidence.

22. My own development of this theme is found in Frederick Schauer, *Playing by the Rules: A Philosophical Analysis of Rule-Based Decision-Making in Law and in Life* (Oxford: Clarendon Press, 1991); idem, "On the Supposed Defeasibility of Legal Rules," in *Current Legal Problems 1998*, ed. M. D. A. Freeman, vol. 51 (Oxford: Oxford University Press, 1998), pp. 223–240; idem, "Prescriptions in Three Dimensions," *Iowa Law Review*, 82 (1997): 911–922; idem, "The Practice and Problems of Plain Meaning," *Vanderbilt Law Review*, 45 (1992): 715–741.

23. The "no vehicles in the park" example originates in H. L. A. Hart, "Positivism and the Separation of Law and Morals," *Harvard Law Review*, 71 (1958): 607.

24. For a good summary of the debates, combined with a critique of currently contemplated regulatory approaches, see Robert W. Hahn and Patrick M. Dudley, "The Disconnect between Law and Policy Analysis: A Case Study of Drivers and Cell Phones," AEI-Brookings Joint Center for Regulatory Studies Working Paper 02-7 (Washington, D.C., May 2002). See also Donald A. Redelmeier and Milton C. Weinstein, "Cost-Effectiveness of Regulations against Using a Cellular Telephone while Driving," *Medical Decision Making*, 19 (1999): 1–8.

25. Much of normative philosophy is properly focused on ideal conditions and presuppositions of strict compliance. See most notably John Rawls, *A Theory of Justice* (Cambridge, Mass.: Harvard University Press, 1971), pp. 8–9, 142–145, 245–246; and from that perspective it might be objected here that my focus on mistaken individuators, however real, is theoretically uninteresting. But if we are in the realm of ideal theory, we would also be able to stipulate that our generalizations would be universal, and not as imprecise as real generalizations usually are. The very fact that we are considering generalizations whose very imprecision is in the realm of nonideal theory authorizes, and indeed demands, that we consider the alternative to generalizations in the realm of nonideal theory as well.

26. I use the word "exclusionary" here to connect with Joseph Raz's important insight that rules operate through the use of exclusionary reasons that exclude other reasons from being part of a decision-making process; Joseph Raz, *The Authority of Law: Essays on Law and Morality* (Oxford: Clarendon Press, 1979); idem, *Practical Reason and Norms* (1975; reprint, Princeton: Princeton University Press, 1990). For an important commentary, see Larry Alexander, "Law and Exclusionary Reasons," *Philosophical Topics,* 18 (1990): 5–22.

A good example of the exclusion of statistically relevant evidence in the service of larger goals is the exclusion of evidence of a defendant's propensity to commit crimes in general, or to commit crimes of a certain type, on the basis of previous convictions for crimes, or crimes of a certain type. Such evidence is statistically relevant—probative, in the language of the law of evidence—but excluded partly in recognition of the value of giving people who have "paid their debt to society" a totally fresh start. For a valuable and skeptical discussion of the traditional exclusion, see Chris William Sanchirico, "Character Evidence and the Object of Trial," *Columbia Law Review,* 101 (2001): 1227–1311.

27. See Frederick Schauer, "Rules and the Rule of Law," *Harvard Journal of Law and Public Policy,* 14 (1991): 645–694.

28. For example, Frank Plumpton Ramsey, *The Foundations of Mathematics and Other Essays* (London: Kegan Paul, 1931). Among the milestones in the modern literature are Willard Van Orman Quine, *Word and Object* (Cambridge, Mass.: MIT Press, 1960); idem, "On the Individuation of Attributes" and "Predicates, Terms and Classes," in *Theories and Things* (Cambridge, Mass.: Harvard University Press, 1981), pp. 100–112; 164–172; Bertrand Russell, "The World of Universals," in *The Problems of Philosophy* (Oxford: Oxford University Press, 1959), pp. 91–100; P. F. Strawson, "Particular and General," in *Logico-Linguistic Papers* (London: Methuen, 1971), pp. 28–52.

## 4. Eighty-Year-Old Pilots and Twelve-Year-Old Voters

1. The rule provides that "no certificate holder may use the services of any person as a pilot on an airplane engaged in [commercial passenger] operations . . . if that person has reached his 60th birthday. No person may serve as a pilot on an airplane engaged in [commercial passenger] operations . . . if that person has reached his 60th birthday"; 14 C.F.R. 121.383(c) (2000).

2. 29 U.S.C. §§621–634 (1994). Technically the act limits employers and not the federal government in its regulatory capacity; see Professional Pilots Association v. FAA, 118 F.3d 758 (D.C. Cir. 1997). But the entire impetus for the regulation is the Federal Aviation Administration's desire to make clear its view that age is a "bona fide occupational qualification," and thus an allowable exception under the act itself; 29 U.S.C. §623(f). For a comprehensive discussion of the history of the Age Sixty Rule and the history of the controversy surrounding it, see Beatrice Kathleen Barklow, "Rethinking the Age Sixty Mandatory Retirement Rule: A Look at the Newest Movement," *Journal of Air Law and Commerce*, 60 (1994): 329–368.

3. The largest pilots' union, the Air Line Pilots Association, over the objection of many of its members, supports the Age Sixty Rule, ostensibly for safety reasons but possibly also because mandatory retirement opens up employment and promotion opportunities for younger pilots.

4. The issue is discussed in Western Air Lines, Inc. v. Criswell, 472 U.S. 400 (1985).

5. A good summary of the evidence is found in Rasberg v. Nationwide Life Insurance Company, 671 F. Supp. 494, 496 (S.D. Ohio 1987), finding that "aging may have an impact on . . . ability to receive and respond to stimuli, reaction time, memory, degree of attention, the ability of the eye to focus on objects at varying distances or to adjust to lower levels of illumination or glare, and the ability to understand speech in the presence of noise." Examples of more recent primary studies include George J. Anderson, John Cisneros, Asad Saidpour, and Paul Atchley, "Age-Related Differences in Collision Detection during Deceleration," *Psychology and Aging*, 15 (2000): 241–252; Filippo Speranza, Meredyth Daneman, and Bruce A. Schneider, "How Aging Affects the Reading of Words in Noisy Backgrounds," ibid., pp. 253–258; Bruce A. Schneider, Meredyth Daneman, Dana R. Murphy, and Sheree Kwong See, "Listening to Discourse in Distracting Settings: The Effect of Aging," ibid., pp. 110–125. Earlier studies include Merrill J. Allen and Johannes J. Vos, "Ocular Scattered Light and Visual Performance as a Function of Age," *American Journal of Optometry and Archives of American Academy of Optometry*, 44 (1967): 717–727; Waneen Wyrick Spirduso and Philip Clifford, "Replication of Age and Physical Activity Effects in Reaction and Movement Time," *Journal of Gerontology*, 33 (1978): 26–30.

6. 14 U.S.C. §621 (a)(2) and (b) (2000).

7. See, for example, Airline Pilots Association, International v. Quesada, 276 F.2d 892 (2d Cir. 1960).

8. As I write this, a debate exists in Massachusetts about the wisdom and justice of a statewide mandatory achievement test for middle-school and high-school students, a test generally known as MCAS. The objectors, led by the largest teachers' union in the state, have argued that it is arbitrary and thus unjust for students who score one point below the passing point not to be allowed to progress to the next grade, a penalty not imposed on students scoring merely one point higher. See Michele Kurtz, "MCAS Facing Major Hurdle," *Boston Globe,* September 5, 2002, p. B1; Steve Rauscher, "MCAS Opponents Rip Test as 'Arbitrary' at Gathering," *Boston Herald,* March 25, 2001, p. 16; "CEO Finds Fault with Standardized Tests," *Boston Globe,* July 29, 2001, p. B7.

9. See Max Black, "Reasoning with Loose Concepts," in *Margins of Precision: Essays on Logic and Language* (Ithaca, N.Y.: Cornell University Press, 1970), pp. 1–13; Willard Van Orman Quine, "What Price Bivalence?" *Journal of Philosophy,* 78 (1981): 90–102; Crispin Wright, "Language-Mastery and the Sorites Paradox," in *Truth and Meaning,* ed. Gareth Evans and John McDowell (Oxford: Clarendon Press, 1976), pp. 223–242.

10. Bertrand Russell, "Vagueness," *Australasian Journal of Philosophy,* 1 (1923): 84–92. See also Roy T. Cook, "Vagueness and Mathematical Precision," *Mind,* 111 (2002): 225–247.

11. Quoted in Antony Flew, *Thinking about Thinking* (Glasgow: Fontana/Collins, 1975), p. 104.

12. As quoted in the *Detroit Free Press,* April 27, 1984, p. F1.

13. As Justice Oliver Wendell Holmes Jr. put it, "where to draw the line . . . is the question in pretty much everything worth arguing in the law"; Irwin v. Gavit, 268 U.S. 161, 168 (1925).

14. Police officers typically allow some leeway, but the upper bounds of the leeway possess the same properties. Thus, if police officers do not stop people unless they are driving more than ten miles per hour above the posted speed limit, those driving at seventy-six are vulnerable in a way that those driving at seventy-five are not.

15. The statement in the text is a slight oversimplification. In reality the change was made by several provisions of the Voting Rights Act Amendments of 1970, Pub. L. 91-285, 84 Stat. 314; but when the Supreme Court ruled that Congress could not change by statute the qualifications for voting in state elections (Oregon v. Mitchell,

400 U.S. 112 [1970]), it became necessary to amend the Constitution to produce the same outcome.

16. See Louisiana v. United States, 380 U.S. 145 (1965); United States v. Duke, 332 F.2d 759 (5th Cir. 1964); United States v. Raines, 189 F. Supp. 121 (M.D. Ga. 1960). Most of this legacy of using literacy and related tests to disenfranchise African Americans was not a question of the disproportionate impact of a facially nondiscriminatory test, but instead typically involved the intentional discriminatory application of the tests by giving challenging tests to African Americans and simple ones to whites.

17. Those who find the comparison offensive should reflect on the fact that the fatal accident rate in automobiles for male drivers between the ages of sixteen and twenty is almost nine times as high as it is for women between the ages of fifty-five and sixty-four, the exact numbers being 86.95 fatalities per 100,000 drivers in the former case and 10.68 fatalities per 100,000 drivers in the latter. *Traffic Safety Facts 2000: A Compilation of Motor Vehicle Crash Data from the Fatality Analysis Reporting System and the General Estimates System* (Washington, D.C.: National Highway Traffic Safety Administration, December 2001), pp. 101–104.

18. For an account of the most recent rebuff by the Federal Aviation Administration (FAA) and the courts of the pilots' arguments for individualized testing, see Yetman v. Garvey, 261 F.3d 664 (7th Cir. 2001). Part of the basis for the FAA's continued adherence to the Age Sixty Rule is its belief that certain age-correlated cognitive disorders cannot be reliably identified by an existing testing procedure.

19. On side constraints and their relationship to the nature of justice and morality, see Ronald Dworkin, *Taking Rights Seriously* (London: Duckworth, 1977), pp. 90–100, 190–97; Robert Nozick, *Anarchy, State, and Utopia* (New York: Basic Books, 1974), pp. 28–34; idem, "Moral Complications and Moral Structures," in *Socratic Puzzles* (Cambridge, Mass.: Harvard University Press, 1997), pp. 201–48; Frederick Schauer, "A Comment on the Structure of Rights," *Georgia Law Review*, 27 (1993): 415–434; Judith J. Thomson, "Some Ruminations on Rights," in *Rights, Restitution, and Risk: Essays in Moral Theory* (Cambridge, Mass.: Harvard University Press, 1986), pp. 49–65.

20. On the philosophical dimensions and complications of the idea of incommensurability, see Ruth Chang, *Making Comparisons Count* (New York: Routledge, 2002); Ruth Chang, ed., *Incommensurabil-*

*ity, Incomparability, and Practical Reasoning* (Cambridge, Mass.: Harvard University Press, 1997); Frederick Schauer, "Instrumental Commensurability," *University of Pennsylvania Law Review,* 146 (1998): 1215–34.

21. I use the word "fundamental" before "injustice," here and elsewhere, not as a way of linguistically pounding my fist on the table, but only to suggest the difference between those injustices that are a consequence of nonconsequentialist side constraints on consequentialist calculations, and those unsound results (which some consequentialists might choose to refer to as "injustices") that are the product of miscalculated consequentialist calculations.

22. See Yetman v. Garvey, 261 F.3d 664 (7th Cir. 2001); Professional Pilots Federation v. FAA, 118 F.3d 758 (D.C. Cir. 1997).

23. Vance v. Bradley, 440 U.S. 93 (1979); Massachusetts Board of Retirement v. Murgia, 427 U.S. 307 (1976). In the latter case, the Supreme Court noted that the elderly are best seen not as a "discrete and insular minority," but instead that aging "marks a stage that each of us will reach if we live out our normal span." For discussion, see Christine Jolls, "Hands-Tying and the Age Discrimination in Employment Act," *Texas Law Review,* 74 (1996): 1813–46.

## 5. The Women of the Virginia Military Institute

1. In the law of evidence, this distinction has traditionally (though less so in the last few decades) been marked by the distinction between *materiality,* which refers to the question whether some fact bears upon something that is actually part of what the plaintiff (or prosecution) or defendant must prove or deny, and *relevance,* which refers to the tendency of a piece of evidence to support some material fact in issue. See United States v. Agurs, 427 U.S. 97 (1976); Charles T. McCormick, *McCormick on Evidence,* ed. Edward W. Cleary, 3d ed. (St. Paul: West, 1984), §§184–185.

2. United States v. Virginia, 518 U.S. 515 (1996).

3. For a comprehensive history of the case and its background, see Philippa Strum, *Women in the Barracks: The VMI Case and Equal Rights* (Lawrence: University Press of Kansas, 2002).

4. On some forms of sex discrimination as representing ends in themselves and not means to other ends, see Deborah Hellman, "Two Types of Discrimination: The Familiar and the Forgotten," *California Law Review,* 86 (1998): 315–357. Hellman maintains that VMI's policy was in reality based on this goal of seeing separation

of the sexes as an end in itself, although, as explained in the text, VMI's legal justification in court for its policy was couched in different terms.

5. This belief is especially clear from the lower court opinions; United States v. Virginia, 44 F.3d 1229, 1232–33 (4th Cir. 1995); United States v. Virginia, 766 F. Supp. 1407 (W.D. Va. 1991). For a close look at the initial trial, see Juliette Kayyem, "The Search for Citizen Soldiers: Female Cadets and the Campaign against the Virginia Military Institute," *Harvard Civil Rights–Civil Liberties Law Review,* 30 (1995): 246–266.

6. See Dianne Avery, "Institutional Myths, Historical Narratives and Social Science Evidence: Reading the 'Record' in the Virginia Military Institute Case," *Southern California Review of Law and Women's Studies,* 5 (1996): 189–223; Mary Anne Case, "'The Very Stereotype the Law Condemns': Constitutional Sex Discrimination Law as a Quest for Perfect Proxies," *Cornell Law Review,* 85 (2000): 1447–91; idem, "Two Cheers for Cheerleading: The Noisy Integration of VMI and the Quiet Success of Virginia Women in Leadership," *University of Chicago Legal Forum,* 1999, pp. 347–380; idem, "Reflecting on Constitutionalizing Women's Equality," *California Law Review,* 90 (2002): 765–790.

7. See Kayyem, "The Search for Citizen Soldiers," pp. 263–264.

8. The name comes from the belief at VMI that rats were "probably the lowest animal on earth"; United States v. Virginia, 766 F. Supp. at 1430–32, n. 4.

9. United States v. Virginia, 44 F.3d at 1232.

10. Although all American colleges and universities, public and private, are subject to statutes prohibiting gender discrimination in admissions, the law contains an explicit exemption for single-sex schools; 20 U.S.C. §1681(a)(5) (2002). As a result, if VMI's men-only policy was not unconstitutional, then it was, at least as a matter of law, entirely permissible.

11. United States v. Virginia, 518 U.S. at 532.

12. The Supreme Court, when it first began to deal with the constitutionality of state-sponsored sex discrimination several decades earlier, had emphasized, but without explanation, that statistical correlation between gender and a legitimate state goal was insufficient by itself to justify a gender-based classification. In Craig v. Boren, 429 U.S. 190 (1976), Justice William Brennan's majority opinion stressed, in a case involving a law that allowed women to drink beer at age eighteen when men were required to wait until age

twenty-one, that statistics showing that women between the ages of eighteen and twenty-one were less likely to abuse alcohol than men, especially while driving, were insufficient to render the law permissible. "Thus, if statistics were to govern the permissibility of state alcohol regulation without regard to the Equal Protection Clause as a limiting principle, it might follow that States could freely favor Jews and Italian Catholics at the expense of other Americans, since available studies regularly demonstrate that the former two groups exhibit the lowest rates of problem drinking."

13. 404 U.S. 71 (1971).

14. See Catherine MacKinnon, "Reflections on Sex Equality under Law," *Yale Law Journal*, 100 (1991): 1293.

15. Bradwell v. Illinois, 83 U.S. (16 Wall.) 130, 142 (1983) (Bradley, J., concurring). The *Bradwell* case is doubly ironic. On Myra Bradwell, a woman who actively and aggressively promoted anti-Semitic causes for much of her life, see Jane M. Friedman, *America's First Woman Lawyer: The Biography of Myra Bradwell* (Buffalo, N.Y.: Prometheus, 1993). Bradwell is an unfortunate symbol of the struggle for equality, as well as a strong counterexample to the 1873 characterization of women as delicate and timid.

16. See, for example, Philip Bishop, Kirk Cureton, and Mitchell A. Collins, "Sex Differences in Muscular Strength in Equally-Trained Men and Women," *Ergonomics*, 30 (1987): 675–692; Stephen T. Pheasant, "Sex Differences in Strength: Some Observations on Their Variability," *Applied Ergonomics*, 414 (1983): 205–211.

17. See Lawrence v. Metro Dade County, 872 F. Supp. 957 (S.D. Fla. 1994), involving a requirement that women who applied for positions with the canine unit of the police force pass a rope-climbing test.

18. On fire departments, see Berkman v. New York, 705 F.2d 584, 598 (2d Cir. 1983), aff'd in part and rev'd in part on other grounds, 812 F.2d 52 (2d Cir. 1987). See also Blake v. Los Angeles, 595 F.2d 1367 (9th Cir. 1979) (police department). On transit police, see Lanning v. SEPTA, 181 F.3d 478 (3d Cir. 1999).

19. On hotel bellpersons, see Thorne v. El Segundo, 726 F.2d 459 (9th Cir. 1982). Dwyer v. Smith, 867 F.2d 184 (4th Cir. 1989), deals with upper-body strength in the context of the ability comfortably to hold and fire a heavy shotgun.

20. 42 U.S.C. §2000e-2(a)(1) (2002). The issue here is explicit exclusion of women on the basis of the generalization, and not the disparate impact on women of applying a facially neutral job qualification

that disproportionately excludes women. On the distinction, centrally important in most actual employment discrimination litigation, see generally Mark Kelman, "Concepts of Discrimination in
'General Ability' Job Testing," *Harvard Law Review,* 104 (1991):
1158–1204.

21. 42 U.S.C. §2000e-2(e) (2002).

22. Although it is true that VMI's policy excluded *all* women, it is also
true that it excluded *all* men with test scores below a certain level,
*all* men who would not receive a high school diploma, and *all* men
who could not pass a standard fitness test. So although there might
be some cases in which gender was a total exclusion but other characteristics merely negative factors, the VMI case is harder precisely
because gender was not the only total exclusion based on a generalization.

23. For a sampling of some of the psychological literature documenting
the overuse of gender in decisionmaking, see Kay Deux and Mari-
anne LaFrance, "Gender," in *The Handbook of Social Psychology,* 4th
ed., ed. Daniel T. Gilbert, Susan T. Fiske, and Gardner Lindzey,
vol. 1 (New York: McGraw-Hill, 1998), pp. 788–827; Kay Deux, "Sex
and Gender," in *Annual Review of Psychology,* ed. Mark R. Rosen-
zweig and Lyman W. Porter (Palo Alto: Annual Review, 1985), pp.
49–81; John T. Jost and Mahzarin R. Banaji, "The Role of Stereotyping in System Justification and the Production of False Consciousness," *British Journal of Social Psychology,* 33 (1994): 1–27;
Bernard Six and Thomas Eckes, "A Closer Look at the Complex
Structure of Gender Stereotypes," *Sex Roles,* 24 (1991): 57–71.

24. On the form of this exaggeration, see Charles M. Judd and
Bernadette Park, "Definition and Assessment of Accuracy in Social
Stereotypes," *Psychological Review,* 100 (1993): 109–128; Carey S.
Ryan, Bernadette Park, and Charles M. Judd, "Accuracy in the
Judgment of In-Group and Out-Group Variability," *Journal of Per-
sonality and Social Psychology,* 69 (1995): 460–481. For more skeptical
views about the extent, if any, of the exaggeration, see A. H. Eagly,
"The Science and Politics of Comparing Women and Men," *Amer-
ican Psychologist,* 50 (1995): 145–158; Janet K. Swim, "Perceived versus
Meta-Analytic Effect Sizes: An Assessment of the Accuracy of
Gender Stereotypes," *Journal of Personality and Social Psychology,* 66
(1994): 21–36.

    Judge Posner castigates the Supreme Court in the *VMI* case for
ignoring (or, more accurately, not caring about) empirical evidence
as to the average differences between men and women with respect

to suitability for VMI's style of instruction; Richard A. Posner, "Against Constitutional Theory," *New York University Law Review,* 73 (1998): 1–22; idem, *The Problematics of Moral and Legal Theory* (Cambridge, Mass.: Harvard University Press, 1999), pp. 182–188. But Posner's reading underestimates the opinion, which more plausibly (and more charitably) is understood as accepting the empirical proposition about average differences but then explaining why in some areas average differences are insufficient to justify total and nonindividuating exclusion. For an incisive response to Posner on different grounds, see Deborah Jones Merritt, "Constitutional Fact and Theory: A Response," *Michigan Law Review,* 97 (1999): 1287–95.

25. "Compensatory" here refers not to compensation in the sense of a remedy or award for past wrongs, although it might be possible to understand various forms of prohibition on nonspurious generalizations in just this way. See David A. Strauss, "The Myth of Colorblindness," *Supreme Court Review,* 1999, pp. 99–134. Rather, I use the notion of compensation in the sense of an adjustment to compensate for a present tendency in the opposite direction, as when we compensate for a car that pulls to the left by steering to the right.

26. This interpretation emerges not only from Justice Ginsburg's opinion in the VMI case, but also from a Supreme Court case a year earlier, J.E.B. v. Alabama ex rel. T.B., 511 U.S. 127 (1994).

27. United States v. Virginia, 518 U.S. at 533.

28. See, for example, Catharine MacKinnon, *Feminism Unmodified: Essays on Life and Law* (Cambridge, Mass.: Harvard University Press, 1987), pp. 32–44; Ruth Colker, "Anti-Subordination above All: Sex, Race, and Equal Protection," *New York University Law Review,* 61 (1986): 1003–44; Sylvia A. Law, "Rethinking Sex and the Constitution," *University of Pennsylvania Law Review,* 132 (1984): 955–1019; Christine A. Littleton, "Does It Still Make Sense to Talk about 'Women'?" *U.C.L.A. Women's Law Journal,* 1 (1991): 15–37.

29. See Case, "'The Very Stereotype the Law Condemns'"; Cass R. Sunstein, "The Anticaste Principle," *Michigan Law Review,* 92 (1994): 2410–55.

30. See New York City Transit Authority v. Beazer, 440 U.S. 568, 592–593 (1979).

# 6. The Profilers

1. Television being what it is, there was a recurring suggestion that the profiler's powers were vaguely psychic, but such "powers" are irrele-

vant to what real profilers do and to what we are considering in this chapter.

2. A bit of revisionist history has given Dr. Brussel a larger role in apprehending Metesky than was actually the case. Although Brussel's profile was remarkably accurate, it was also the case that the bomber had provided increasingly incriminating and self-identifying facts in his letters to the *New York Journal-American*, and it is likely that Metesky would have been apprehended even without the profile. Compare the Brussel-centered account in John Douglas and Mark Olshaker, *Mindhunter: Inside the FBI's Serial Crime Unit* (New York: Scribner, 1995), with the accounts in Lyn Bixby, "'Mad Bomber' of Waterbury Terrorized New York for 17 Years," *Hartford Courant*, July 2, 1995, p. A6; and Frank Lombardi, "The Sad 'Mad Bomber,'" *New York Daily News*, April 14, 1996, p. 50.

3. A good and recent summary of current issues and events can be found in Samuel R. Gross and Debra Livingston, "Racial Profiling under Attack," *Columbia Law Review*, 102 (2002): 1413–38. See also "Symposium: Racial Profiling: A New Road Hazard," *Rutgers Race and Law Review*, 3 (2001): 1–296. For a wide-ranging attack on racial profiling, see David A. Harris, *Profiles in Injustice: Why Racial Profiling Cannot Work* (New York: New Press, 2002).

4. The actual audit rate is now slightly lower than one-third of one percent.

5. This is an oversimplification, because it is also well known that "risk-preferring individuals are more deterred from crime by a higher probability of conviction than by severe punishments"; Gary S. Becker, *Accounting for Tastes* (Cambridge, Mass.: Harvard University Press, 1996), p. 144. But when high-probability punishment is logistically impossible, as it is in the tax system, higher punishments produce higher levels of compliance even at low levels of apprehension. See generally Gary S. Becker, "Crime and Punishment: An Economic Approach," *Journal of Political Economy*, 76 (1968): 169–208; Isaac Ehrlich, "Participation in Illegitimate Activities: A Theoretical and Empirical Investigation," *Journal of Political Economy*, 81 (1973): 521–565; William M. Landes and Richard A. Posner, "The Private Enforcement of Law," *Journal of Legal Studies*, 4 (1974): 1–46; George J. Stigler, "The Optimum Enforcement of Laws," *Journal of Political Economy*, 78 (1970): 526–536.

6. See generally Barbara Goodwin, *Justice by Lottery* (Chicago: University of Chicago Press, 1992); Lewis A. Kornhauser and Lawrence G. Sager, "Just Lotteries," *Social Science Information*, 27 (1988): 483–

502. For an example of skepticism about the justice of even the fairest of lotteries, see Einer Elhauge, "Allocating Health Care Morally," *California Law Review,* 82 (1989): 1500–02.

7. See Michael Hirsh, "Behind the IRS Curtain," *Newsweek,* October 6, 1997, p. 28; David Cay Johnston, "Some New Tricks to Help Filers Avoid an Old Audit Trap," *New York Times,* February 25, 1996, sec. 3, p. 26.

8. The major recent controversy has been about the methods used to collect the data necessary to create and then to update the Discriminant Function formulas. Because examining only audited returns would produce a highly distorted sample, the Internal Revenue Service has in the past used, and has more recently proposed using again, a Taxpayer Compliance Measurement Program (TCMP), most recently updated in 1988, which obtains its data by subjecting 50,000 or more randomly selected taxpayers to an extremely thorough audit. Because the burdens on these 50,000 taxpayers are high, however, and also because of budget cuts, a proposed new TCMP, conceivably involving as many as 90,000 random thorough audits, has not been put into practice. For background, see the various statements before the Subcommittee on Oversight of the House Ways and Means Committee, as reported in the *Federal News Service,* July 18, 1995. The Current Market Segment Specialization Program (MSSP) is designed to replace some elements of the still-stalled TCMP.

9. See Florida v. Bostick, 501 U.S. 429 (1991); Elmore v. United States, 595 F.2d 1036 (5th Cir. 1979); Mark K. Kadish, "The Drug Courier Profile: In Planes, Trains, and Automobiles: And Now in the Jury Box," *American University Law Review,* 46 (1997): 747–791.

10. See Alabama v. White, 496 U.S. 325 (1990); United States v. Sharpe, 470 U.S. 675 (1985); Florida v. Royer, 460 U.S. 491 (1983); United States v. Mendenhall, 446 U.S. 544 (1980); Terry v. Ohio, 392 U.S. 1 (1968). More generally, see Wayne R. La Fave, *Search and Seizure,* 3d ed., vol. 4 (St. Paul: West, 1996), §9.4(a), pp. 137–143. The "reasonable suspicion" necessary and sufficient to justify a "stop" is a lesser showing than the "probable cause" necessary and sufficient to justify a "search."

11. 490 U.S. 1 (1989).

12. United States v. Mendenhall, 446 U.S. 544 (1980); United States v. McCaleb, 552 F.2d 717 (6th Cir. 1977).

13. See Sarah Barlow, "Patterns for Arrest for Misdemeanor Narcotics

Possession: Manhattan Police Practices, 1960–62," *Criminal Law Bulletin*, 4 (1968): 549–583; Christopher Slobogin, "Testilying and What to Do about It," *University of Colorado Law Review*, 67 (1996): 1037–60; People v. McMurty, 314 N.Y.S.2d 194 (N.Y. Crim. Ct. 1970).

14. See Tung Yin, "The Probative Values and Pitfalls of Drug Courier Profiles as Probabilistic Evidence," *Texas Forum of Civil Liberties and Civil Rights*, 5 (2000): 141–190.

15. 490 U.S. at 13 (Marshall, J., dissenting).

16. In the legal literature, the choice between rigid and possibly mistaken rules, on the one hand, and flexible and possibly misguided discretion, on the other, is often discussed under the rubric of rules versus standards. See Louis Kaplow, "Rules versus Standards: An Economic Analysis," *Duke Law Journal*, 42 (1992): 557–602; Duncan Kennedy, "Form and Substance in Private Law Adjudication," *Harvard Law Review*, 89 (1976): 1685–1747; Carol M. Rose, "Crystals and Mud in Property Law," *Stanford Law Review*, 40 (1988): 577–612; Frederick Schauer, "Prescriptions in Three Dimensions," *Iowa Law Review*, 82 (1997): 911–922; Kathleen M. Sullivan, "The Justices of Rules and Standards," *Harvard Law Review*, 106 (1992): 22–91.

## 7. The Usual Suspects

1. "I have a dream my four little children will one day live in a nation where they will be judged not by the color of their skin but by the content of their character"; Martin Luther King Jr., "I Have a Dream" (1963), in *A Testament of Hope: The Essential Speeches and Writings of Martin Luther King, Jr.,* ed. James M. Washington (San Francisco: Harper San Francisco, 1991), p. 217.

2. On the legal side, see, for example, Sameer M. Ashar, "Immigration Enforcement and Subordination: The Consequences of Racial Profiling after September 11," *Connecticut Law Review*, 34 (2002): 1185–99; R. Richard Banks, "Race-Based Suspect Selection and Colorblind Equal Protection Doctrine and Discourse," *UCLA Law Review*, 48 (2001): 1075–1114; Brandon Garrett, "Remedying Racial Profiling," *Columbia Human Rights Law Review*, 33 (2001): 41–148; Samuel Gross and Debra Livingston, "Racial Profiling under Attack," *Columbia Law Review*, 102 (2002): 1413–38; David A. Harris, "The Stories, the Statistics, and the Law: Why 'Driving while Black' Matters," *Minnesota Law Review*, 84 (1999): 265–301; Kevin Johnson, "The Case against Racial Profiling in Immigration En-

forcement," *Washington University Law Quarterly*, 78 (2000): 675–736; Tracey Maclin, "Race and the Fourth Amendment," *Vanderbilt Law Review*, 51 (1998): 333–362; Jerome H. Skolnick and Abigail Caplovitz, "Guns, Drugs, and Profiling: Ways to Target Guns and Minimize Racial Profiling," *Arizona Law Review*, 43 (2001): 413–441; Anthony C. Thompson, "Stopping the Usual Suspects: Race and the Fourth Amendment," *New York University Law Review*, 74 (1999): 956–1006.

3. See United States General Accounting Office, Pub. No. GAO/GGD-00-38, *United States Customs Service: Better Targeting of Airline Passengers for Personal Searches Could Produce Better Results* (Washington, D.C.: Government Printing Office, 2000). See also John Gibeaut, "Marked for Humiliation," *American Bar Association Journal*, February 1999, pp. 46–48; David A. Harris, "Factors for Reasonable Suspicion: When Black and Poor Means Stopped and Frisked," *Indiana Law Journal*, 69 (1994): 659–683; David Rudovsky, "Law Enforcement by Stereotypes and Serendipity," *University of Pennsylvania Journal of Constitutional Law*, 3 (2001): 296–366.

4. United States v. Sokolow, 490 U.S. 1, 13 (1989) (Marshall, J., dissenting).

5. See Richard Thaler, *Quasi-Rational Economics* (New York: Russell Sage Foundation, 1991); Cass R. Sunstein, "Probability Neglect: Emotions, Worst Cases, and Law," *Yale Law Journal*, 112 (2002): 61–107. The literature is collected and applied in W. Kip Viscusi and Richard J. Zeckhauser, "The Denominator Blindness Effect: Accident Frequencies and the Misjudgment of Recklessness," John M. Olin Center for Law Economics and Business Discussion Paper no. 387, Harvard Law School, October 2002.

6. See Daniel Bar-Tal, Carl F. Graumann, Avie W. Kruglanski, and Wolfgang Stroebe, eds., *Stereotyping and Prejudice: Changing Conceptions* (New York: Springer-Verlag 1989); Faye Crosby, Stephanie Bromley, and Leonard Saxe, "Recent Unobtrusive Studies of Black and White Discrimination and Prejudice: A Literature Review," *Psychological Bulletin*, 87 (1980): 546–563; David L. Hamilton and Steven J. Sherman, "Perceiving Persons and Groups," *Psychological Review*, 103 (1996): 336–355. For applications of this literature to the law, see Jody Armour, "Stereotypes and Prejudice: Helping Legal Decisionmakers Break the Prejudice Habit," *California Law Review*, 83 (1995): 733–772; Martha Chamallas, "Deepening the Legal Understanding of Bias: On Devaluation and Biased Prototypes," *Southern California Law Review*, 74 (2001): 747–806; Linda Hamil-

ton Krieger, "The Content of Our Categories: A Cognitive Bias Approach to Discrimination and Equal Employment Opportunity," *Stanford Law Review,* 47 (1995): 1161–1248.

7. In this form, and thus when defined as the inclusion of race as one among a considerably larger number of factors that combine to produce the formula, racial profiling has been held by the Supreme Court to be constitutionally permissible. See Whren v. United States, 517 U.S. 806 (1996); United States v. Martinez-Fuente, 428 U.S. 543 (1976); United States v. Briononi-Ponce, 422 U.S. 873 (1975). For a critique, see Alberto B. Lopez, "Racial Profiling and When: Searching for Objective Evidence of the Fourth Amendment on the Nation's Roads," *Kentucky Law Review,* 90 (2002): 75–122.

8. Psychologists have been studying the roots of this kind of irrational prejudice for generations. Among the landmarks are Gordon W. Allport, *The Nature of Prejudice* (Reading, Mass.: Addison-Wesley, 1954); John B. Harding, Harold Proshansky, Bernard Kutner, and Isidor Chein, "Prejudice and Ethnic Relations," in *The Handbook of Social Psychology,* ed. Gardner Lindzey and Eliot Aronson, 2d ed., vol. 5 (Reading, Mass.: Addison-Wesley, 1969), pp. 1–76. See also John F. Dovidio and Samuel L. Gaertner, eds., *Prejudice, Discrimination, and Racism* (San Diego: Academic, 1986).

9. On the importance of this distinction in the specific context of racial profiling, see Arthur Isak Applbaum, "Response: Racial Generalization, Police Discretion, and Bayesian Contractualism," in *Handled with Discretion: Ethical Issues in Police Decision Making,* ed. John Kleinig (New York: Rowman and Littlefield, 1996), pp. 145–157. Compare, in the same volume, David Wasserman, "Racial Generalizations and Police Discretion," pp. 115–130; and Howard McGary, "Police Discretion and Discrimination," pp. 131–144.

10. An unusually insightful and balanced post–September 11 discussion can be found in William J. Stuntz, "Local Policing after the Terror," *Yale Law Journal,* 111 (2002): 2162–80.

11. Even putting aside the question of which social groups should be described in terms of "race," there is an obvious overlap between those whose ethnicity would be described as "Arab" and those whose national origin would be described as "Middle Eastern." Despite the overlap, however, there *is* a difference. The internment during World War II in the United States and Canada of those with Japanese heritage has been properly condemned, but part of the condemnation is premised on the noninternment of Americans with German heritage, a group presumably as likely as the group of

Americans with Japanese heritage to contain people with divided loyalties during time of war between their country of citizenship and their country of national origin. When the factor that is part of the profile is nationality or national origin rather than race, therefore, the issues may be at least slightly different.

12. *Report of the White House Commission on Aviation Safety and Security* (Washington, D.C.: U.S. Department of Transportation, 1998), ¶3.19.

13. See "Remarks of Honorable Norman Y. Maneta at Arab Community Center for Economic and Community Services, Detroit, April 20, 2002," http://www.gov.affairs/042002sp.htm, condemning "profiling based solely on race," reliance "exclusively on race," and the use of "race alone," but avoiding saying whether the nonexclusive use of race or ethnicity was, is, or should be a component of the screening process.

14. See Tom Held, "Keating Endorses Profiling for Airport Searches," *Milwaukee Journal Sentinel*, March 12, 2002, http://www.jsonline.com/news/attack/mar02/2667.asp.

15. See David Armstrong and Joseph Pereira, "Nation's Airlines Adopt Aggressive Measures for Passenger Profiling," *Wall Street Journal*, October 23, 2001, p. A1.

16. See Peter H. Schuck, "A Case for Profiling," *American Lawyer*, January 2002, p. 61.

17. See Bar-Tal et al., *Stereotyping and Prejudice;* Howard J. Ehrlich, *The Social Psychology of Prejudice* (New York: John Wiley, 1973); David L. Hamilton, ed., *Cognitive Processes in Stereotyping and Intergroup Behavior* (Hillsdale, N.J.: Lawrence Erlbaum, 1981); Birt L. Duncan, "Differential Social Perception and Attribution of Intergroup Violence: Testing the Lower Limits of Stereotyping of Blacks," *Journal of Personality and Social Psychology*, 34 (1976): 690–723.

18. This phenomenon is, in part, a manifestation of the well-known "availability heuristic." See Amos Tversky and Daniel Kahneman, "Judgment under Uncertainty: Heuristics and Biases," in *Judgment under Uncertainty*, ed. Daniel Kahneman, Paul Slovic, and Amos Tversky (Cambridge: Cambridge University Press, 1982), pp. 3–24. The consequences of the availability heuristic are compounded by the phenomenon of informational cascades—see David Hirshleifer, "The Blind Leading the Blind: Social Influence, Fads, and Informational Cascades," in *The New Economics of Human Behav-*

*ior,* ed. Mariano Tommasi and Kathryn Ierulli (Cambridge: Cambridge University Press, 1995), pp. 188–213; Timur Kuran and Cass R. Sunstein, "Availability Cascades and Risk Regulation," *Stanford Law Review,* 51 (1999): 683–768—such that information overvalued by virtue of the availability heuristic will become even more so as a result of the interaction of numerous people all using the availability heuristic.

19. Susan T. Fiske, "Stereotyping, Prejudice, and Discrimination," in *Handbook of Social Psychology,* ed. Daniel T. Gilbert, Susan T. Fiske, and Gardner Lindzey (New York: McGraw-Hill, 1998), p. 391.

20. For accounts of the phenomenon, see Dana Canedy and Katherine E. Finkelstein, "A Nation Challenged: Flight Crews," *New York Times,* December 28, 2001, p. B5; Laurie Goodstein, "A Nation Challenged: Civil Rights," *New York Times,* November 10, 2001, p. B6; Michael Janofsky, "Vigilance and Memory," *New York Times,* September 12, 2002, p. B5; "When Fear and Paranoia Take Wing," *Business Week Online,* October 8, 2001.

21. This is an oversimplification of one of the central lines of argument, when applied to race and the police, in Randall Kennedy, *Race, Crime, and the Law* (New York: Pantheon, 1997). Kennedy is also concerned with what he describes as a "racial tax," the fact that using race as part of a profile even when it is statistically rational to do so turns out to create more of an imposition on innocent African-American citizens than on innocent white ones. Yet describing the impact on innocent African Americans as a racial tax may beg the central question. If using a statistically rational profile that includes race imposes a tax on innocent African Americans, then the Age Sixty Rule imposes an age tax on fit older pilots, the actuarial practices of insurance companies impose a Massachusetts tax on safe Massachusetts drivers, and the exclusion of well-behaved English soccer fans imposes an English tax on them. Kennedy is perceptive in identifying the consequences of being an innocent member of an actuarially targeted group as a "tax," but that identification alone does not tell us which of these taxes are socially and morally inappropriate and which are not.

There is an important question to be asked about whether the analysis is the same when the decisions are individual rather than institutional. See R. Kent Greenawalt, *Law and Objectivity* (New York: Oxford University Press, 1992), especially chap. 7. If the decision is about whom I should avoid when walking down the street rather than what algorithms should be given to law-enforcement officials, the calculus of (my) security versus the fact and perception of stigmatization and isolation that I impose by using race to decide when to steer well clear of a group of strangers may produce a different outcome. Nevertheless, there is no reason to suppose that the basic analysis is different, and we may well decide not to use a personal-avoidance algorithm of which race is nonspuriously one of many components because of awareness of our own tendencies to overuse race, or because we are, ideally, willing to make some personal sacrifices in order to reduce the race-based stigmatization of others.

22. A significant complicating factor is the fact that flying, even after September 11, is considerably safer than driving. If increased delays at airports, or an increase in ticket costs from airlines' passing on to passengers the costs of increased security measures, results in more people driving, then the tradeoff becomes one in which there are indeed lives to be lost on both sides of the equation.

23. See Jerome H. Skolnick and Abigail Caplovitz, "Guns, Drugs, and Profiling: Ways to Target Guns and Minimize Racial Profiling," *Arizona Law Review*, 43 (2000): 413–437; Sherry Lynn Johnson, "Race and the Decision to Detain a Suspect," *Yale Law Journal*, 93 (1983): 214–248; William J. Stuntz, "Terry and Legal Theory: Terry's Impossibility," *St. John's Law Review*, 72 (1998): 1213–29.

24. See State v. Soto, 734 A.2d 350 (N.J. Super. Ct. Law Division 1996); David Kocieniewski, "Study Suggests Racial Gap in Speeding in New Jersey," *New York Times*, March 21, 2002, p. B1; David Kocieniewski and Robert Hanley, "An Inside Story of Racial Bias and Denial," *New York Times*, December 3, 2000, p. 53; David Kocieniewski, "Trenton Charges 2 Troopers with Falsifying Drivers' Race," *New York Times*, April 20, 1999, p. B1; Iver Peterson and David M. Halbfinger, "New Jersey Agrees to Pay $13 Million in Profiling Suit," *New York Times*, February 3, 2001, p. A1.

25. See David Harris, *Profiles in Injustice: Why Racial Profiling Cannot Work* (New York: New Press, 2002); idem, *Driving while Black: Racial Profiling on Our Nation's Highways* (New York: American Civil Liberties Union, 1999); Kenneth Meeks, *Driving while Black: What to Do If You Are a Victim of Racial Profiling* (New York: Broadway Books, 2000); Katheryn C. Russell, "'Driving while Black': Corollary Phenomenon and Collateral Consequences," *Boston College Law Review*, 40 (1999): 717–754.

26. I am grateful to William Stuntz for pointing this out to me.

27. That the implicit statistical basis for the previous practice was probably mistaken is supported by the fact that when race was enforceably excluded from the factors that could justify a stop for a minor traffic violation in the hope of finding contraband, the rate at which such contraband was found increased. See Monitors' Fifth Report, Long Term Compliance Audit, Civil Number 99–5970 (MLC), United States District Court for the District of New Jersey, January 18, 2002. The implications of this conclusion are slightly unclear, however, because the report attributes the increase, in part, to "improved training and supervision" (p. vi). As a result, the increase in the "find rate" could be due in part to the increase in training, and it is at least possible that the same increase in training without excluding race from the profile would have produced an even greater increase in the find rate.

## 8. Two Cheers for Procrustes

1. For example, see Anthony Flew, *The Politics of Procrustes: Contradictions of Enforced Equality* (Buffalo: Prometheus, 1981).

2. See ibid.; J. R. Lucas, "Against Equality Again," *Philosophy*, 52 (1977): 255–280.

3. For a thorough historical background and philosophical examination of the idea, see Kenneth I. Winston, "On Treating Like Cases Alike," *California Law Review*, 62 (1974): 1–39.

4. See H. L. A. Hart, *The Concept of Law*, 2d ed. (Oxford: Clarendon Press, 1994), p. 159; Jurgen Habermas, "Reply to Symposium Participants," *Cardozo Law Review*, 17 (1996): 1550; Joseph Raz, "The Relevance of Coherence," *Boston University Law Review*, 72 (1992): 301.

5. I am grateful to Walter Sinnott-Armstrong for the example.

6. Aristotle, *Ethica Nicomachea* 5.1131a10–b15, trans. W. D. Ross (Oxford: Oxford University Press, 1925) (on treating people who are equal equally, commonly understood, though perhaps erroneously so, to be the equivalent of treating like cases alike); ibid., 1131a15–25 (on giving equal shares to those who are equal and unequal shares to those who are not); Aristotle, *Magna Moralia* 1.1193b–1194b, trans. W. D. Ross (Oxford: Oxford University Press, 1925) (on justice as equality); Aristotle, *Politics* 3.1280a8–15, 1282b18–23, trans. Ernest Barker (Oxford: Oxford University Press, 1946) (repeating the idea of equality for equal and inequality for unequal, and again

connecting equating equality with justice). For exegesis and discussion, see Wolfgang von Leyden, *Aristotle on Equality and Justice: His Political Argument* (London: Macmillan, 1985).

7. See Elizabeth Wolgast, *Equality and the Rights of Women* (Ithaca, N.Y.: Cornell University Press, 1980), pp. 77–78; R. Kent Greenawalt, "How Empty Is the Idea of Equality?" *Columbia Law Review,* 83 (1983): 1174–75; A. M. Honoré, "Social Justice," *McGill Law Journal,* 8 (1962): 83–84.

8. See Peter Westen, "The Empty Idea of Equality," *Harvard Law Review,* 95 (1982): 537–584, with the ideas subsequently developed (and qualified) in idem, *Speaking of Equality: An Analysis of the Rhetorical Force of "Equality" in Moral and Legal Discourse* (Princeton: Princeton University Press, 1990), pp. 185–229. See also Kenneth Cauthen, *A Passion for Equality* (Totowa, N.J.: Rowman and Littlefield, 1987), p. 5.

9. Hart, *The Concept of Law,* p. 159. To the same effect, see Chaim Perelman, *Justice, Law, and Argument: Essays on Moral and Legal Reasoning,* trans. John Petrie (London: Routledge and Kegan Paul, 1963), pp. 1–23.

10. See Richard E. Flathman, "Equality and Generalization: A Formal Analysis," in *Equality,* ed. J. Roland Pennock and John W. Chapman (*NOMOS* XX) (New York: Atherton, 1967), pp. 38–60; Norman C. Gillespie, "On Treating Like Cases Differently," *Philosophical Quarterly,* 25 (1975): 151–158.

11. See Hans Kelsen, *General Theory of Law and State* (Cambridge, Mass.: Harvard University Press, 1945), p. 439; idem, "Aristotle's Theory of Justice," in *What Is Justice?* (Berkeley: University of California Press, 1957), p. 134.

12. Gary L. Francione, *Introduction to Animal Rights: Your Child or the Dog?* (Philadelphia: Temple University Press, 2000), p. 144.

13. In suggesting that "the day may come" when animals would be included in the utilitarian calculus of each to count for one and none for more than one, Bentham observed, famously, that "the question is not, Can they reason? Nor, Can they talk? But, Can they suffer?"; Jeremy Bentham, *An Introduction to the Principles of Morals and Legislation,* ed. James H. Burns and H. L. A. Hart (London: Athlone, 1970), p. 283.

14. In addition to Westen, *Speaking of Equality,* see Christopher Peters, "Equality Revisited," *Harvard Law Review,* 110 (1997): 1210–64; idem, "Foolish Consistency: On Equality, Integrity, and Justice in Stare Decisis," *Yale Law Journal,* 105 (1996): 2057–73; Kenneth I.

Winston, "Justice and Rules: A Criticism," in *Proceedings of the World Congress for Legal and Social Philosophy* (Brussels, 1971), pp. 177–182.

15. H. L. A. Hart, "Positivism and the Separation of Law and Morals," *Harvard Law Review*, 71 (1958): 623–624. To the same effect, see Joseph Raz, *The Morality of Freedom* (Oxford: Clarendon Press, 1986), p. 220; Alf Ross, *On Law and Justice* (Berkeley: University of California Press, 1959), pp. 273–274; Honoré, "Social Justice," p. 82.

16. See chapter 2 and also Frederick Schauer, *Playing by the Rules: A Philosophical Examination of Rule-Based Decision-Making in Law and in Life* (Oxford: Clarendon Press, 1991).

17. 29 U.S.C. §§621–634 (2000). Although the act itself dates from 1967, mandatory retirement was not ended until the upper age limit of the act's coverage was ended with the passage of the Age Discrimination in Employment Act of 1986, Pub. L. No. 99-592, §2, 100 Stat. 3342 (1986).

18. On antidiscrimination laws in general as imposing the cost of inability to use rational proxies, see Larry Alexander and Kevin Cole, "Discrimination by Proxy," *Constitutional Commentary*, 14 (1997): 456. See also Larry Alexander, "What Makes Wrongful Discrimination Wrong?: Biases, Preferences, Stereotypes, and Proxies," *University of Pennsylvania Law Review*, 141 (1992): 203–208.

19. See John J. Donahue III and Peter Siegelman, "The Changing Nature of Employment Discrimination Litigation," *Stanford Law Review*, 43 (1991): 983–1026; Samuel Issacharoff and Erica Worth Harris, "Is Age Discrimination Really Age Discrimination?: The ADEA's Unnatural Solution," *New York University Law Review*, 72 (1997): 780–840.

20. The claim here is about employees who would have been compelled to retire because of demonstrably reduced skills, and is not a claim about employees who would have been forced to retire because they did not demonstrate an increase in skills commensurate with their age-linked increase in wages, a consequence of what is now known as the life-cycle model of employment. See Robert Hutchens, "Delayed Payment Contracts and a Firm's Propensity to Fire Older Workers," *Journal of Labor Economics*, 4 (1986): 439–454; Edward Lazear, "Why Is There Mandatory Retirement?" *Journal of Political Economy*, 87 (1979): 1261–74.

21. Recent legal changes, often requiring periodic testing for older but not younger drivers, are summarized in Insurance Institute for Highway Safety, "U.S. Driver Licensing Renewal Procedures for

Older Drivers," http://www.hwysafety.org/safety_facts/state_laws/ older_drivers.html (May 2002). See also Loren Staplin, Kathy H. Lococo, Joseph Stewart, and Lawrence E. Decina, "Safe Mobility for Older People Notebook," U.S. Department of Transportation/ National Traffic Highway Safety Administration Publication No. DOT HS 808853 (Washington, D.C., 1999); and the five-part series on older drivers by Brian C. Jones in *AAA Horizons,* 32, nos. 5–9 (2002).

22. The issue is hardly without controversy. See the dispute about using racial differences in diagnosing and treating heart disease in the *New England Journal of Medicine,* 344, nos. 1 (pp. 351, 357) and 3 (pp. 558, 565) (May 2001); and also Sally Satel, "I Am a Racially Profiling Doctor," *New York Times Magazine,* May 5, 2002. The issues become even more complex when conditions that are distributed disproportionately by race or ethnicity are themselves part of a stigmatizing characterization, as with alcoholism among American Indians. See Malcolm H. Holmes and Judith A. Antell, "The Social Construction of American Indian Drinking: Perceptions of American Indian and White Officials," *Sociological Quarterly,* 42 (2001): 151–173; Philip A. May, "The Epidemiology of Alcohol Abuse among American Indians: The Mythical and Real Properties," *American Indian Culture and Research Journal,* 18 (1994): 121–143.

23. See Joel Feinberg, *Social Philosophy* (Englewood Cliffs, N.J.: Prentice-Hall, 1973), p. 90; Westen, *Speaking of Equality,* pp. 59–92; Kent Greenawalt, "'Prescriptive Equality': Two Steps Forward," *Harvard Law Review,* 110 (1997): 1265–1303.

24. See the illuminating discussion in Jeremy Waldron, "Two Essays on Basic Equality" (colloquium paper, New York University Law School, 1999), available at http://www.law.law.nyu.edu./clppt/ papers/basicequality.pdf.

25. The move from a shared characteristic to prescriptive equality does not require that the shared characteristic be shared equally—that all its possessors hold it to the same degree. See Waldron, "Two Essays on Basic Equality," usefully developing the idea of a "range property" earlier set out in John Rawls, *A Theory of Justice* (Cambridge, Mass.: Harvard University Press, 1971), pp. 505–508.

26. See the highly controversial opinion by then Associate Justice William Rehnquist in General Electric Company v. Gilbert, 429 U.S. 125 (1976).

27. Anatole France, *The Red Lily* (New York: Modern Library, 1917), p. 75.

## 9. Ships with Altered Names

1. Jeremy Bentham, *Principles of the Penal Code,* book 4, chap. 15, in *The Theory of Legislation,* trans. Richard Hildreth from Etienne Dumont, ed. C. K. Ogden (London: Kegan Paul, Trench, Trubner, 1931), pp. 425–427.

2. Possessing a weapon with an obliterated serial number is, however, a federal crime in the United States; 18 U.S.C. §922(k)(1994). Another of Bentham's examples, possession of stolen property as an offense on the basis of a presumption that the possessor was the thief, is still a quite common offense worldwide.

3. 31 U.S.C. §5316 (2002). Details are contained in 31 C.F.R. §103.23(a) (2002). For a discussion of the point of the statute, see United States v. Bajakajian, 524 U.S. 321 (1998), holding that requiring Bajakajian to forfeit $357,144 for nonreporting was excessive given the fine specified in the statute and in the Federal Sentencing Guidelines and given that Bajakajian was "not a money launderer, a drug trafficker, or a tax evader"; 524 U.S. at 338.

4. The fact that reporting the transaction prevents criminal liability appears to prevent a "major" injustice, but the requirement that innocent people must still report these transactions is more than a momentary inconvenience, making the "penalty" of reporting perhaps a minor injustice in itself. The requirement of reporting even innocent transactions is a form of punishment for engaging in an innocent transaction, in part because the very fact of reporting raises the level of government scrutiny of all one's actions above what it would otherwise have been and above what it is for most ordinary citizens. Here I speak from personal experience. In 1992 I traveled to Estonia on behalf of the U.S. Information Agency. Because the stay was a lengthy one, because I was expected to employ drivers and translators, because restaurants and hotels accessible to Americans charged Western prices, and because neither credit cards nor traveler's checks were commonly accepted at the time in Estonia, the U.S. government provided me with approximately $12,000 in cash for the aforesaid transactions. Having dutifully reported to customs officials that I was leaving the United States with more than $10,000 in cash, and having explained in writing the reason for my doing so, I was surprised and angered a year later by a special request from the Internal Revenue Service requesting that I detail all the large cash transactions in which I had engaged in the previous year, a request rarely issued to ordinary taxpayers. Plainly,

even my obedience to a law equally plainly not designed for me had placed me on the Internal Revenue Service's "persons needing to be watched carefully" list, an honor I would just as soon have avoided.

5. A good example is the Florida law providing that anyone possessing more than 28 grams of cocaine is guilty of *trafficking* in cocaine; Florida Statutes §893.135(1)(b)(1) (Supp. 2002).

6. For example, Michie's West Virginia Code, chap. 60A-4-403a (2000), which makes criminal all knowing possession of paraphernalia "primarily useful as drug devices," with the logical implication that even possession of devices for purposes encompassed by the logical space between "primarily" and "exclusively" is nonetheless a crime.

7. Most devices used for burglaries, such as crowbars, glass cutters, and even lock picks, have significant lawful uses, and thus the typical burglar-tools conviction involves someone possessing a combination of individually less suspicious implements, but whose presence in combination is extremely unlikely to have a lawful use. Good examples include the simultaneous possession of a crowbar and a bent coathanger (Burgess v. Bintz, 2002 U.S. Dist. LEXIS 7168); of a crowbar, a hacksaw, and a lock pick (People v. Trimmer, 2002 Cal. App. Unpub. LEXIS 6520); and of six porcelain pieces from automobile spark plugs (People v. O. M., 2002 Cal. App. Unpub. LEXIS 6565) (apparently, jagged porcelain pieces are highly suitable for the quiet breaking of windows).

8. 18 U.S.C. §922(4) (2000).

9. People v. Bunis, 9 N.Y.2d 1, 210 N.Y.S.2d 505, 172 N.E.2d 273 (1961). There is some reason to believe that Mr. Bunis was engaged in the sale of pornographic magazines, a type of magazine that typically retains more of its value for its intended audience well after its publication date than, say, *Newsweek, Sports Illustrated,* or the *Times Literary Supplement.*

10. To the same effect is Delmonico v. State, 155 So. 2d 368 (Fla. 1963), in which the Supreme Court of Florida invalidated a law prohibiting possession of spearfishing equipment within a designated area. Although the court acknowledged that most people possessing such equipment in that area were likely to be engaged in illegal spearfishing, the fact that such a likely inference was not inevitable invalidated a statute that prohibited all possession even though most of it would have been for unlawful purposes.

11. Vlandis v. Kline, 412 U.S. 441 (1973).

12. Weinberger v. Salfi, 422 U.S. 749 (1975).

13. See, for example, Cleveland Board of Education v. LaFleur, 414 U.S. 632 (1974); United States Department of Agriculture v. Murry, 413 U.S. 508 (1973). Commentators had recognized this untenability from the outset. See [Student] Note, "Irrebuttable Presumptions: An Illusory Analysis," *Stanford Law Review,* 27 (1975): 449–473; [Student] Note, "The Irrebuttable Presumption Doctrine in the Supreme Court," *Harvard Law Review,* 87 (1974): 1534–56.

14. Of interest here is United States v. Fior D'Italia, Inc., 122 S. Ct. 2117 (2002), in which the Supreme Court upheld an aggregation estimate approach to imposing social security (FICA) taxes on the tip income of restaurant waiters, with Justice Breyer, speaking for the majority, noting that there is no reason to believe that "individualized employee assessments will inevitably lead to a more 'reasonable' assessment of employer liability than an aggregate estimate"; 122 S. Ct. At 2125.

15. Securities and Exchange Act of 1934, §16(b), 15 U.S.C. §78p(b) (2000).

16. See State v. Rolle, 560 So. 2d 1154 (Fla. 1990).

17. See Douglas N. Husak, "Reasonable Risk Creation and Overinclusive Legislation," *Buffalo Criminal Law Review,* 1 (1998): 599–644.

18. Indeed, the Supreme Court continues on occasion to invalidate criminal laws that rest too overtly on irrebuttable presumptions, or even on presumptions that have the effect of shifting the burden of proof from prosecution to defense for an essential element of the offense. Mullaney v. Wilbur, 421 U.S. 684 (1975), expresses the basic idea, but it is roughly contemporaneous with the irrebuttable presumption cases and thus may embody the same instincts. And although the retreat from *Mullaney* in Patterson v. New York, 432 U.S. 197 (1977), was less dramatic than the retreat in the irrebuttable presumption cases, the parallel is noteworthy. For more recent ebbs and flows of the basic idea, see Apprendi v. New Jersey, 120 S. Ct. 2348 (2000); Francis v. Franklin, 471 U.S. 307 (1985); Sandstrom v. Montana, 442 U.S. 510 (1979). For analysis, see Claire Finkelstein, "Positivism and the Notion of an Offense," *California Law Review,* 88 (2000): 335–394; John C. Jeffries Jr. and Paul B. Stephan, "Defenses, Presumptions, and Burden of Proof in Criminal Law," *Yale Law Journal,* 88 (1979): 1325–52; Nancy J. King and Susan R. Klein, "Essential Elements," *Vanderbilt Law Review,* 54 (2001): 1467–1555.

19. As the New York Court of Appeals itself seemed to recognize some years later. Although the court had relied on the *Bunis* case in 1983 in striking down a law prohibiting the public possession of an

opened alcoholic beverage container—People v. Lee, 58 N.Y.2d 491, 448 N.E.2d 1328, 462 N.Y.S.2d 417 (1983)—by 1988 the Court of Appeals, while never actually overruling *Bunis,* was redescribing it as a case solely involving insufficient notice of what conduct was unlawful; People v. Bright, 71 N.Y.2d 376, 520 N.E.2d 1355, 526 N.Y.S.2d 66 (1988).

20. On the circumstances under which a person is charged with knowing the legal requirements even if he did not in fact know them, an instructive example is United States v. Freed, 401 U.S. 601 (1971), in which the U.S. Supreme Court concluded, not surprisingly, that a defendant might have been on notice that the law did not treat the possession of hand grenades as "an innocent act"; 401 U.S. at 609. On the issue generally, see, for example, Sharon L. Davies, "The Jurisprudence of Wilfullness: An Evolving Theory of Excusable Ignorance," *Duke Law Journal,* 48 (1998): 341–374.

21. Perhaps we would want to avoid the problem of compound probabilities, however, by having a slightly higher standard of proof for presumed offenses. Assume that proof beyond a reasonable doubt is equivalent to at least 99 percent certainty. That being the case, then if the offense is not a presumed one—if it is defined in such a way that it cannot be committed innocently—there is no greater than a one percent chance that someone convicted of, say, burglary (it is really hard to be an innocent burglar) has done nothing wrong. But if 99 percent rather than 100 percent of the sellers of coverless magazines are engaged in genuinely wrongful behavior, and if one can be convicted of the crime of selling a coverless magazine on proof to a 99 percent certainty, then there is almost a 2 percent possibility $(1 - [.99 \times .99])$ that someone not doing anything genuinely wrong will be convicted. Perhaps the notice issue alleviates much of the problem, but if it does not, then one solution would be to require a higher burden of proof in presumed offense cases than in nonpresumed offense cases.

22. See People v. Munoz, 103 Ill. App. 3d 1080, 432 N.E.2d 370 (3rd Dist. 1982); People v. Atencia, 113 Ill. App. 3d 247, 446 N.E.2d 1243 (1st Dist. 1983).

23. See Edna Ullman-Margalit, "On Presumption," *Journal of Philosophy,* 80 (1983): 143–162; Edna Ullman-Margalit and Avishai Margalit, "Analyticity by Way of Presumption," *Canadian Journal of Philosophy,* 12 (1982): 435–452.

24. The example is part of the rhetorical arsenal of American trial

lawyers, and is typically employed to demonstrate to jurors the frequent reliability of so-called circumstantial evidence.

25. Here I transpose to a different context and a different lesson the famous example from James Q. Wilson and George L. Kelling, "Broken Windows: The Police and Neighborhood Safety," *Atlantic Monthly*, March 1982, pp. 32–36.

26. The assumption here is that it is possible for a workplace to have a large number of accidents for reasons other than the lack of safety of the workplace itself—it could be an unusual month, or the workers might be unusually clumsy—but that in most cases the high accident rate will be both indicative of and caused by unsafe workplace conditions.

27. An important analysis of punishing the innocent more generally is Alan Wertheimer, "Punishing the Innocent—Unintentionally," *Inquiry*, 20 (1978): 45–65.

28. Chief among these goals is the goal of punishing the genuinely guilty, and "to insure [that] the probability of convicting the innocent really reaches zero may require the willingness to accept a probability of conviction for the guilty which is considerably less than one"; Lester Thurow, "Equity versus Efficiency in Law Enforcement," *Public Policy*, 18 (1970): 468.

## 10. The Generality of Law

1. See Michael Davis, *To Make the Punishment Fit the Crime* (Boulder: Westview, 1992).

2. For reports of earlier studies, as well as contemporary research, see Celesta Albonetti, "Race and the Probability of Pleading Guilty," *Journal of Quantitative Criminology*, 6 (1990): 315–351; Shawn D. Bushway and Anne Morrison Piehl, "Judging Judicial Discretion: Legal Factors and Racial Discrimination in Sentencing," *Law and Society Review*, 35 (2001): 733–764; Terance D. Miethe and Charles A. Moore, "Socioeconomic Disparities under Determinate Sentencing Systems: A Comparison of Preguideline and Postguideline Practices in Minnesota," *Criminology*, 23 (1985): 337–363; Ilene H. Nagel and John L. Hagan, "The Sentencing of White-Collar Criminals in Federal Courts: A Socio-Legal Explanation of Disparity," *Michigan Law Review*, 80 (1982): 1427–64; Barbara Meierhoefer, "The Role of Offense and Offender Characteristics in Federal Sentencing," *Southern California Law Review*, 66 (1992): 367–399.

3. See Marvin Frankel, *Criminal Sentences: Law without Order* (New York: Hill and Wang, 1972); idem, "Lawlessness in Judging," *University of Cincinnati Law Review*, 41 (1972): 1–54.

4. For a sampling of many studies documenting this disparity, see Celesta A. Albonetti, "Direct and Indirect Effects of Case Complexity, Guilty Pleas, and Offender Characteristics on Sentencing for Offenders Convicted of a White-Collar Offense prior to Sentencing Guidelines," *Journal of Quantitative Criminology*, 14 (1998): 353–378; Stanton Wheeler, David Weisburd, and Nancy Bode, "Sentencing the White-Collar Offender: Rhetoric and Reality," *American Sociological Review*, 47 (1982): 641–659; John Hagan, Irene Nagel, and Celesta Albonetti, "The Differential Sentencing of White-Collar Offenders in Ten Federal District Courts," *American Sociological Review*, 45 (1980): 802–820.

5. See William Rhodes, "Federal Criminal Sentencing: Some Measurement Issues with Application to Pre-Guideline Sentencing Disparity," *Journal of Criminal Law and Criminology*, 81 (1991): 1002–33.

6. A significant initial impetus for reform came from (Judge) Frankel, *Criminal Sentencing*. Also influential was then Judge and now Justice Stephen Breyer. See Stephen Breyer, "The Federal Sentencing Guidelines and the Key Compromises on Which They Rest," *Hofstra Law Review*, 17 (1988): 1–50.

7. Pub. L. No. 98-473, 98 Stat. 1837, 2017, codified as 18 U.S.C. §§3551–3673, 28 U.S.C. §§991–998 (2002).

8. Under the statute, new sentencing commissions are appointed periodically with the task of updating the Sentencing Guidelines. See Diana E. Murphy, "Inside the United States Sentencing Commission: Federal Sentencing Policy in 2001 and Beyond," *Iowa Law Review*, 87 (2002): 359–399.

9. See Michael Tonry, "The Success of Judge Frankel's Commission," *University of Colorado Law Review*, 64 (1993): 713–722.

10. Mistretta v. United States, 488 U.S. 361 (1989). A good discussion of judicial antagonism to the guidelines is found in Marc Miller, "Rehabilitating the Federal Sentencing Guidelines," *Judicature*, 78 (1995): 180–203. Among the longest and angriest denunciations of the guidelines is a book coauthored by José Cabranes, formerly a district judge and now a judge of the U.S. Court of Appeals for the Second Circuit; Kate Stith and José A. Cabranes, *Fear of Judging: Sentencing Guidelines in the Federal Courts* (Chicago: University of Chicago Press,

1998) (an earlier version, whose title efficiently announces the author's views, is Jose A. Cabranes, "Sentencing Guidelines: A Dismal Failure," *New York Law Journal*, 207 [February 11, 1992]: 2–6. Other criticisms include Albert W. Alschuler, "The Failure of Sentencing Guidelines: A Plea for Less Aggregation," *University of Chicago Law Review*, 58 (1991): 901–951; Daniel J. Freed, "Federal Sentencing in the Wake of the Guidelines: Unacceptable Limits on the Discretion of Sentencers," *Yale Law Journal*, 101 (1992): 1681–1754; Gerald Heaney, "The Reality of Sentencing Guidelines: No End to Disparity," *American Criminal Law Review*, 28 (1991): 161–232; Stephen Schulhofer, "Assessing the Federal Sentencing Process: The Problem Is Uniformity, Not Disparity," ibid., 29 (1992): 833–873; Kate Stith and Steve Y. Koh, "The Politics of Sentencing Reform: The Legislative History of the Federal Sentencing Guidelines," *Wake Forest Law Review*, 28 (1993): 223–290. For rare defenses of the guidelines, see Frank O. Bowman III, "The Quality of Mercy Must Be Restrained, and Other Lessons in Learning to Love the Federal Sentencing Guidelines," *Wisconsin Law Review*, 1996, pp. 679–749; Ronald F. Wright, "Complexity and Distrust in Sentencing Guidelines," *University of California at Davis Law Review*, 25 (1992): 617–637.

Judicial hostility to the guidelines is often intertwined with hostility to mandatory minimums for various crimes, minimums that often come from legislative anger about certain types of crimes and not from the guidelines. On the problems with mandatory minimums, see Gerard E. Lynch, "Sentencing Eddie," *Journal of Criminal Law and Criminology*, 91 (2001): 547–566.

11. See, for example, A. Abigail Payne, "Does Inter-Judge Disparity Really Matter? An Analysis of the Effects of Sentencing Reforms in Three Federal District Courts," *International Review of Law and Economics*, 17 (1997): 337–366; Chantale LaCasse and A. Abigail Payne, "Federal Sentencing Guidelines and Mandatory Minimum Sentences: Do Defendants Bargain in the Shadow of the Judge?" *Journal of Law and Economics*, 42 (1999): 245–269; Jennifer Reinganum, "Sentencing Guidelines, Judicial Discretion, and Plea Bargaining," Vanderbilt University Department of Economics Working Paper No. 96-W05 (1996).

12. See Joseph E. Kennedy, "Making the Crime Fit the Punishment," *Emory Law Journal*, 51 (2002): 753–876.

13. See Michael Tonry, *Sentencing Matters* (New York: Oxford University Press), pp. 72–99. Tonry's principal point is that many of the ac-

tual and perceived deficiencies of the federal guidelines are specific to flaws in the design of those guidelines and the way in which they are implemented, with state guidelines having been substantially more successful. See also James M. Anderson, Jeffrey R. Kling, and Kate Stith, "Measuring Interjudge Sentencing Disparity: Before and After the Federal Sentencing Guidelines," *Journal of Law and Economics*, 42 (1999): 271–307; Paul J. Hofer, Kevin R. Blackwell, and R. Barry Ruback, "The Effect of the Federal Sentencing Guidelines on Inter-Judge Sentencing Disparity," *Journal of Criminal Law and Criminology*, 90 (1999): 239–322. On the various state guidelines, see "Symposium on Sentencing Reform in the States," *University of Colorado Law Review*, 64 (1993): 645–847.

14. A comprehensive examination of contemporary issues and research can be found in "Symposium: Legal Issues and Sociolegal Consequences of the Federal Sentencing Guidelines," *Iowa Law Review*, 87 (2002): 357–804.

15. As Bill Stuntz has pointed out to me, the aggravating aspects of a defendant's personal history—criminal record, especially—may be more susceptible to being reduced to formal guidelines than are mitigating aspects such as modesty, courage, and hardship. Insofar as this is true, then to move from discretion to rules may have the (possibly) unintended consequence of making mercy more difficult and sentences therefore more severe.

16. An increase in discretion is not logically linked to an increase in mercy, but that connection has both psychological and philosophical appeal. See Martha C. Nussbaum, "Equity and Mercy," *Philosophy and Public Affairs*, 22 (1993): 83–125.

17. 18 U.S.C. § 922(g)(1)(2002).

18. United States v. Barstow, 110 F.3d 754 (11th Cir. 1997).

19. The guidelines not only preclude otherwise appropriate mercy, but also at times preclude otherwise appropriate sentence *in*creases. In United States v. Bakhtiari, 913 F.2d 1053 (2d Cir. 1990), for example, the defendant's sentence for a weapons violation was increased under the guidelines on account of his possession of a silencer with an "obliterated serial number." But because Mr. Bakhtiari had manufactured his own silencer, and had manufactured it, not surprisingly, without a serial number, he had not technically "obliterated" anything, and thus the appellate court felt compelled to order the reduction of his sentence; 913 F.2d at 1063.

20. The process is not all that simple, since the grid encapsulates in-

structions that run to some 400 pages (U.S. Sentencing Commission, Federal Sentencing Guidelines Manual [St. Paul: Westgroup, 2001]), and which after those 400 pages are still in need of yet further instructions in order to use them effectively. See Roger W. Haines Jr., Frank O. Bowman III, and Jennifer C. Woll, *Federal Sentencing Guidelines Handbook: Text and Analysis* (St. Paul: Westgroup, 2001) (1914 pages). But the complexity of the guidelines still serves to reduce rather than increase discretion, and to eliminate rather than to add considerations, in much the same way that the thousands of pages making up the Internal Revenue Code are more discretion-limiting and fact-excluding than would be a mandate to the Internal Revenue Service to levy a "fair" tax on each taxpayer.

21. See David Dolinko, "Justice in the Age of Sentencing Guidelines," *Ethics*, 110 (2000): 585.

22. See Patti B. Saris, "Below the Radar Screens: Have the Sentencing Guidelines Eliminated Disparity? One Judge's Perspective," *Suffolk University Law Review*, 30 (1997): 1027–66.

23. See John E. Coons, "Consistency," *California Law Review*, 75 (1987): 59–113.

24. 1 Kings 3:16.

25. See Frederick Schauer, "Judging in a Corner of the Law," *Southern California Law Review*, 61 (1988): 1717–34. The problem with taking judging as too representative of law is the problem of the selection effect, pursuant to which only those cases in which two parties holding mutually exclusive positions believe it worthwhile to litigate. As a result, the easy cases never get to court, and the population of court cases is thus the skewed population consisting only of hard cases. On this, the locus classicus is George Priest and William Klein, "The Selection of Disputes for Litigation," *Journal of Legal Studies*, 13 (1984): 1–55.

26. 26 U.S.C. 5845(a).

27. United States v. Lam, 20 F.3d 999 (9th Cir. 1994).

28. Philip K. Howard, *The Death of Common Sense: How Law Is Suffocating America* (New York: Random House, 1994). A substantially more sophisticated dissent from law's rule-based orientation is Cass R. Sunstein, "Problems with Rules," *California Law Review*, 83 (1995): 953–1026.

29. For a sampling of the voluminous literature, see Rupert Cross and J. W. Harris, *Precedent in English Law*, 4th ed. (Oxford: Clarendon Press, 1990); Laurence Goldstein, ed., *Precedent in Law* (Oxford:

Clarendon Press, 1987); Larry Alexander, "Constrained by Precedent," *Southern California Law Review*, 63 (1989): 1–64; Stephen R. Perry, "Judicial Obligation, Precedent and the Common Law," *Oxford Journal of Legal Studies*, 7 (1987): 215–232; Frederick Schauer, "Precedent," *Stanford Law Review*, 39 (1987): 571–605.

30. [1932] S.C. 31 (H.L.).

31. See Michael C. Dorf, "Courts, Reasons, and Rules," in *Rules and Reasoning: Essays in Honour of Fred Schauer*, ed. Linda Meyer (Oxford: Hart, 1999), pp. 129–146; James L. H. Sprague, "Remedies for the Failure to Provide Reasons," *Canadian Journal of Administrative Law and Practice*, 13 (2000): 209–223; N. R. Campbell, "The Duty to Give Reasons in Administrative Law," *Public Law*, 1994, pp. 184–191; Alex Samuels, "Giving Reasons in the Criminal Justice and Penal Process," *Journal of Criminal Law*, 45 (1981): 51–58.

32. The requirement of reason-giving is elaborated in a crossnational context in Paul R. Verkuil, "Crosscurrents in Anglo-American Administrative Law," *William and Mary Law Review*, 27 (1986): 701–705.

33. Frederick Schauer, "Giving Reasons," *Stanford Law Review*, 47 (1995): 633–659.

34. The mandate to generalize takes an especially concrete form in the prohibition on bills of attainder (legislative punishments directed at identifiable individuals) in the U.S. Constitution, art. 1, sec. 9 (as to the federal government) and art. 1, sec. 10 (as to the states). For one of the few cases interpreting the attainder clauses, see United States v. Lovett, 328 U.S. 303 (1946). For an overview, see [Student] Note, "The Bounds of Legislative Specification: A Suggested Approach to the Bill of Attainder Clause," *Yale Law Journal*, 72 (1962): 330–358.

35. Burnet v. Coronado Oil & Gas Co., 285 U.S. 393, 406 (1932) (Brandeis, J., dissenting).

36. See Joseph Raz, *The Authority of Law: Essays on Law and Morality* (Oxford: Clarendon Press, 1979); Joseph Raz, ed., *Authority* (New York: New York University Press, 1990); Frederick Schauer, "The Questions of Authority," *Georgetown Law Journal*, 81 (1992): 95–115.

37. On authority as being essentially and necessarily content independent (and thus necessarily general), see H. L. A. Hart, "Commands and Authoritative Legal Reasons," in *Essays on Bentham: Jurisprudence and Political Theory* (Oxford: Clarendon Press, 1982), pp. 243–268.

## 11. Generality, Community, and the Wars of the Roqueforts

1. *Newsweek,* October 1, 1962, quoted in James B. Simpson, *Simpson's Contemporary Quotations* (Boston: Houghton Mifflin, 1988), p. 287.

2. On the American restrictions and their effect on European cheese-making, see Burkhard Bilger, "Raw Faith: The Nun and the Cheese Underground," *New Yorker,* August 19, 2002, pp. 150–162.

3. Most of the controversy centers on a single directive, identified as 92/46 EC. There is not yet a "Remember the Maine" or "54–40 or Fight" slogan encapsulating opposition to 92/46 EC, but one cannot be too far away.

4. In part because American restrictions on raw-milk cheeses make the United States a convenient foil, references to Velveeta and Cheez-Whiz crop up frequently in the European debates.

5. *Terroir* is literally translated as "soil," but the word is used by the French people to describe the full glory, history, and charm of the French local agricultural tradition.

6. Among the more important explorations of this theme is Joseph H. H. Weiler, "The Transformation of Europe," *Yale Law Journal,* 100 (1991): 2403–83.

7. The eleven languages are Sepedi, Sesotho, Setswana, siSwati, Tshivenda, Xitsonga, Afrikaans, English, sisNdebele, isiXhosa, and isiZulu. Constitution of the Republic of South Africa, chap. 1, sec. 6(1). In addition, the constitution creates a Pan South African Language Board charged with promoting and encouraging respect for three other indigenous languages (Khoi, Nama, and San), sign language, the languages of various ethnic communities (German, Greek, Gujarati, Hindi, Portuguese, Tamil, Telegg, and Urdu), and the languages of religious communities (Arabic, Hebrew, Sanskrit, and other unlisted religious languages); chap. 1, sec. 6(5).

8. See Russell E. Neuman, Marion R. Just, and Ann N. Crigler, *Common Knowledge: News and the Construction of Political Meaning* (Chicago: University of Chicago Press, 1992).

9. See, for example, Åke E. Anndersson, Björn Hårsman, and John M. Quigley, eds., *Government for the Future: Unification, Fragmentation, and Regionalism* (Amsterdam: Elsevier, 1997); John D. Donahue, *Disunited States* (New York: Basic Books, 1997); Jonathan Potter, *Devolution and Globalisation: Implications for Local Decision-Makers* (Paris: OECD, 2001).

10. See J. Nicholas Entikin, "Political Community, Identity and Cosmopolitan Place," *International Sociology*, 14 (1999): 269–282.

11. On the identity-creating characteristics of community, see Michael Sandel, *Liberalism and the Limits of Justice* (Cambridge: Cambridge University Press, 1982).

12. For good overviews, see John W. Chapman and Ian Shapiro, eds., *Democratic Community (NOMOS XXXV)* (New York: New York University Press, 1993); Michael J. Sandel, ed., *Liberalism and Its Critics* (Cambridge: Cambridge University Press, 1984); Stephen A. Gardbaum, "Law, Politics, and the Claims of Community," *Michigan Law Review*, 90 (1992): 685–760.

13. Not surprisingly, the South African analogue to the cheesemakers of Roquefort are the white Afrikaaner speakers of Afrikaans, for they are the ones who believe most strongly, perhaps with some justification, that their culture and their identity are at grave risk in the new South Africa.

14. For the full development of the argument of which the sentence here is but the conclusion, see Frederick Schauer, "Giving Reasons," *Stanford Law Review*, 47 (1995): 633–661.

15. See Frederick Schauer, "Rights as Rules," *Law and Philosophy*, 5 (1987): 115–121; also Marcus G. Singer, *Generalization in Ethics* (New York: Alfred A. Knopf, 1961).

16. See Church of the American Knights of the Ku Klux Klan v. Safir, 1999 U.S. App. LEXIS 28106 (2d Cir., October 22, 1999); McIntyre v. Ohio Elections Commission, 514 U.S. 334 (1995); Talley v. California, 362 U.S. 60 (1960).

17. This is intended as an entirely innocuous claim, designed to steer well clear of the view that most or all of our categories are socially constructed as opposed to being antecedent to human categorization. On some of these issues, see John Searle, *The Construction of Social Reality* (New York: Free Press, 1992).

18. See, for example, Mary Ann Glendon, *Rights Talk: The Impoverishment of Political Discourse* (Cambridge, Mass.: Harvard University Press, 1991).

19. As Jeremy Waldron points out in "An Essay on Basic Equality" (colloquium paper, New York University Law School, 1999), available at http://www.law.nyu.edu/clppt/papers/basicequality.pdf, the idea that prescriptive equality is a product of community is most often associated with Hannah Arendt. See Hannah Arendt, *On Revolution* (Harmondsworth: Penguin, 1977), pp. 30–31. As Waldron

puts it, "By nature we may be utterly different from one another in background, abilities and character; but by political convention we *hold* ourselves to be one another's equals," thereby "mak[ing] possible a form of political community that we could not otherwise have"; Waldron, p. 23.

## Coda

1. The obligatory and entirely appropriate citation is John Rawls, *A Theory of Justice* (Cambridge, Mass.: Harvard University Press, 1971).